The Art of Robert Frost

The Art of
Robert Frost

TIM KENDALL

Yale

UNIVERSITY PRESS

New Haven and London

Published with assistance from the Mary Cady Tew Memorial Fund.

Yale University Press books may be purchased in quantity for educational, business, or promotional use. For information, please e-mail sales.press@yale.edu (U.S. office) or sales@yaleup.co.uk (U.K. office).

Designed by Sonia Shannon. Set in Monotype Bulmer type by Duke & Company, Devon, Pennsylvania. Printed in the United States of America.

Library of Congress Cataloging-in-Publication Data
Kendall, Tim, 1970–
The art of Robert Frost / Tim Kendall.
p. cm.
Includes bibliographical references and index.
Includes the entirety of Frost's North of Boston (1914); selections from A boy's will (1913); generous selections from Mountain Interval (1916) and New Hampshire (1923); and a selection of lyrics in the section titled Later poems, from West-running brook (1928), A further range (1936), A witness tree (1942), and Steeple bush (1947).
ISBN 978-0-300-11813-1 (cloth : alk. paper) 1. Frost, Robert, 1874–1963—Criticism and interpretation. 2. Frost, Robert, 1874–1963—Aesthetics. I. Frost, Robert, 1874–1963. Poems. Selections. II. Title.
PS3511.R94Z7585 2012
811'.54—dc23
2011041416

A catalogue record for this book is available from the British Library.

This paper meets the requirements of ANSI/NISO Z39.48-1992 (Permanence of Paper).

10 9 8 7 6 5 4 3 2 1

A poem is best read in the light of all the other poems ever written. We read A the better to read B (we have to start somewhere; we may get very little out of A). We read B the better to read C, C the better to read D, D the better to go back and get something more out of A. Progress is not the aim, but circulation. The thing is to get among the poems where they hold each other apart in their places as the stars do.

—Robert Frost, "The Prerequisites" (1954)

Contents

Acknowledgments xi
A Note on the Texts xii
List of Abbreviations xvi
Introduction 3

A Boy's Will (1913)   13

Into My Own   16
Ghost House   19
Rose Pogonias   23
Mowing   27
The Trial by Existence   30
The Tuft of Flowers   36
Reluctance   40

North of Boston (1914)   45

The Pasture   47
Mending Wall   49
The Death of the Hired Man   54
The Mountain   64
A Hundred Collars   72
Home Burial   82
The Black Cottage   90
Blueberries   98
A Servant to Servants   104
After Apple-Picking   113
The Code   117

The Generations of Men   124

The Housekeeper   136

The Fear   149

The Self-Seeker   156

The Wood-Pile   168

Good Hours   173

Mountain Interval (1916)   177

The Road Not Taken   179

Christmas Trees   183

An Old Man's Winter Night   187

In the Home Stretch   191

Meeting and Passing   202

Hyla Brook   205

The Oven Bird   208

Birches   211

Putting in the Seed   216

The Cow in Apple Time   219

An Encounter   222

The Bonfire   225

"Out, Out—"   232

The Gum-Gatherer   237

The Vanishing Red   241

The Sound of the Trees   246

New Hampshire (1923)   251

A Star in a Stone-boat   253

Maple   260

The Axe-Helve   270

The Grindstone   277

Paul's Wife   282

Place for a Third   290

Two Witches
  I. The Witch of Coös 296
  II. The Pauper Witch of Grafton 305
Fire and Ice 312
To E. T. 315
Stopping by Woods on a Snowy Evening 319
For Once, Then, Something 324
The Onset 328
A Hillside Thaw 331
The Need of Being Versed in Country Things 334

Later Poems 339
  Acquainted with the Night 340
  Two Tramps in Mud Time 343
  Desert Places 350
  Neither Out Far Nor In Deep 354
  Design 357
  The Silken Tent 362
  The Most of It 365
  The Subverted Flower 369
  The Gift Outright 374
  Directive 378

Bibliography 385
Index 389

Acknowledgments

I COULD NOT HAVE WRITTEN this book without the assistance of a great many individuals and institutions. It is a pleasure to have the opportunity to thank them here.

Much of my research was carried out while I was in receipt of a Philip Leverhulme Award from the Leverhulme Trust, to which I am hugely grateful. Mimi Ross at Henry Holt and Co., LLC, and Sarah McMahon at Random House in London have been generous and helpful in dealing with my request for permission to quote Frost's poems. The University of Exeter allowed me the time to finish this book, and my colleagues Jo Gill and Jane Spencer gave me the encouragement that I occasionally needed. I have benefited from conversations over many years with fellow Frostians Rachel Buxton and John Redmond. Bysshe Coffey read the typescript and suggested improvements. Profound thanks to John Kulka for commissioning the project, to Jennifer Banks for her patience and expertise, and to Alison MacKeen, Niamh Cunningham, Piyali Bhattacharya, and Dan Heaton for bringing it safely to publication.

To Fiona, Charlie, Milly, and Rosie I am grateful for everything else.

A Note on the Texts

~⁂~

FROST MADE SMALL REVISIONS to his poems for the various selected
and collected editions published in his lifetime. I have preferred to use
the early versions as given in the first edition of each volume of new
poetry. The poems which I have included from *A Boy's Will* (London:
David Nutt, 1913), *North of Boston* (London: David Nutt, 1914), *Mountain
Interval* (New York: Henry Holt, 1916), *New Hampshire* (New York:
Henry Holt, 1923), *West-Running Brook* (New York: Henry Holt, 1928),
A Further Range (New York: Henry Holt, 1936), *A Witness Tree* (New
York: Henry Holt, 1942), and *Steeple Bush* (New York: Henry Holt, 1947)
are printed here as in those editions, except for the following alterations
made in line with Frost's own editorial practices: I have changed Brit-
ish to American spellings; I have made consistent the use of single and
double quotation marks within poems; and I have consulted subsequent
editions in order to correct clear typographical errors. By focusing on
the first editions, I have been able to restore some of the peculiarities of
Frost's punctuation, such as the two-em dash (——), which he uses in
North of Boston when a speaker is interrupted midsentence.

The following list of corrections gives the page number, the poem title,
the line as it appears in this edition, and after the square bracket the line
as it was printed in the first edition.

64 "The Mountain"
The mountain held the town as in a shadow.] The mountain
held the town as in a shadow

72 "A Hundred Collars"
And cars that shock and rattle—and *one* hotel.] And cars that shook and rattle—and *one* hotel.

90 "The Black Cottage"
Anyway they won't have the place disturbed."] Anyway they won't have the place disturbed.
"That was the father as he went to war.] That was the father as he went to war.
He fell at Gettysburg or Fredericksburg,] He fell at Gettysburg or Fredricksburg,
There are bees in this wall." He struck the clapboards,] "There are bees in this wall." He struck the clapboards,

98 "Blueberries"
Not forcing her hand with harrow and plow."] Not forcing her hand with harrow and plow. [*I have added a stanza break after this line, as in later editions.*]
"I wish you had seen his perpetual bow—] I wish you had seen his perpetual bow—
And they looked so solemn-absurdly concerned."] And they looked so solemn-absurdly concerned.
Some strange kind—they told me it hadn't a name."] Some strange kind—they told me it hadn't a name.
It was all he could do to keep a straight face."] It was all he could do to keep a straight face.
As talking—you stood up beside me, you know."] As talking—you stood up beside me, you know.

104 "A Servant to Servants"
Cruel—it sounds. I s'pose they did the best] Cruel—it sounds. I 'spose they did the best
I s'pose I've got to go the road I'm going:] I 'spose I've got to go the road I'm going:

Bless you, of course you're keeping me from work,] Bless you,
of course you'rt keeping me from work,

117 "The Code"
"To cock the hay?—because it's going to shower?] "To cock the
hay?—because it's going to shower?"

136 "The Housekeeper"
He must have changed his mind and gone to Garland's.] He
must have changed his mind and gone to Garlands.

149 "The Fear"
The woman spoke out sharply, "Whoa, stand still!] The woman
spoke out sharply, "Whoa, stand still!"
I saw it just as plain as a white plate,"] "I saw it just as plain as
a white plate,"
It touched, it struck, it clattered and went out.] It touched, it
struck it, clattered and went out.

156 "The Self-Seeker"
You! crumpling folks's legal documents.] You! crumpling folkses
legal documents.

191 "In the Home Stretch"
Its seeming bad for a moment makes it seem] It's seeming bad for
a moment makes it seem
[*I have indented "'What kind of years?'" and added linespaces
each time that the speaker changes. This follows revisions made
in later editions.*]

241 "The Vanishing Red"
But he gave no one else a laugher's license.] But he gave no one
else a laughter's license.

260 "Maple"
[*I have added linespaces after "Maple is right" and "There's*
no such name." This follows revisions made in later editions.]
(The arrangement made a pleasant sunny cellar.)] (The arrang-
ment made a pleasant sunny cellar.)

277 "The Grindstone"
Spheroid that kicked and struggled in its gait,] Spheroid that
kicked and struggled in its gate,

305 "The Pauper Witch of Grafton"
And I don't mean just skulls of Rogers' Rangers] And I don't
mean just skulls of Roger's Rangers

Abbreviations

CPP&P   *Collected Poems, Prose, and Plays,* edited by Richard
         Poirier and Mark Richardson. New York: Library of
         America, 1995.

CPr   *The Collected Prose of Robert Frost,* edited by Mark
         Richardson. Cambridge: Belknap Harvard, 2007.

LU   *The Letters of Robert Frost to Louis Untermeyer,* edited by
         Louis Untermeyer. New York: Holt, Rinehart and Winston,
         1963.

N   *The Notebooks of Robert Frost,* edited by Robert Faggen.
         Cambridge: Belknap Harvard, 2006.

SL   *Selected Letters of Robert Frost,* edited by Lawrance
         Thompson. New York: Holt, Rinehart and Winston, 1964.

The Art of Robert Frost

Introduction

TOWARD THE END OF *The Shawshank Redemption,* one convict gives another a set of instructions to follow after release from prison: he must make his way to a hayfield near Buxton and retrieve a buried object. To the response "Lots of hayfields there," the first convict elaborates: "One in particular. Got a long rock wall with a big oak at the north end. Like something out of a Robert Frost poem." That description suffices for filmgoers and convicts alike. Life prisoners in 1960s America—differentiated in this case by age, race, class, and educational background— are all expected to recognize a Frost landscape when they see one. For no other poet after Wordsworth would the same assumption be safely made. Imagine the absurdity if the object had been concealed in an urban wasteland, "like something out of a T. S. Eliot poem."

Frost set out with the ambition "to be a poet for all sorts and kinds" (*SL,* 98). That he succeeded is proven by the frequency of casual allusions to his work, from *The Shawshank Redemption* to *The Simpsons* to cups and tea towels and postcards. *How* he succeeded, and with what losses as well as gains, is a story dramatized in the poems themselves. From the outset, he valued above all else in poetry what he called "the pleasure of ulteriority"—that is, "saying one thing and meaning another, saying one thing in terms of another" (*CPr,* 147). His double speaking allowed him to address multiple audiences at the same time. Lawrance Thompson recounts a talk Frost gave in 1953:

> He said that in writing a poem, he was aware of saying two things at once; but of wanting to say the first thing so well that any reader who liked that part of the poem might feel free to settle for that part of the poem as sufficient in itself. But, he

3

added, it was of the nature of poetry to say two things at once, and it was of the nature of literary appreciation to perceive that an ulterior meaning had been included in the particular meaning. (*CPr*, 279)

In "Maple," a poem about ulteriority which is itself sophisticatedly ulterior, Frost provides an architecture for his strategies: he describes a house which is "one story high in front, three stories / On the end it presented to the road." Approaching his work from the front, Frost's readers are encouraged but not compelled to perceive the many "stories" hidden under the visible surface, the ulterior beyond the particular.

Occasionally, Frost expressed disapproval of parts of his audience who had missed the point. He complained about readers who had not taken his hints: "I hate to think I cant [*sic*] count on people to know when I am being figurative and when I am not being" (*N*, 487). Yet his strategy *required* that some would not understand: to have an ulterior motive is to conceal, mislead, and deceive. Where there is no deception, there is no ulteriority. Frost's late masterpiece "Directive," as well as other notebooks and public talks, referred approvingly to Christ's defense of parable as a way of excluding some people from salvation: "That seeing they may see, and not perceive, and hearing they may hear, and not understand, lest at any time they should be converted, and their sins should be forgiven them" (Mark 4:12). The failings of others could not easily be forgiven. Exasperated by what he believed to be continued misreadings of one of his best-known poems, "The Road Not Taken," Frost conveyed his regret to one audience: "I can't mark [the hints]—there's no way of marking them. I have to leave it to nice people to know the difference" (Thompson 1970, 547). There is little sense in these examples that Frost genuinely tolerated any reader who settled for the particular at the expense of the ulterior. Yet he was equally harsh on those readers who followed a hint where none had been intended. As far as Frost was concerned, the best "literary appreciation" was that which traveled far enough, but no farther, and in the right direction. This he considered to be "the ultimate refinement" (*CPr*, 166).

Frost's emphasis on the ability of poetry to say one thing and mean another created tensions between his audiences, most publicly in 1959 after Lionel Trilling had spoken at a dinner in celebration of the poet's eighty-fifth birthday. Trilling confessed himself alienated by Frost's "great canon" of poetry because it "seemed to denigrate the work of the critical intellect or . . . gave to its admirers the ground for making the denigration" (Trilling, 155). A number of respondents used the pages of the *New York Times* to criticize the scholar for—among other crimes—failing to know "when he is out of his field or his depth," and being part of a New York critical movement which had "gone whoring after European gods." That two constituencies of admirers should have turned on each other so prominently indicates both the breadth of Frost's appeal and the risks of its fracture. Many of the contradictions in the poet's public image were caused by the struggle to remain a favorite both of a broad reading public and of the university professors. Here was a plain-speaking Yankee, and a riddling mischief maker with an ulterior motive whose literary career had begun in England; a critic of "much that goes on in college" as being "against the spirit" (*CPr*, 176), but who spent most of his adulthood teaching and lecturing there; and a baiter of academics, who nevertheless admitted that "to be studied is the great thing in life" (*CPr*, 322). In person as in poetry, Frost seems to have developed the same quality which Thomas Hardy detected in Biblical narratives—"the simplicity of the highest cunning" (Hardy, 170).

As the terms of the disagreement between Trilling and his detractors laid bare, Frost's poetry invests heavily in a myth of nationhood which eschews the city in favor of the frontier and the homestead. Let urban sophisticates go whoring after strange European gods. Frost focuses *his* attention on isolated individuals and small communities which—there being no American Arcadia—struggle to subsist amid the harsh grandeur of the natural landscape. The "bookish tones" which Frost regularly condemned and took pains to avoid are replaced in his poetry by what Wordsworth had called "a selection of language really used by men." Those men (and, so often in Frost's work, women) were the vibrantly unschooled, whose speech was alive with rhythms and idioms which an excess of education might have removed. Frost would have found little to dispute in Wordsworth's argument that poets "separate themselves from the sympathies of men" to the extent to which they "indulge in arbitrary and capricious habits of expression" at the expense of the "simple and unelaborated." This need not entail an anti-intellectualism of the kind which concerned Trilling: a classicist like Frost who experiments with Catullan hendecasyllabics is in no position to dismiss the benefits of learning. Rather, the attention to speech rhythms has an ulterior purpose of exposing and capturing wrinkles of character, and by doing so, extending "the sympathies of men."

In a letter of March 1915, Frost described a journey from misanthropy toward such sympathies as he looked back over the phases of his adult life and the poetry which had accompanied them. His first volume, *A Boy's Will* (1913), had been the record of a time (for ten years from the age of eighteen) when he thought that he "preferred stocks and stones to people." There followed a "conscious interest in people" which was "no more than an almost technical interest in their speech." Finally, in "The Death of the Hired Man," he made the discovery that he was "interested in neighbors for more than merely their tones of speech—and always had been" (*SL,* 158–159). Written around 1905 and collected almost a decade later in *North of Boston,* "The Death of the Hired Man" marked a shift into poetry as a drama of everyday lives—and deaths. Encouraging her husband to look kindly on a laborer who has returned sick to their farm, having previously abandoned them, Mary persuades not through elaborate argument but through nuances of rhythm and repetition which amount to a cunning simplicity:

> "Warren," she said, "he has come home to die:
> You needn't be afraid he'll leave you this time."
>
> "Home," he mocked gently.
>
>   "Yes, what else but home?
> It all depends on what you mean by home.

Of course he's nothing to us, any more
Than was the hound that came a stranger to us
Out of the woods, worn out upon the trail."

"Home is the place where, when you have to go there,
They have to take you in."

"I should have called it
Something you somehow haven't to deserve."

The word "home" occurs five times, as Mary and Warren contest its definition. Mary wins because she is able to incorporate it more fluently into other kinds of repetition: "come" and "came" call out to "home," compelling the return; "to us" and, again, "to us" make the destination seem inevitable; "Out of the woods, worn out upon the" is an echo chamber so insistent that it almost seems like chiasmus. Contrast the heavily accented clunk in Warren's repetitions: " 'Home is the place where, when you have to go there, / They have to take you in.' " The crashing internal rhyme of "where" and "there," the collision of "where" and "when," the awkward stresses on "have"—Warren's definition sounds too unpleasantly grudging to win support. His heart is not in it. The case is immediately defeated by Mary's fleet-footedness: "have" loses its stress ("I should have called it"), and "haven't" negates Warren's previous insistence on obligation. Mary's definition will never find its way into a dictionary: the repetition in "Something" and "somehow" draws attention to its vagueness. But that is her point and her strategy: "home" is something (and somehow) *felt*, not rationalized and defined. The rhythm and the harmony belonging to her description of home overwhelm Warren's resistance.

"The Death of the Hired Man" is probably the earliest successful embodiment of Frost's theory of the "sound of sense," the impression of which (he tells one correspondent in 1913) can be gained by listening to "voices behind a door that cuts off the words." This is "the abstract vitality of our speech," and it explains why Frost always felt that no sentence ever exists wholly on the page; it requires the intonations of voice for it to come alive and be understood by the hearing imagination. Without that quality, a poem remains embalmed in bookish tones. Frost goes on to explain that the poet must "learn to get cadences by skillfully breaking the sounds of sense . . . across the regular beat of the metre" (*SL*, 80). Those cadences can be deliberately awkward (Warren's definition of home), or can be engaging and persuasive (Mary's definition), but they amount to the essential drama of Frost's work. "The possibilities for tune from the dramatic tones of meaning struck across the rigidity of a limited meter are endless," he states in his best-known essay, "The Figure a Poem Makes" (*CPr*, 131). These discussions of meter and rhythm parallel Frost's concern with the ulteriority of poetry. Just as rhythm exists beyond, and engages variously with, the poem's meter, so one or many meanings exist beyond the "particular meaning." The emphasis on the interaction of meter and rhythm explains a lifelong suspicion of free verse, which is like a poem without ulteriority, unnatural and impoverished. Having deprived itself of a grid on which to measure its rhythms, free verse becomes—as one of Frost's most famous aphorisms has it—akin to playing tennis with the net down.

"I am as sure that the colloquial is the root of every good poem as I am that the national is the root of all thought and art" (*SL*, 228). Frost's comment to Régis Michaud in January 1918 offers yet another defense of the sound of sense against bookish tones; it also implies an equation between the colloquial and the national, or a belief that the colloquial is the means by which the national might be realized. Yet the colloquial as heard by Frost is local or, at most, regional. Calling his fourth volume *New Hampshire*, Frost pledges allegiance to that state as a major source of the landscape and speech rhythms which inspire his work. In doing so, he offers himself as an example of a poet who, as Auden would later say, hopes to be "like some valley cheese, local, but prized elsewhere." New Hampshire becomes a synecdoche for a nation which is otherwise too unmanageably large and various.

These concerns over metrical traditions and colloquiality become bound up for Frost, as for Walt Whitman before him, with ideas of nation building and nationhood. John Hollander has justly described Frost as "that most un-Whitmanian of major twentieth-century American poets" (Hollander 1997b, 179), and Frost's own references to Whitman are almost uniformly negative. Whitman, Frost argued, had sacrificed art in favor of scope; and in that criticism can be distantly heard the self-justification of a writer who chose to advertise so prominently his regional attachments. Yet those two unlike-minded poets share preoccupations even while they reach opposing solutions. Their attitudes to meter are overtly expressed in terms of national identity. Whitman believed that "authorities, poems, models, laws, names, imported into America, are useful to America today to destroy them, and so move disencumbered to great works, great days." The Whitmanian long line mimicked the measureless expanse of his nation's geography. "Old forms," Whitman announced, seemed "haggard, dwarfed, ludicrous," when compared with the democratic immensity of the United States: "The truest and greatest poetry . . . can never again, in the English language, be express'd in arbitrary and rhyming meter." Frost could not have agreed less. He considered that measure gave the poet freedom within bounds (which was the only meaningful freedom), and insisted that only two meters were permitted—"strict iambic and loose iambic"; a line might be any length up to six feet (*CPr,* 149). Rebuking his troublesome predecessor, he complained that "when a man sets out consciously to tear up forms and rhythms and measures, then he is not interested in giving you poetry. He just wants to perform, he wants to show you his tricks" (Lathem, 52–53).

Frost advocated an American poetry more openly receptive to European traditions than Whitman ever allowed or acknowledged. Ralph Waldo Emerson, their shared progenitor, had stated that "all educated Americans, first or last, go to Europe"; Frost, characteristically, chose to go first. From September 1912 to February 1915, he and his family lived in England. There he met Ezra Pound, Robert Graves, and the "only brother [he] ever had," Edward Thomas (*SL,* 217); he wrote many of the poems which would be published in his second and third books, *North of Boston* and *Mountain Interval;* he heard the poet laureate, Robert

Bridges, holding forth on the virtues of quantitative meter and was inspired to formulate his theory of the "sound of sense" as a rebuttal; and the publication of *A Boy's Will* by a small English firm led directly to a contract with Holt for *North of Boston*. "I seem in a fair way to become an Englishman," Frost wrote to Susan Hayes Ward in May 1913, before adding, as if reassuringly, "we are very very homesick in this English mud" (*SL*, 73). He had reason to look forward to his homecoming; having left the United States as an unknown, he returned a literary sensation.

Frost would later joke—in all seriousness—that he had never seen New England so clearly as when he had been in old England. The United States supplanted Britain as the world's superpower during Frost's lifetime. Yet in 1948 he could still refer, with a twinkling eye, to the need for good relations between the United States and the "Mother Country" (his own mother having been Scottish). Addressing the Americans and British together, he expressed the hope that they would continue to listen to each other across the Atlantic gulf. "Remember," he told them, "the future of the world may depend on your keeping in practice with each other's quips and figures" (*CPr*, 160). This book is intended as one small contribution to that project.

I have included the entirety of *North of Boston* (1914), a volume which, Frost professes, "was not written as a book nor towards a book" (*CPr*, 196). Even so, its structure and its recurring motifs create a coherence which constitutes more than the sum of its parts. Whereas *A Boy's Will* (1913), which Frost disparaged in later years, is more modestly represented, I have made generous selections from *Mountain Interval* (1916) and *New Hampshire* (1923). After *New Hampshire*, Frost continued to write great poems but (by the high standards of earlier work) not great books. The section titled "Later Poems" comprises an anthology-in-miniature of lyrics successfully lodged by Frost "where they will be hard to get rid of" (*CPP&P*, 744).

I have chosen poems according to two criteria: their quality and their variety. My desire to give a sense of Frost's range has occasionally entailed the exclusion of poems on grounds other than my opinion of their merit. All books have to end somewhere, but I especially regret not having found space for "The Vantage Point," "The Hill Wife," "The Star-Splitter," "Once by the Pacific," "Provide, Provide," and "Iris by Night."

"A poem," Frost tells us, "is best read in the light of all the other poems ever written" (*CPr*, 174). Returning mischief for mischief, we might reasonably respond: why stop at "all the other poems," or for that matter, why stop at what is *written?* Interpretation of poems as complex as Frost's must necessarily remain incomplete, but I have tried to draw on whatever contexts the poems seem to require. I have learned a great deal from previous scholars of Frost's work, and even where I disagree with them, my debt is clear. Like Frost himself, I have remained mindful of the need to serve different kinds of audience. Some will want only the poems, others will want commentaries on particular poems, and still others will read from beginning to end. This book is designed to have something to offer all its readers. My priorities have been, first, to produce a reliable text accounting for editorial decisions which may differentiate it from other available versions; and, second, to pursue the same journey which Frost claims for all great poetry: "It begins in delight and ends in wisdom" (*CPr*, 132). While I hope that my commentaries travel at least some of the way, I have not let them forget their origins in that sense of delight which Frost's work continues to give me.

A BOY'S WILL

~⁊⁊~

ROBERT FROST'S first full-length collection, *A Boy's Will,* was slow in the making. Published in 1913, it contained poems written over the previous two decades, the majority of which had not appeared in print before. Having brought his poems across to England in September 1912, Frost finally determined to shape them into a book, and the manuscript was accepted by the first publisher which he approached: a London firm, David Nutt and Company. The volume would not appear in the United States until 1915, when Holt issued it alongside Frost's next book, *North of Boston.*

Frost took his title from Henry Wadsworth Longfellow's poem, "My Lost Youth": "A boy's will is the wind's will, / And the thoughts of youth are long, long thoughts." The wind's will is a force of nature which cannot be resisted, but it is also inconsistent and subject to sudden change. The allusion to Longfellow therefore provided an apology for Frost's own lost youth, which the poems mapped in all its variousness. "Call it a study in a certain kind of waywardness" (*SL*, 60), Frost wrote on Christmas Day 1912, and later he described the volume as "pretty near being the story of five years of [his] life" (*SL*, 66). Ignoring the order in which the poems had been written, he enforced this autobiographical narrative by dividing the volume into three sections as different phases of a spiritual and intellectual journey, and arranging the poems so that they followed an arc of departure and return. The list of poems on the contents page was accompanied by explanatory glosses—"He is in love with being misunderstood," "He is afraid of his own isolation," and so on—which Frost dropped from later editions. (I have appended, below, the glosses for each of the poems included here; "Reluctance" was not glossed.) The coherence of *A Boy's Will* was essential: although he had already finished several of the dramatic monologues which would eventually be published in *North of Boston* or his third book, *Mountain Interval,* Frost does not seem to have been tempted to include any of them here.

A Boy's Will was widely and positively reviewed, and a number of influential figures championed Frost's cause. Ezra Pound wrote a laudatory review for *Poetry,* but made Frost jittery by excoriating American editors for having failed to discover Frost themselves. W. B. Yeats was reported to have called *A Boy's Will* "the best poetry written in America for a long time" (Walsh, 96). Frost himself described it, with a modesty not entirely false, as "a good book in spots" (*SL,* 73), and although in later years he retained his enthusiasm for "the few lyrics [he] ever really liked in [his] first book" (*SL,* 248), he warned that the others should not be read "on any account" (*CPP&P,* 684).

Among the seven poems included here, only "Mowing" and "The Tuft of Flowers" bear comparison with Frost's best work. Even so, it is remarkable how many themes and motifs span his writing career. "Into My Own" and "Reluctance," the first and last poems of *A Boy's Will,* establish a pattern of departure and return which will be repeated in book after book; "Ghost House" marks the first appearance of the ruined homestead which will reappear so much more powerfully in later poems like "The Generations of Men" and "Directive"; and "Rose Pogonias" joins with "Mowing" and "The Tuft of Flowers" as early expressions of Frost's interlinked concerns over ownership and poetic originality.

INTO MY OWN *The youth is persuaded that he will be rather more than less himself for having forsworn the world.*
GHOST HOUSE *He is happy in society of his choosing.*
ROSE POGONIAS *He is no dissenter from the ritualism of nature[.]*
MOWING *He takes up life simply with the small tasks.*
THE TRIAL BY EXISTENCE *[He resolves] to know definitely what he thinks about the soul[.]*
THE TUFT OF FLOWERS *[and] about fellowship[.]*
RELUCTANCE

Into My Own

One of my wishes is that those dark trees,
So old and firm they scarcely show the breeze,
Were not, as 'twere, the merest mask of gloom,
But stretched away unto the edge of doom.

I should not be withheld but that some day
Into their vastness I should steal away,
Fearless of ever finding open land,
Or highway where the slow wheel pours the sand.

I do not see why I should e'er turn back,
Or those should not set forth upon my track
To overtake me, who should miss me here
And long to know if still I held them dear.

They would not find me changed from him they knew—
Only more sure of all I thought was true.

The first poem of a first collection provides a crucial opportunity to persuade potential readers to buy the book—or at least to turn the page. It also establishes some rules of engagement; more accurately, in this case, disengagement. By placing "Into My Own" at the start of *A Boy's Will*, Frost introduces himself to the world by turning his back on it. Perhaps recognizing a strategic error, his second thoughts were to prove more hospitable. Starting with his *Selected Poems* of 1923, and for all collected and complete editions, the poet welcomes his audience with "The Pasture," an eight-line poem which invites us into his work with the reassuring promise of a shared journey: "You come too." "The Pasture" had first been published as the introductory poem in Frost's second volume, *North of Boston* (1914). Using it as the gatekeeper for his various collected editions, Frost ensures that its appeal will counteract the less alluring tone of those poems from *A Boy's Will* which it is made to precede.

Another reason why Frost should have come to feel shy of "Into My Own" may be that he would not have wanted to head his collected editions with anything less than his best work. On that score, "Into My Own" fails to qualify. Even the first rhyme—"trees"/"breeze"—sets itself up to be mocked: "Where'er you find the cooling Western Breeze," wrote Alexander Pope in his *Essay on Criticism,* "In the next Line, it whispers thro' the Trees." Frost's couplets rhyme too predictably, with heavy end-stops accentuating the fact not only that "Trees" must rhyme with "breeze," but "gloom" with "doom." (The phrase "edge of doom" is taken from Shakespeare's Sonnet 116, as the tyro sonneteer pays homage to the Master.) To these qualms should be added that the expression is verbose and archaic: "I do not see why I should e'er turn back,/Or those should not set forth upon my track." But this is only to elaborate on the reasons why Frost would soon dismiss *A Boy's Will* (with the exception of "Mowing" and a handful of others) as markedly inferior to his later work. "Into My Own" merits attention because it broaches, for the first time, themes and metaphors which will be more subtly explored elsewhere.

Frost's authorial note in the table of contents described "Into My Own" as a poem in which "The youth is persuaded that he will be rather more than less himself for having forsworn the world." Having written "Into My Own" in 1909, aged thirty-five, he would have long since given up hope of being described as a "youth." Yet the poem's first-person voice, and the title's emphatic possessives, do suggest an autobiographical impulse. *A Boy's Will* is Frost's oblique portrait of the artist as a young man, with "Into My Own" representing what he is reported to have called "his first desire to escape from something, his fear of something" (Sergeant, 57).

Fear is one of Frost's great subjects. This poem's fear of fear is portrayed through the wish-fulfilling fantasy of the self-reliant individual's "Fearless" escape into the dark trees. Lost in the midst of a dark wood, Dante could rely on an emissary to guide him on his journey. Frost's speakers, by contrast, are typically isolated and must fall back on their own resources. The forswearing of human society with its associated fears, and the consequent journey into wilderness which is also an inner journey toward knowledge, are commonly replayed in Frost's work, comprising his own version of what Harold Bloom has called "the American religion": "What the American self has found . . . is its own freedom—from the world, from time, from other selves" (Bloom, 21). "Into My Own" foreshadows a later and greater poem like "Stopping by Woods on a Snowy Evening," in which "those dark trees" have become the "lovely, dark, and deep" woods of the poem's title, or "The Sound of the Trees," with its vague yet nagging desire to "set forth" (that phrase again) for "somewhere" and, in doing so, to "make the reckless choice." As Frost would argue in an essay from 1959 on Emerson: "Freedom is nothing but departure—setting forth—leaving things behind, brave origination of the courage to be new" (*CPr*, 203).

From the perspective of *A Boy's Will*, those poetic departures lie in the future. For now, escape remains safely hypothetical, expressed by "Into My Own" as nothing more than "One of my wishes"; and the sonnet's fourteen lines couch their assertions among five sturdy negatives (not to mention the hedging use of the conditional) as if to make emphatically clear that no action will be required. Even the "trees" / "breeze" rhyme functions to reverse usual expectations: the breeze, this time, "scarcely" ruffles the trees. This is stay-at-home poetry, poetry which does not seek disruption. The speaker remains as rooted as those "old and firm" trees. For all the rhetorical posturing, he does not really forswear the world or plan to "steal away." His argument cancels the need: he claims to know that if he were to make the journey, the truth of what he already believes would be proven. It would be a journey of confirmation, not discovery.

Ghost House

I dwell in a lonely house I know
That vanished many a summer ago,
    And left no trace but the cellar walls,
    And a cellar in which the daylight falls,
And the purple-stemmed wild raspberries grow.

O'er ruined fences the grape-vines shield
The woods come back to the mowing field;
    The orchard tree has grown one copse
    Of new wood and old where the woodpecker chops;
The footpath down to the well is healed.

I dwell with a strangely aching heart
In that vanished abode there far apart
    On that disused and forgotten road
    That has no dust-bath now for the toad.
Night comes; the black bats tumble and dart;

The whippoorwill is coming to shout
And hush and cluck and flutter about:
    I hear him begin far enough away
    Full many a time to say his say
Before he arrives to say it out.

It is under the small, dim, summer star,
I know not who these mute folks are
    Who share the unlit place with me—
    Those stones out under the low-limbed tree
Doubtless bear names that the mosses mar.

They are tireless folk, but slow and sad,
Though two, close-keeping, are lass and lad,—

With none among them that ever sings,
   And yet, in view of how many things,
As sweet companions as might be had.

"Into My Own" had fantasized about "steal[ing] away" from human company into the wilderness. "Ghost House" acts out that fantasy, but in unexpected ways. "He is happy in society of his choosing," Frost's authorial note informs the reader. That society is no society at all, consisting of birds, bats, and ghosts found among the ruins of a "lonely house."

Only the reference to the speaker's "strangely aching heart," and the suggestion of a transferred epithet in the phrase "lonely house," hint at any regret for a solitude otherwise presented as entirely desirable. Cleansed of the human stain, nature has reestablished its bounty with free-growing "purple-stemmed wild raspberries" and "grape-vines" which "shield" the ruined fences originally erected to protect and support them. Fields, once mown, have been reclaimed by woods, and a new copse has sprung up where once there was merely an "orchard tree." "The footpath down to the well is healed"—that is to say, the tracks left by man were a wound in the landscape which time has made good. Even those lingering monuments to man's presence, the gravestones "out under the low-limbed tree," are "Doubtless" being repossessed. Names have been "marred" by moss, their intention to memorialize frustrated, and yet that marring is viewed as a necessary redress and return. The poem's locus amoenus, set apart from the trappings of civilization, exposes the vanity of—as well as the temporary damage caused by—human wishes. Ghosts may linger, but their names will be lost. The "lass and lad" are no Adam and Eve, despite the paradisal connotations of the orchard tree; Eden can be Eden only in the absence of mankind. "The Ghost House," then, is an early example of what Randall Jarrell identified as one of Frost's perennial subjects: "the wiping-out of man, his replacement by the nature out of which he arose" (Jarrell 1952, 537).

Although the speaker's own situation is never made explicit, he is presumably a ghost like the "mute folk" who are his "sweet compan-ions." "I dwell in a lonely house I know," he begins, and the reason why "I know" is not redundant is that he can remember what the house was like before it "vanished many a summer ago." Literally a "ghost house" and not just because it is haunted, the house continues to exist in the present even after its physical disappearance. The motif of the vanished house will recur in Frost's work, from the "old cellar-hole in a by-road" which is the origin of the Stark family in "The Generations of Men," to the late masterpiece "Directive," with its "house that is no more a house." The image carries no consistent meaning from example to example, but it joins with the springs and flowers and walls and trees to create Frost's hinterland—a hinterland as distinctive as any in modern poetry.

Frost conceded that "You will find me [in *A Boy's Will*] using the traditional clichés" (Mertins, 187), not all of which "Ghost House" manages to avoid. There is something too studied about "dwell" (used twice—after all, a ghost can hardly be said to "live" in a house) and "O'er" and "abode," and phrases like "Full many a time" and "I know not." When Frost told Sidney Cox that "Words exist in the mouth not in books" (*SL*, 108), he was criticizing just this kind of lexis. Equally poetical is the "slow and sad" measure of the poem's four-beat lines; and the desire to shun the world of human interaction is couched in overly familiar terms. The polysyndeton of the first stanza ("And . . . And . . . And") brings to mind Yeats's "The Lake Isle of Innisfree," with its six uses of the conjunction in its first eight lines. Even though Frost worried that Yeats came "perilously near" to believing in fairies, he admired the older poet and considered him to be "the greatest talker" he had ever met (Francis, 78). Yeats is a major influence not just here but throughout *A Boy's Will:* the authorial notes sound like the titles of early Yeats poems.

"Ghost House" comes toward the start of a volume which traces Frost's gradual realization that he "liked people even when [he] believed [he] detested them" (*SL*, 158). Consequently, it cultivates deprivation and isolation rather than the complex tones of the speaking voice which characterize Frost's second book, *North of Boston*—a "book of people," as the dedication puts it. "Ghost House" conspicuously lacks people, offering instead an impoverished and dehumanized mindscape in which the poet's imagination self-denyingly squats: even the ghosts are "mute folk." "There came a day about ten years ago," Frost wrote in 1915, "when I made the discovery that though sequestered I wasnt [*sic*] living without reference to other people" (*SL*, 159). That discovery seems to have post-dated "Ghost House," a poem which willingly sequesters itself without any such reference. Only by learning to act on the instinct of that "aching heart"—an instinct sufficiently embattled by circumstance to seem "strange"—will Frost's poetry accommodate the people and the speech rhythms which make his great work memorable.

Rose Pogonias

A saturated meadow,
Sun-shaped and jewel-small,
A circle scarcely wider
Than the trees around were tall;
Where winds were quite excluded,
And the air was stifling sweet
With the breath of many flowers,—
A temple of the heat.

There we bowed us in the burning,
As the sun's right worship is,
To pick where none could miss them
A thousand orchises;
For though the grass was scattered,
Yet every second spear
Seemed tipped with wings of color,
That tinged the atmosphere.

We raised a simple prayer
Before we left the spot,
That in the general mowing
That place might be forgot;
Or if not all so favored,
Obtain such grace of hours,
That none should mow the grass there
While so confused with flowers.

Orchises seem to be Frost's flowers of choice, occurring here and in "Mowing," "The Self-Seeker," and "The Quest of the Purple-Fringed." This particular species, the rose pogonia, is native to North America, and as such it begins Frost's treatment of New World subjects unburdened by the weight of the European literary tradition. (The oven bird in the poem of that title and the frogs of "Hyla Brook" provide prominent later examples.) But problems of ownership and entitlement preoccupy the poem, because just as the speaker picks startling quantities of flowers the rights to which remain unclear, so the poet's claim to his subject is haunted by prior claims. Of Frost's "Mowing"—a sonnet which appears seven poems later in *A Boy's Will*—John Hollander has doubted whether "even a specific moment of actual mowing [can] escape the shadow of metaphor" (Hollander 1997a, 11). This is what Frost called "the pleasure of ulteriority" (*CPr*, 147), but it may not be *only* or *always* a pleasure that (for example) mowing brings Death the Mower to mind. "Rose Pogonias," similarly, must recognize precedence even as it attempts to stake out its own virgin territory. Frost acknowledged as much in his argument that "a poem is best read in the light of all the other poems ever written" (*CPr*, 174).

Such a tall order implies that any reading of a given poem must remain necessarily incomplete and open to revision; and yet "Rose Pogonias," like "Mowing" after it, is less the victim of boundless ulteriority than the exploiter of particular metaphoric traditions for its own enrichment. At first, the terrain colonized by the poem seems intimate and self-sufficient—"Sun-shaped and jewel-small"—but before long the circumscribed atmosphere becomes "stifling" as the flowers prove to be too much of a good thing. For all that it rhymes, this "heat" is anything but "sweet." Frank Lentricchia has argued that the poem's description of enclosed space is "also a figuration for a psychological 'place,' for a mental enclosure that frees the poet from the penetrations of dangerous psychic experience" (Lentricchia, 34). However, this overlooks the suffocating nature of the "enclosure," and does not account for what is, amid the larger context of *A Boy's Will*, the surprising presence of a companion or companions. For once, human society does not seem to have been entirely forsworn: "we" appears three times, emphasizing that "worship" at the "temple" is on this occasion at odds with the volume's inclination toward solitude. Where Lentricchia finds in the clearing's figuration a mental enclosure, others have been convinced—by references to the "saturated meadow," the sweetly stifling atmosphere, the burning, and the worship—that the poem is an allegory of sexuality, its landscape a disguised bodyscape. That would also explain the poem's use of the first-person plural.

Even so, such figurative readings are compelling only inasmuch as they draw support from the poem's literal meanings. Although Frost defined ulteriority as "saying one thing and meaning another, saying one thing in terms of another" (*CPr*, 147), it is better to think of it as a way of meaning two things at once, or of saying one thing in terms of another thing which is also said. Whatever else may concern it, "Rose Pogonias" is a poem concerned with picking rose pogonias. That sense of entitlement to the flowers informs the ulterior meaning: "Rose Pogonias" makes literal—except that nothing in Frost's work is ever *wholly* literal—Montaigne's humble admission that in his essays he had "gathered a posie of other men's flowers, and nothing but the thread which binds them is [his] own." (Behind that metaphor lies the word "anthology," derived from the Greek for "flower-gathering"; and to direct the reader toward this ulterior meaning in which flowers are emblems of art, the previous poem in *A Boy's Will* happens to be titled "Flower-Gathering.") Frost's speaker claims those flowers as his inalienable right. The orchids may stifle him with their sweetness and their number, making it impossible to remain in such a rarefied atmosphere for long, but he feels able to remove them from the temple for his own purposes. Ironically, even his justification for this desecration, that he picks flowers only "where none could miss them" (with its potential to mean either that they will be missed or that they will not), borrows from Thomas Gray's "Elegy in a Country Churchyard": "Full many a flower is born to blush unseen."

Hollander's point about the inescapable presence of death in poems of mowing is especially pertinent to the final stanza, in which the "general mowing" evokes Death as Mower and Leveler. All flesh is grass; so the mowing of the grass offers a figure for the way of all flesh. The prayer that the "place might be forgot" is therefore (paradoxically) a prayer that the place should survive oblivion, or "if not all so favored," at least survive for a time. Flowers, by a quirk of rhyme, have a tendency to last or to be enjoyed for "hours" rather than days and months. Richard Poirier quotes Henry Vaughan's "The Retreat" ("When on some gilded cloud or flower / My gazing soul would dwell an hour, / And in those weaker glories spy / Some shadows of eternitie") (Poirier, 208–209), and probably more familiar to Frost would have been Marvell's "The Garden": "How could such sweet and wholesome hours / Be reckoned but with herbs and flowers!" Frost uses "sweet" as well as that clinching rhyme "hours" / "flowers"; and Marvell's phrase "Ensnared with flowers," earlier in the poem, may be echoed in Frost's phrase "confused with flowers."

But "confused" encourages its own confusion, as befits a poem so thoroughly anxious about ownership rights. Is the grass "so confused with flowers," or is it rather those anonymous potential mowers who are confused? The grammar does not clarify. And does "so confused" mean "as confused as the poem's speaker," thereby introducing a note of self-criticism? The poem also draws on the various meanings of "confuse": to mix together, to overthrow, to cause mental perplexity. Giving none priority, Frost ensures that each reading speaks differently to the relationship between poetic tradition and the modern poet, and between the brevity of human life and the longevity of art. As he told John Cournos, in reply to those skeptics who did not believe that speech tones could "survive long on paper": "They'll probably last as long as the finer meanings of words. And if they don't last more than a few hundred years that will be long enough for me—much longer than I can hope to be read" (*SL*, 130).

Mowing

There was never a sound beside the wood but one,
And that was my long scythe whispering to the ground.
What was it it whispered? I knew not well myself;
Perhaps it was something about the heat of the sun,
Something, perhaps, about the lack of sound—
And that was why it whispered and did not speak.
It was no dream of the gift of idle hours,
Or easy gold at the hand of fay or elf:
Anything more than the truth would have seemed too weak
To the earnest love that laid the swale in rows,
Not without feeble-pointed spikes of flowers
(Pale orchises), and scared a bright green snake.
The fact is the sweetest dream that labor knows.
My long scythe whispered and left the hay to make.

"Mowing" is, by its author's and by common consent, the most impres-
sive poem in *A Boy's Will* (*SL*, 141). It is also the most enigmatic. Frost
wrote "Mowing" in or around 1900 and later called it his first "talk song"
(Poirier, 34). In that respect it would not look out of place in *North of
Boston*. What it talks about is a whisper (derivatives of which appear
four times: "whispering," "whispered," "whispered," "whispered").
That whisper can never be properly overheard or understood even by
the poet himself. Frost's delight in the poet's gift for saying one thing
and meaning another is here allegorized, albeit with little confidence in
the poet's ability to control the ulterior meaning. His "labor" creates a
whisper which proves enigmatic; he is both the originator of it and the
first audience for its mystery.

   "There was never a sound beside the wood but one": "never" is
absolutist, signaling that the landscape of "Mowing" is not real but lit-
erary and imaginary. The sounds of nature—the singing of birds, the

wind in the trees—are nowhere to be heard, a point stressed in line five's "lack of sound." Only the instrument of the poet's solitary work breaks the silence, making a whisper the meaning of which he can merely guess at: "Perhaps . . . perhaps." But his guesses, which assume "more than the truth" in thinking that the scythe is capable of whispering anything humanly meaningful, may be revealing. Like "Into My Own," "Mowing" is a sonnet which broadcasts an allusion to Shakespeare: "the heat of the sun" recalls "Fear no more the heat o'the sun," the death song of *Cymbeline;* and together with the familiar connotations of mowing and scythes, the allusion encourages the impression of a poem much possessed with death. As the *Book of Common Prayer* puts it, "Man that is born of woman hath but a short time to live and is full of misery. He cometh up and is cut down, like a flower." "Death thou art a Mower too," ends Andrew Marvell's "Damon the Mower" (a poem which has in common with Frost's "Mowing" the scythes, the sun's heat, snakes, and hay). "Mowing," the authorial note tells us, "takes up life simply with the small tasks," but the poem itself is anything but simple. It cannot escape ulteriority, and that ulterior meaning is insisted on by the weight of religious and poetic tradition.

"Mowing" also encourages readers to think about love: the poem refers to "the earnest love that laid the swale in rows." Jay Parini's claim that mowing equals lovemaking (Parini, 77–79) may at first glance seem far-fetched, yet it finds support from a traditional folk song called "The Mower," which makes exactly that erotic parallel. There is supporting textual evidence in Frost's poem, too. For a landscape so literary as to be filled with poetic allusions, the reference to "Pale orchises" seems suspiciously precise, and with good reason: etymologically, "orchis" is derived from the Greek for "testicle." That, in turn, makes the reader wonder about those phallic "spikes of flowers." The "bright green snake," a fitting creature for a poem of such whispering sibilance, is an escapee from Coleridge's "Christabel," where it had appeared in a dream wrapped round an innocent white dove; it had symbolized the threat to innocence posed by sexual temptation.

So by taking mowing as his ostensible subject, Frost invites and encourages interpretations which center on those staple constituents of ulterior meaning, Eros and Thanatos. Yet to claim that "Mowing" is *about* sexual desire, or about death, or even about sex and death together, is to diminish the poem's achievement. Rather than provide the simple answers—the "easy gold"—Frost explores the *process* by which ulteriority is created, and tries consciously to raise to the surface what must remain concealed even from himself. As he admitted late in life: "A poet builds better than he knows" (Richardson 2001, 214). His protagonist's concern is with "the truth" and "the fact" of the mowing: "Anything more than the truth would have seemed too weak." Those who come in the aftermath will be rewarded. Normally, the poet himself is the "maker," harking back to the archaic term still current (as "makar") in the Scottish homeland of Frost's mother. But he leaves "the hay to make" for others. They are the readers who will enjoy the rewards, making hay figuratively and literally with the product of the poet's labor.

The Trial by Existence

Even the bravest that are slain
    Shall not dissemble their surprise
On waking to find valor reign,
    Even as on earth, in paradise;
And where they sought without the sword
    Wide fields of asphodel fore'er,
To find that the utmost reward
    Of daring should be still to dare.

The light of heaven falls whole and white
    And is not shattered into dyes,
The light for ever is morning light;
    The hills are verdured pasture-wise;
The angel hosts with freshness go,
    And seek with laughter what to brave;—
And binding all is the hushed snow
    Of the far-distant breaking wave.

And from a cliff-top is proclaimed
    The gathering of the souls for birth,
The trial by existence named,
    The obscuration upon earth.
And the slant spirits trooping by
    In streams and cross- and counter-streams
Can but give ear to that sweet cry
    For its suggestion of what dreams!

And the more loitering are turned
    To view once more the sacrifice
Of those who for some good discerned
    Will gladly give up paradise.
And a white shimmering concourse rolls

Toward the throne to witness there
The speeding of devoted souls
    Which God makes his especial care.

And none are taken but who will,
    Having first heard the life read out
That opens earthward, good and ill,
    Beyond the shadow of a doubt;
And very beautifully God limns,
    And tenderly, life's little dream,
But naught extenuates or dims,
    Setting the thing that is supreme.

Nor is there wanting in the press
    Some spirit to stand simply forth,
Heroic in its nakedness,
    Against the uttermost of earth.
The tale of earth's unhonored things
    Sounds nobler there than 'neath the sun;
And the mind whirls and the heart sings,
    And a shout greets the daring one.

But always God speaks at the end:
    "One thought in agony of strife
The bravest would have by for friend,
    The memory that he chose the life;
But the pure fate to which you go
    Admits no memory of choice,
Or the woe were not earthly woe
    To which you give the assenting voice."

And so the choice must be again,
    But the last choice is still the same;
And the awe passes wonder then,

And a hush falls for all acclaim.
And God has taken a flower of gold
    And broken it, and used therefrom
The mystic link to bind and hold
    Spirit to matter till death come.

'Tis of the essence of life here,
    Though we choose greatly, still to lack
The lasting memory at all clear,
    That life has for us on the wrack
Nothing but what we somehow chose;
    Thus are we wholly stripped of pride
In the pain that has but one close,
    Bearing it crushed and mystified.

Frost's best poetry, Randall Jarrell has argued, is "at once wonderfully different and wonderfully alike" (Jarrell 1952, 535). Initially, the peculiarities of "The Trial by Existence" appear more striking than any familial resemblances to the rest of Frost's work. A poet's first collection will often contain false starts and roads never subsequently taken. Certainly, there is nothing quite like "The Trial by Existence" anywhere else in Frost's writing career. Yet the poem broaches a subject—the responsibility of individuals for their own actions—which will concern him for the rest of his life.

"The Trial by Existence" is, like much of Frost's poetry, sustained by a classical source, in this case Plato's *Republic*. "Pity some would say to think a thing out," Frost would write several decades later, "only to find that Plato or St. Thomas had thought it out before" (*N*, 465). Plato "thought out" the source for "The Trial by Existence" in his myth of Er at the end of *Republic*, his purpose being to illustrate the existence of free will, the advantages of leading a moral life, and the rewards and punishments of the afterlife. Frost would also have been familiar with Wordsworth's "Immortality Ode," in which preexistence is given its most famous poetic expression. Wordsworth subsequently argued that the doctrine remained "far too shadowy a notion to be recommended to faith." Frost appears to have felt a similar anxiety about his subject, which his authorial note described as the protagonist's attempt "to know definitely what he thinks about the soul." An apparent cooling in relations with his teaching colleagues at Pinkerton Academy, immediately after his "poem about the heretofore" had appeared, was first (and, Frost soon discovered, wrongly) put down to the likelihood that "The Trial by Existence" had "led them to question [his] orthodoxy." But the poem mimics its source in *Republic* so closely as to seem like an act more of translation than of faith. Although a knowledge of Frost's source dispels some of the poem's strangeness, it also draws particular attention to the significance of his additions, changes, and omissions.

"The Trial by Existence" begins with those who have died on the battlefield: "the bravest that are slain." The reference is to Plato's Er, a "brave" soldier killed in battle who, miraculously, came back to life twelve days later. What Er witnessed in that intervening period becomes, with significant variations, the eschatology of Frost's poem. Er sees the dead judged according to their merits and, consequently, sent on a route either up through the sky or down into the earth. He also sees others returning to begin the cycle once more, after their thousand-year journey of delight or pain. Having taken turns to choose the lives available, they pass through the Plain of Oblivion and drink from the River of Neglect. They are then ready to be reincarnated.

Frost follows his source both in its broad outline and in several of its details. The fields of asphodel are found in Homer and various other classical texts (Plato happens to be less botanically specific), but Frost's description of the bright morning light of heaven is directly inspired by Er's account of "a straight shaft of light stretching from on high through the heavens and the earth; the light was like a pillar, and it was just like a rainbow in colour, except that it was brighter and clearer" (Plato, 374). Similarly, the spirit which "stand[s] simply forth, / Heroic in its nakedness," and which is attracted by "The tale of earth's unhonored things," seems to shadow Er's description of the soul of Odysseus. According to

Er, Odysseus is the last to choose a new life, and remembering all the hardship his heroism and ambition had brought him previously, he seeks out an unhonored destiny as a "non-political private citizen" (Plato, 378). It is even possible that the choice of verbs in the otherwise weak line, "And the mind whirls and the heart sings," is punningly prompted by merging the "whorls" seen by Er on the "spindle of Necessity" and the song of the Sirens which is heard as the spindle turns.

Despite these connections, Frost has lightly disguised his source by declassicizing much of the poem. The names of the various protagonists have been removed, along with the spindle and the Sirens, and Necessity has been replaced by God and angels. But the biggest changes occur in relation to the poem's key themes: memory and choice. Whereas Plato makes little fuss about the obliviousness of the living to their former existences, for Frost it becomes the dominant motif—so much so that God is ushered in to deliver a grim speech on the topic. Already the poem's third stanza had referred, with regular iambic emphasis, to "The obscuration upon earth"; but God's more substantial intervention seems chiefly designed to upset those who are about to be reborn. His reference to "agony of strife"—which, fittingly for this context, is made to rhyme with "life"—suggests a view of existence far bleaker than anything in Plato, for whom happiness remains attainable if the right choices are made. (Another of Frost's crucial rhymes is "sacrifice"/"paradise," as the usual religious intimations of "sacrifice" are inverted: sacrifice becomes the giving up of paradise, not the means by which to achieve it.) Plato's long accounts of hellish penalties for the wicked after death disappear from Frost's poem, only to reemerge as the indiscriminate pains of life itself. Memory may be the sole quality capable of easing the burden, yet it is denied to the sufferers of "earthly woe." In case that divine message should be missed, the voice of the poet concludes by repeating the argument, that in the midst of our human pain we lack a "lasting memory" of having chosen it ourselves.

Plato lingers over the ability of souls to choose different kinds of life. In Frost's poem the choosing of life itself causes the inevitable suffering. We "somehow chose": that puzzled "somehow" indicates Frost's problems with free will and responsibility. It is as if the poem wants to make us responsible for our actions—each of us chose our life—but offers no way in which our choice could have been different. We are "crushed" by the pain which we are supposed to have chosen, and lack the consolation of remembering that we chose. Frost's final word—"mystified"—is the cruelest cut of all, because it hints at a solace only to deny it. This is no spiritual mystification, but merely another allusion to human ignorance. The poem's cold comfort is that, by recounting what we cannot remember, it reveals our ignorance to us.

The Tuft of Flowers

I went to turn the grass once after one
Who mowed it in the dew before the sun.

The dew was gone that made his blade so keen
Before I came to view the leveled scene.

I looked for him behind an isle of trees;
I listened for his whetstone on the breeze.

But he had gone his way, the grass all mown,
And I must be, as he had been,—alone,

"As all must be," I said within my heart,
"Whether they work together or apart."

But as I said it, swift there passed me by
On noiseless wing a 'wildered butterfly,

Seeking with memories grown dim o'er night
Some resting flower of yesterday's delight.

And once I marked his flight go round and round,
As where some flower lay withering on the ground.

And then he flew as far as eye could see,
And then on tremulous wing came back to me.

I thought of questions that have no reply,
And would have turned to toss the grass to dry;

But he turned first, and led my eye to look
At a tall tuft of flowers beside a brook,

A leaping tongue of bloom the scythe had spared
Beside a reedy brook the scythe had bared.

I left my place to know them by their name,
Finding them butterfly weed when I came.

The mower in the dew had loved them thus,
By leaving them to flourish, not for us,

Nor yet to draw one thought of ours to him,
But from sheer morning gladness at the brim.

The butterfly and I had lit upon,
Nevertheless, a message from the dawn,

That made me hear the wakening birds around,
And hear his long scythe whispering to the ground,

And feel a spirit kindred to my own;
So that henceforth I worked no more alone;

But glad with him, I worked as with his aid,
And weary, sought at noon with him the shade;

And dreaming, as it were, held brotherly speech
With one whose thought I had not hoped to reach.

"Men work together," I told him from the heart,
"Whether they work together or apart."

"The Tuft of Flowers" is among Frost's earliest poems, having been written before 1897. It marks a culmination in the development of *A Boy's Will*. Frost pointed out that in the opening poem, "Into My Own," he "went away from people (and college)," and in "The Tuft of Flowers" he "came back to them" (*SL*, 66). This risks making the order of the poems sound unduly neat and programmatic, not least because "Into My Own" is voiced for a persona who only fantasizes about escape. Nevertheless, after so many poems of isolation—not to say loneliness—"The Tuft of Flowers" is singled out as constituting a return to human society. That return had earlier been promised but not achieved. "If tired of trees I seek again mankind," "The Vantage Point" had begun promisingly, only for the search to amount to a few hours spent lying on a slope to watch in the distance the homes of men and the graveyard behind them. By the end of that sonnet, Frost's persona has turned his attention back to the flowers and the ants.

Only by comparison with that hint of misanthropy does "The Tuft of Flowers" qualify as a sociable poem, but at least it looks for connections with humankind where previously in the volume solitude had often been preferred. According to the authorial note, Frost's persona resolves to consider his views on "fellowship." The poem carries out this exploration by offering itself as a sequel or reply to "Mowing" (which, despite having been written much later, appears earlier in *A Boy's Will*). The link is established by a shared line. "And hear his long scythe whispering to the ground" recalls and almost recapitulates the second line of "Mowing": "And that was my long scythe whispering to the ground." And while "Mowing" ends by leaving "the hay to make," "The Tuft of Flowers" begins that process of making with the intention to "toss the grass to dry." Engaged so closely with its precursor, "The Tuft of Flowers" is primarily a meditation on the nature of subsequence. How ought the work of the past to be read and appreciated? What relationship can be established across time and across generations? These may look suspiciously like "questions that have no reply"; but the poem enacts an answer because it represents art as created out of an endeavor which consciously draws strength from its predecessors.

At its simplest, "The Tuft of Flowers" maps a reversal of understanding. Initially, the emphasis falls on the laborer's essential solitude: whether they work in company or not, people work "alone." This bleak philosophy is overtaken by events, allowing the poem to clinch (or at least, to propose) a far more positive conclusion: "'Men work together,' . . . 'Whether they work together or apart.'" Such a reversal, and in such a short space, dodges accusations of sentimentality because it relies on a profound insight into the nature of tradition, and in particular, poetic tradition: toward the end of his life, Frost admitted that this poem contained a "definition of poetry" (*CPr*, 214). Sociability no longer requires the spending of time in physical proximity with others. Contemporaries, in fact, hardly matter; and in that respect butterflies and flowers seem to be preferred to men. It is the sense of a shared enterprise, carrying on the job begun by predecessors, which provides consolation and inspiration to the solitary worker.

The mower is first depicted as absent and untrackable, having "gone his way" indifferent to successors: he had left the tuft of flowers to flourish "not for us, // Nor yet to draw one thought of ours to him. / But from sheer morning gladness at the brim." The effect of his actions, however, is very different, because although the mower is considered to have made no attempt to communicate by means of the flowers, they serve as "a message from the dawn" bringing news of him. (Frost makes a similar point in his essay "The Constant Symbol": "A poem is the emotion of having a thought while the reader waits a little anxiously for the success of dawn" (*CPr*, 149).) As a consequence, the "one whose thought I had not hoped to reach" can now be addressed in "brotherly speech" and treated as "a spirit kindred to my own" who "aid[s]" the successor's work. This benign pretense is Frost's gift to his audience. His first-person voice had made him seem a mere continuator, but by calling his poem "The Tuft of Flowers," he also becomes its vanished maker, leaving this "leaping tongue of bloom" for his readers to do with as they choose.

Reluctance

Out through the fields and the woods
    And over the walls I have wended;
I have climbed the hills of view
    And looked at the world, and descended;
I have come by the highway home,
    And lo, it is ended.

The leaves are all dead on the ground,
    Save those that the oak is keeping
To ravel them one by one
    And let them go scraping and creeping
Out over the crusted snow,
    When others are sleeping.

And the dead leaves lie huddled and still,
    No longer blown hither and thither;
The last lone aster is gone;
    The flowers of the wich-hazel wither;
The heart is still aching to seek,
    But the feet question "Whither?"

Ah, when to the heart of man
    Was it ever less than a treason
To go with the drift of things,
    To yield with a grace to reason,
And bow and accept the end
    Of a love or a season?

This, the final poem of *A Boy's Will*, remained one of Frost's favorites, although he was quick to concede that it could hardly be said to herald "a new force in literature" (*SL*, 47). "Reluctance" marks the end of a book and a journey. *A Boy's Will* had begun with a poem fantasizing about escape into the vastness of "those dark trees." "Reluctance" seems to remember such an escape having taken place—"Out through the fields and the woods / And over the walls I have wended." But whereas the speaker of "Into My Own" had seen no reason why he "should e'er turn back," the circle of departure and return now looks to be completed after all: "I have come by the highway home, / And lo, it is ended."

Ended in one sense, because the book is now finished, but the poem itself finds no satisfactory resolution. As a character from a later poem, "In the Home Stretch," puts it: "End is a gloomy word." Accordingly, Frost's decision to conclude *A Boy's Will* with a wintry admission of failure (failure of the poet and his protagonist alike) is offset by the poem's refusal to "accept the end," and its desire for another beginning. Glancing back over the imaginative terrain crossed by *A Boy's Will*, "Reluctance" also looks forward to new prospects which the "heart is still aching to seek." (The heart is a hardworking organ in Frost's early poetry: "Ghost House" had also referred to a "strangely aching heart.") This contains the promise of Frost's second book, *North of Boston*, which will follow the same pattern of departure (its opening poem, "The Pasture") and return (its last, "Good Hours").

Not merely because each of its last two stanzas culminates in a question, "Reluctance" is a fundamentally perplexed poem. The aching heart which encourages further journeyings does not tell the feet (with a familiar play on poetic feet) which direction they should travel or what their destination should be. After all, the landscape, with its dead leaves, "crusted snow" and withering flowers, mocks poetic inspiration and confirms poetic failure, so that those "others" who "are sleeping" may prove to be acting more sensibly. And regret is perfectly expressed in the rhythm's dying fall created from the alternation of masculine endings ("woods," "view," "home," and so on) and feminine rhymes ("wended"/"descended"/"ended"—words which themselves trace a revealing trajectory).

Nevertheless, reluctance to "accept the end" grows into resistance. The landscape, at once "dead" and abrasive ("scraping"), demands rebuttal, and although that rebuttal arrives in the form of a question, the question is so loaded as to seem rhetorical:

> Ah, when to the heart of man
>   Was it ever less than a treason
> To go with the drift of things,
>   To yield with a grace to reason,
> And bow and accept the end
>   Of a love or a season?

"Ah" is the knowing expression of one who trumps a limited with a superior wisdom. To "go with the drift of things" may be the reasonable option, but its quietism offends the heart's instinct: "reason," after all, rhymes with (and is the large part of) "treason." Frost would later observe that he would never have committed himself "to the treason-reason-season rhyme-set . . . if [he] had been blasé enough to know that these three words about exhausted the possibilities" (*CPr*, 151); and, in fact, the inevitable rhyme with "season" does cause difficulties. Refusing to accept "the end/Of a love" is a different matter altogether from refusing to accept the end of "a season." The parallel drawn between the human heart and the cycles of the natural world only risks encouraging a new fatalism.

Frost once proposed that in "Reluctance," as in "The Tuft of Flowers," he had explored his "position . . . between socialism and individualism" (Parini, 240). That imposes on the poem a political dimension which the text nowhere justifies. Better to replace those binaries with others like "solitude" and "society," because the desire to leave behind the world of men and the gradual return to it are the volume's most prominent themes. But "Reluctance" is a strange augury of Frost's later achievement, because the continuing attractions of a peripatetic solitude run counter to the inspiration which his poetry will learn to find at home and among people. There can be few, if any, more important words in *North of Boston* than "home." The next phase of Frost's work, "Reluctance" does not yet seem to realize, lives most fully in the very place which the speaker of *A Boy's Will* commonly desires to evade.

NORTH OF BOSTON

"I T IS SUCCESS ENOUGH," Frost argued, "if your first book does well enough to get you a publisher for the second" (*SL*, 98). Proving keen to continue the relationship with its author, David Nutt and Company published *North of Boston* for a British market in 1914; the volume was distributed in the United States courtesy of Holt, which brought out the first American edition the following year. Reviews were almost entirely laudatory, with Frost's new friend Edward Thomas celebrating "one of the most revolutionary books of modern times" (Spencer, 16) and Ford Madox Ford finding Frost's poetry "superior even to that of Whitman" (Walsh, 172). Frost was confident of his achievement, calling *North of Boston* "epoch making" (*SL*, 151). Still considered by many readers to be Frost's masterpiece, it contains some of the best, certainly best-loved, poems of the twentieth century: "Mending Wall," "The Death of the Hired Man," "Home Burial," "A Servant to Servants," "After Apple-Picking," "The Wood-Pile."

Late in life, Frost recalled that *North of Boston* had been written neither "as a book nor towards a book." Rather, "it gathered itself together in retrospect" (*CPr*, 196). That account gives a slightly misleading impression of a volume which, having been carefully crafted from an early stage, rewards being read in its entirety. Several of its poems date from 1905 or 1906, but most were written (or, at least, finished) in England after Frost had secured a contract for *A Boy's Will*. Deciding to overlook poems like "The Death of the Hired Man" as unsuited to the lyric autobiography of that first book, Frost already had in mind a further volume, his working titles revealing a unity of purpose: *Farm Servants and Other People; New England Eclogues; New Englanders; New England Hill Folk.* The eventual title was taken from newspaper advertisements for property located "north of Boston" (Thompson 1966, 434). If that suggested a rural simplicity beyond the immediate circles of urban erudition, the poems themselves were anything but unlearned. *North of Boston* represents Frost's attempt "to Anglicize Virgil's versification, dactylic hexameter" (*CPr*, 196). These New England pastorals offer more than an updating of Virgil's eclogues; nevertheless, *North of Boston* remains the book in which Frost's classical learning is most consistently felt.

That the volume has been painstakingly ordered is apparent from the outset. The italics of the first and last poems set them apart as preface and afterword, and draw attention to the same pattern of departure and return which was followed in *A Boy's Will*. The importance of inner and outer space is stressed via recurring motifs of doors and windows, and the poems chart a seasonal progression from spring ("The Pasture," "Mending Wall"), through fall ("After Apple-Picking"), to winter ("The Wood-Pile," "Good Hours"). Still more conspicuous is Frost's use of what he called "a language absolutely unliterary," born out of his ambition not to use any phrase which he had not himself heard in "running speech" (*SL*, 102). The auditory drama of the poems comes from Frost's ability to bring into strained relation the irregular rhythms of the spoken voice—in all its incoherence, garrulity, and sporadic eloquence—and the regular meter of blank verse. This is why *North of Boston* exemplifies the "hearing imagination" which Frost valued even above the "seeing imagination" (though, he added, as if keen not to tempt fate, "I should not want to be without the latter"; *SL*, 130).

The Pasture

I'm going out to clean the pasture spring;
I'll only stop to rake the leaves away
(And wait to watch the water clear, I may):
I sha'n't be gone long.—You come too.

I'm going out to fetch the little calf
That's standing by the mother. It's so young,
It totters when she licks it with her tongue.
I sha'n't be gone long.—You come too.

First published in italic font as the introductory poem of *North of Boston,* "The Pasture" was subsequently recruited as prologue to Frost's 1923 *Selected Poems* and all later selected and collected editions. Without its parentheses, the third line became the epigraph to Frost's final volume, *In the Clearing* (1962), thereby drawing attention to the poem's continued relevance across his long writing career.

"The Pasture" is, on the face of it, a beguiling invitation to accompany the poet on an excursion into the landscape of his work. The journey will not take long, and the soothing vowel-music of the repeated phrase "You come too" promises an undemanding experience. Frost represents his poetry as something natural, familiar, and wholesome: like farming, it works the land and keeps in touch with the seasonal cycles of birth (the young calf) and death (the fallen leaves).

Yet "The Pasture" is much more complex than may at first be apparent. Although Frost would later reveal that the model for *North of Boston* had been Virgil's *Eclogues* (*CPP&P*, 849), "The Pasture" already advertises a poetry steeped in classical education. Just as Greek antiquity associated the Muses with springs, so Frost locates and tends the pastoral source of his poetic inspiration in his own "pasture spring." The presence of the calf is another nod to Virgil, whose *Eclogues* are otherwise known as the *Bucolics*—from the Greek for "on care of cattle."

The poem's two stanzas are therefore linked by their repetitions and by their attachment to an ancient pastoral tradition signaled even by the title. Yet "You come too" is more than mere insistence; the phrase is repeated because it invites two different audiences, each with its own expectations. A poet's activities, like a farmer's, may be many and varied. The first stanza emphasizes cleaning and clarifying, the second nurturing. The first is studied, the second sentimental—to the point of tweeness—in the redundant phrase "licks it *with her tongue*" (my italics). Frost appeals to the sophisticated and the naïve alike, writing for "all sorts and kinds" (*SL,* 98). The task is to reassure potential readers with the promise that his is a poetry for them.

Although "The Pasture" is now rarely considered in its original context as the opening poem of *North of Boston,* its motifs are particular to that volume in one further respect: the movement from inside to out ("I'm going out") prefigures a group of poems concerned with the interplay of open and enclosed spaces, with windows and doorways, with walls built and breached, and with barriers between people. Those on the inside look out; those on the outside look in. The opening of doors and crossing of thresholds, as obliquely registered in "The Pasture," is common throughout *North of Boston.*

"The Pasture" is also a fitting introduction to Frost's work more generally, because it conveys his ambition to bring very dissimilar audiences with him. But that desire for inclusivity is challenged by the poem's stanza break. "I think that's two poems, don't you?" he asked in 1959, having just read "The Pasture" in a public lecture. The question that his poetry (and its reception) constantly poses is whether there may be a style capable of reconciling those audiences without the need to address them separately.

Mending Wall

Something there is that doesn't love a wall,
That sends the frozen-ground-swell under it,
And spills the upper boulders in the sun;
And makes gaps even two can pass abreast.
The work of hunters is another thing:
I have come after them and made repair
Where they have left not one stone on stone,
But they would have the rabbit out of hiding,
To please the yelping dogs. The gaps I mean,
No one has seen them made or heard them made,
But at spring mending-time we find them there.
I let my neighbor know beyond the hill;
And on a day we meet to walk the line
And set the wall between us once again.
We keep the wall between us as we go.
To each the boulders that have fallen to each.
And some are loaves and some so nearly balls
We have to use a spell to make them balance:
"Stay where you are until our backs are turned!"
We wear our fingers rough with handling them.
Oh, just another kind of out-door game,
One on a side. It comes to little more:
There where it is we do not need the wall:
He is all pine and I am apple orchard.
My apple trees will never get across
And eat the cones under his pines, I tell him.
He only says, "Good fences make good neighbors."
Spring is the mischief in me, and I wonder
If I could put a notion in his head:
"*Why* do they make good neighbors? Isn't it
Where there are cows? But here there are no cows.
Before I built a wall I'd ask to know

What I was walling in or walling out,
And to whom I was like to give offense.
Something there is that doesn't love a wall,
That wants it down." I could say "Elves" to him,
But it's not elves exactly, and I'd rather
He said it for himself. I see him there
Bringing a stone grasped firmly by the top
In each hand, like an old-stone savage armed.
He moves in darkness as it seems to me,
Not of woods only and the shade of trees.
He will not go behind his father's saying,
And he likes having thought of it so well
He says again, "Good fences make good neighbors."

One of the most loved and anthologized of Frost's poems, "Mending Wall" was written in England probably during the latter half of 1913. It has enjoyed an extensive critical afterlife. Read by the octogenarian poet in his 1962 visit to Soviet Russia, it seemed like an appropriate critique of the Berlin Wall: "Before I built a wall I'd ask to know / What I was walling in or walling out, / And to whom I was like to give offense." The poem also lends itself to debates about nationhood and internationalism, selfhood, neighborliness, the rituals of labor, the interactions between man and nature, and any number of related subjects which, according to context, can seem equally possible and equally partial. But allegorical readings ought not to overwhelm the poem's precisely physical descriptions. "Mending Wall" (a title so unfussily functional that it refuses even to stretch to an indefinite article) also happens to be about mending a wall.

The challenge of reading "Mending Wall" afresh, without the encumbrance of prior interpretations, is complicated by the fact that even the poem's first audience enjoyed no such luxury. "Mending Wall" is the only poem in *North of Boston* to be prefaced by an authorial note:

"*Mending Wall* takes up the theme where *A Tuft of Flowers* [*sic*] in *A Boy's Will* laid it down." Frost had previously characterized "The Tuft of Flowers" as a poem "about fellowship," but there are also other connections. The metaphors of taking up and laying down reinforce the sense of continuity from poem to poem and from Frost's first book to his second—the laying down of mown grass in one poem, and the picking up of fallen stones in the next. "The Tuft of Flowers" had developed a laborer's new understanding of community, as he renounced his initial belief that men work alone "Whether they work together or apart" and came to trust that, whether in company or apart, "Men work together." Similar paradoxes are at play in "Mending Wall," where men work together in order to maintain the wall which keeps them apart, and where the construction of a wall may be anything but constructive.

The poem is framed by two aphorisms: "Something there is that doesn't love a wall" occurs twice, and is thought and spoken by the poem's first-person voice; "Good fences make good neighbors," spoken by the neighbor who lives "beyond the hill," also occurs twice. Each man uses his aphorism combatively, as a retort to the other; neither acknowledges that both may be simultaneously true. Frost's classical education would have taught him that the word "aphorism" has its roots in the Greek for "boundary." As the men mend their own boundary, each uses aphorisms to fight off or even colonize his neighbor: "Spring is the mischief in me, and I wonder / If I could put a notion in his head." Small wonder that the barely repressed antagonism comes out in metaphor, as the neighbor is compared (in an example of transference) to "an old-stone savage armed." It is hard to find much sign of "fellowship" there.

The rivalry may have its origins in Frost's acknowledged source throughout *North of Boston:* Virgil's *Eclogues.* Robert Faggen has stated that "Mending Wall" reanimates "a kind of poem found in Virgil's ten *Eclogues,* known as amoebaean dialogue, a type of competition between shepherds" (Faggen 2001b, 53). Yet "Mending Wall" ensures that the competition becomes a rout, the dialogue virtually a monologue. The neighbor is allowed only the drab reiteration of an aphorism (which is, anyway, his father's and not his own, and which Frost elsewhere attributed to the Spartans [*N*, 637]); he is associated with savagery and an unnatural darkness "Not of woods only and the shade of trees"; and he insists on mending a wall where no wall is even needed—"He is all pine and I am apple orchard." The portrayal is of a dullard unable to "go behind" the hand-me-down wisdom of his "father's saying" as the speaker teases and outwits him. But the poem is not quite so straightforward in its sympathies. Frank Lentricchia argues that while the speaker "moves in a world of freedom," by contrast his neighbor, "unaware of the value of the imagination, must live his unliberated life without it" (Lentricchia, 106). There is no doubt that the speaker, claiming to play an "outdoor game" while his neighbor merely and stolidly works, encourages that interpretation; but he also confesses to a "mischief" which marks him out as an untrustworthy narrator. There is a good textual reason why his account should not be wholly accepted: for all his mockery of the officious neighbor, it is the speaker himself who instigates the annual mending of the wall.

"The more I say I," Frost once observed in a conversation about "Mending Wall," "the more I always mean somebody else" (Cook 1974, 82). Although the comment comes with its own unraveling mischief, it recognizes the truth that lyric poems are always dramatic. The style of "Mending Wall" is designed to reassure, its familiar blank verse and plain diction causing no concerns: remarkably, there are only two words in the poem—"another" and "exactly"—with more than two syllables. ("I dropped to an everyday level of diction that even Wordsworth kept above," Frost wrote about *North of Boston* [*SL*, 83–84].) The speaker soothes his audience into agreement; and yet when he states that his neighbor "moves in darkness *as it seems to me*" (my italics), the frank admission of subjectivity ought to raise the possibility that there is as much of Frost in the opaque, taciturn neighbor as in the judgmental and rather self-satisfied speaker. Although the title of "Mending Wall" insists on construction and reparation, the unnamed "Something" which doesn't love a wall and which "sends the frozen-ground-swell under it," with its cluster of stresses complementing the upsurge, is, punningly, *frost* itself (or himself). (A later poem, "Two Tramps in Mud Time," spells out "The lurking frost in the earth beneath.") "I am both wall-builder and wall-destroyer," Frost told his friend and fellow poet Charles Foster (Parini, 139). The protagonists are two sides of the human instinct to make and break boundaries.

On the evidence of his notebooks, Frost came back to "Mending Wall" regularly in later life, and even tried to redeploy its opening line for a new poem. Tidied of errors and deletions, one draft begins:

> Something there is that doesn't love a wall
> Something there is that does and after all
> Oh guileless children house and pastures
> Can't you be taught that since the world began
> All life upon it has been cellular
> Inside and outside cells are all we are.

$$(N, 612)$$

Walls are inherent in creation and creativity. While critical attention has tended to focus on the macrocosmic possibilities for readings of "Mending Wall"—such as wars and the nation state—Frost here and elsewhere in his notebooks dwells on the microcosmic, the cellular. "One chief disposition of life living," he comments in a prose entry, "is cell walls breaking and cell walls making," with health being "a period called peace in the balance of the two" (N, 281). "Mending Wall" seems even more precarious and prone to sudden change: "We have to use a spell to make [the boulders] balance." But it is that dynamic balance which is key to the poem—a balance which is achievable only if the speaker and his neighbor work together to keep themselves apart.

The Death of the Hired Man

Mary sat musing on the lamp-flame at the table
Waiting for Warren. When she heard his step,
She ran on tip-toe down the darkened passage
To meet him in the doorway with the news
And put him on his guard. "Silas is back."
She pushed him outward with her through the door
And shut it after her. "Be kind," she said.
She took the market things from Warren's arms
And set them on the porch, then drew him down
To sit beside her on the wooden steps.

"When was I ever anything but kind to him?
But I'll not have the fellow back," he said.
"I told him so last haying, didn't I?
'If he left then,' I said, 'that ended it.'
What good is he? Who else will harbor him
At his age for the little he can do?
What help he is there's no depending on.
Off he goes always when I need him most.
'He thinks he ought to earn a little pay,
Enough at least to buy tobacco with,
So he won't have to beg and be beholden.'
'All right,' I say, 'I can't afford to pay
Any fixed wages, though I wish I could.'
'Someone else can.' 'Then someone else will have to.'
I shouldn't mind his bettering himself
If that was what it was. You can be certain,
When he begins like that, there's someone at him
Trying to coax him off with pocket-money,—
In haying time, when any help is scarce.
In winter he comes back to us. I'm done."

"Sh! not so loud: he'll hear you," Mary said.

"I want him to: he'll have to soon or late."

"He's worn out. He's asleep beside the stove.
When I came up from Rowe's I found him here,
Huddled against the barn-door fast asleep,
A miserable sight, and frightening, too—
You needn't smile—I didn't recognize him—
I wasn't looking for him—and he's changed.
Wait till you see."

        "Where did you say he'd been?"

"He didn't say. I dragged him to the house,
And gave him tea and tried to make him smoke.
I tried to make him talk about his travels.
Nothing would do: he just kept nodding off."

"What did he say? Did he say anything?"

"But little."

      "Anything? Mary, confess
He said he'd come to ditch the meadow for me."

"Warren!"

      "But did he? I just want to know."

"Of course he did. What would you have him say?
Surely you wouldn't grudge the poor old man
Some humble way to save his self-respect.
He added, if you really care to know,

He meant to clear the upper pasture, too.
That sounds like something you have heard before?
Warren, I wish you could have heard the way
He jumbled everything. I stopped to look
Two or three times—he made me feel so queer—
To see if he was talking in his sleep.
He ran on Harold Wilson—you remember—
The boy you had in haying four years since.
He's finished school, and teaching in his college.
Silas declares you'll have to get him back.
He says they two will make a team for work:
Between them they will lay this farm as smooth!
The way he mixed that in with other things.
He thinks young Wilson a likely lad, though daft
On education—you know how they fought
All through July under the blazing sun,
Silas up on the cart to build the load,
Harold along beside to pitch it on."

"Yes, I took care to keep well out of earshot."

"Well, those days trouble Silas like a dream.
You wouldn't think they would. How some things linger!
Harold's young college boy's assurance piqued him.
After so many years he still keeps finding
Good arguments he sees he might have used.
I sympathize. I know just how it feels
To think of the right thing to say too late.
Harold's associated in his mind with Latin.
He asked me what I thought of Harold's saying
He studied Latin like the violin
Because he liked it—that an argument!
He said he couldn't make the boy believe
He could find water with a hazel prong—

Which showed how much good school had ever done him.
He wanted to go over that. But most of all
He thinks if he could have another chance
To teach him how to build a load of hay——"

"I know, that's Silas' one accomplishment.
He bundles every forkful in its place,
And tags and numbers it for future reference,
So he can find and easily dislodge it
In the unloading. Silas does that well.
He takes it out in bunches like big birds' nests.
You never see him standing on the hay
He's trying to lift, straining to lift himself."

"He thinks if he could teach him that, he'd be
Some good perhaps to someone in the world.
He hates to see a boy the fool of books.
Poor Silas, so concerned for other folk,
And nothing to look backward to with pride,
And nothing to look forward to with hope,
So now and never any different."

Part of a moon was falling down the west,
Dragging the whole sky with it to the hills.
Its light poured softly in her lap. She saw
And spread her apron to it. She put out her hand
Among the harp-like morning-glory strings,
Taut with the dew from garden bed to eaves,
As if she played unheard the tenderness
That wrought on him beside her in the night.
"Warren," she said, "he has come home to die:
You needn't be afraid he'll leave you this time."

"Home," he mocked gently.

"Yes, what else but home?
It all depends on what you mean by home.
Of course he's nothing to us, any more
Than was the hound that came a stranger to us
Out of the woods, worn out upon the trail."

"Home is the place where, when you have to go there,
They have to take you in."

                    "I should have called it
Something you somehow haven't to deserve."

Warren leaned out and took a step or two,
Picked up a little stick, and brought it back
And broke it in his hand and tossed it by.
"Silas has better claim on us you think
Than on his brother? Thirteen little miles
As the road winds would bring him to his door.
Silas has walked that far no doubt to-day.
Why didn't he go there? His brother's rich,
A somebody—director in the bank."

"He never told us that.

                    "We know it though."

"I think his brother ought to help, of course.
I'll see to that if there is need. He ought of right
To take him in, and might be willing to—
He may be better than appearances.
But have some pity on Silas. Do you think
If he'd had any pride in claiming kin
Or anything he looked for from his brother,
He'd keep so still about him all this time?"

"I wonder what's between them."

"I can tell you.
Silas is what he is—we wouldn't mind him—
But just the kind that kinsfolk can't abide.
He never did a thing so very bad.
He don't know why he isn't quite as good
As anyone. He won't be made ashamed
To please his brother, worthless though he is."

"*I* can't think Si ever hurt anyone."

"No, but he hurt my heart the way he lay
And rolled his old head on that sharp-edged chair-back.
He wouldn't let me put him on the lounge.
You must go in and see what you can do.
I made the bed up for him there to-night.
You'll be surprised at him—how much he's broken.
His working days are done; I'm sure of it."

"I'd not be in a hurry to say that."

"I haven't been. Go, look, see for yourself.
But, Warren, please remember how it is:
He's come to help you ditch the meadow.
He has a plan. You mustn't laugh at him.
He may not speak of it, and then he may.
I'll sit and see if that small sailing cloud
Will hit or miss the moon."

It hit the moon.
Then there were three there, making a dim row,
The moon, the little silver cloud, and she.

Warren returned—too soon, it seemed to her,
Slipped to her side, caught up her hand and waited.

"Warren," she questioned.

"Dead," was all he answered.

~❧~

Like "Mending Wall," "The Death of the Hired Man" is a rhetorical contest, except that now the antagonism has been replaced by love. It is the poem's great irony that while husband and wife (Warren and Mary) debate at considerable length how best to deal with Silas, an unreliable hired man who has returned sick to the farm, the hired man dies alone in the next room. By the time they are agreed that they should help him, he is beyond help.

Richard Poirier has described "The Death of the Hired Man" as "essentially a marriage idyll," in which "what to do about a difficult old man is in every way made subordinate" (Poirier, 107–108). That is true, but perhaps not "in every way." Although Silas is never seen except through the reports and reminiscences of Warren and Mary, the title serves as an insistent reminder that the poem's drama is not only *how* they talk but *what* they talk about, and what is happening while they talk. (The reader knows from the title what Warren and Mary don't: that the hired man is doomed.) Their talking is a kind of action, inasmuch as Mary's persuasion of Warren represents also the gentlest and most skillful of seductions. But it is also a fatal delaying of action; when Silas most needs companionship and possibly even medical intervention, they are busy next door exchanging aphorisms about the meaning of home.

Only in the title is Silas referred to as a "hired man"; Warren and Mary always call him by his name. By subsuming identity into functionality, Frost raises questions of value and cost. Is a man who can be bought worth anything beyond the going rate? Warren's reaction on hearing of Silas's return is to ask the same: "What good is he?" A hired man who can do "little," and whose little "there's no depending on," is worse than useless. "Good" occurs on four subsequent occasions, merging or muddling the ethical and the economic. Mary teaches Warren that Silas may indeed be "no good"—may even be (she agrees) "worthless"—but that the financial assessment is only partial. She "took the market things from Warren's arms / And set them on the porch": the description is more than literal, because Mary's task is to remove the burden of the marketplace from her husband and draw his attention to more important values. Silas, she points out, has "self-respect," and "won't be made ashamed to please his brother." He may not know the reasons why he "isn't quite as good / As anybody," but he is also keen to improve others according to his own standards. If he could only show the bookish Harold Wilson (student of Latin for the economically absurd reason that he likes it) how to build a load of hay, then the boy might yet be "Some good perhaps to someone in the world." It is Mary's ability to argue that even hired men who are no good have some value, and that even their betrayed employers have obligations to them, which finally persuades Warren to "Be kind." "Kind" has its etymological roots in kinship: Warren will be more of a brother to Silas than the rich banker whom Silas is too proud to visit. Blood and money can be barriers to kinship. Silas's death does not prove these kind intentions entirely futile. Rather, they seem like versions of Harold's desire to study Latin: impractical, worthless, and good.

The poem's most famous passage crystallizes debates about prerogative and deserving. After Mary explains that Silas has "come home to die," Warren's response initiates an attempt by each (without the aggression of "Mending Wall") to out-aphorize the other:

> "Home is the place where, when you have to go there,
> They have to take you in."
>
>   "I should have called it
> Something you somehow haven't to deserve."

Frost would later characterize the first position (spoken by Warren) as the manly and Republican way, and the second as maternal and Democratic

(Poirier, 234–235). Taking the hint, one of Frost's best recent scholars, Mark Richardson, has complained that the passage sums up the poem's attitude to gender, in which masculinity includes "justice and reason" and femininity "mercy and emotion" (Richardson 1997, 50); and Richardson attributes the popularity of the poem in "genteel American culture" to that distinction. But this may be to overstate contrasts where, as John Hollander has pointed out, similarities are more striking (Hollander 1997b, 65). Warren, like Mary, sees home as "Something you somehow haven't to deserve"; after all, "They have to take you in." Mary is the most nuanced rhetorician in *North of Boston;* and her genius here is to turn the coldness of third-person obligation ("They have to") into the reassurance of unearned entitlement. Home is home, she comes close to arguing, only *because* it isn't deserved. Silas has let Warren down, and therefore Warren (by his own as well as his wife's argument) must take him in.

To associate Mary with mercy and emotion *to the exclusion of* justice and reason is to miss the sophistication of her speech. Warren briefly dominates the exchanges; Mary's news that "Silas is back" and her encouraging him to "Be kind" inspire a twenty-line explanation of why he refuses to "have the fellow back." But Mary gently takes control, and by the end her husband has become her pupil (" 'I wonder what's between them.' / 'I can tell you' "). Mary's is the subtlest of victories: she wins the argument without explicitly requiring Warren to concede defeat. Her diction being loftier than Warren's, it prompts Poirier's accusation that the poem belongs to Frost's "elevated mode" and is marred by an obnoxious gentility (Poirier, 108). Undoubtedly, there is something too precious about her waiting to see whether " 'that small sailing cloud / Will hit or miss the moon.' " ("Never larrup an emotion," Frost once advised; "Set yourself against the moon. Resist the moon" (Poirier, 279).) There is also something too self-satisfied about the prim repetitiveness of "And nothing to look backward to with pride, / And nothing to look forward to with hope." These are tones of fine writing, not of speech. However, such faults are mitigated by the air of otherworldliness clinging to Mary, whose name implies a pure maternal instinct later confirmed by a passage of heightened lyrical description:

Part of a moon was falling down the west,
Dragging the whole sky with it to the hills.
Its light poured softly in her lap. She saw
And spread her apron to it. She put out her hand
Among the harp-like morning-glory strings,
Taut with the dew from garden bed to eaves,
As if she played unheard some tenderness
That wrought on him beside her in the night.

The poem's sympathy with Mary is indicated by such descriptive passages, which align themselves stylistically with her own sensitivity to her environment. The focus here is on Mary's fertility, from her gesture of consent as the light of the moon (the goddess of childbirth) pours into her lap, to the references to "bed" and to the tenderness "wrought" on her husband "beside her in the night." (It is tempting to wonder whether the moon goddess in Sylvia Plath's last poem, "Edge," was inspired by Frost: "Her blacks crackle and drag.") Mary and Warren meet with things dying, but there remains at least the strong implication—not quite consolation—that things newborn await them.

The Mountain

The mountain held the town as in a shadow.
I saw so much before I slept there once:
I noticed that I missed stars in the west,
Where its black body cut into the sky.
Near me it seemed: I felt it like a wall
Behind which I was sheltered from a wind.
And yet between the town and it I found,
When I walked forth at dawn to see new things,
Were fields, a river, and beyond, more fields.
The river at the time was fallen away,
And made a widespread brawl on cobble-stones;
But the signs showed what it had done in spring;
Good grass-land gullied out, and in the grass
Ridges of sand, and driftwood stripped of bark.
I crossed the river and swung round the mountain.
And there I met a man who moved so slow
With white-faced oxen in a heavy cart,
It seemed no harm to stop him altogether.

"What town is this?" I asked.

                              "This? Lunenburg."

Then I was wrong: the town of my sojourn,
Beyond the bridge, was not that of the mountain,
But only felt at night its shadowy presence.
"Where is your village? Very far from here?"

"There is no village—only scattered farms.
We were but sixty voters last election.
We can't in nature grow to many more:
That thing takes all the room!" He moved his goad.

The mountain stood there to be pointed at.
Pasture ran up the side a little way,
And then there was a wall of trees with trunks:
After that only tops of trees, and cliffs
Imperfectly concealed among the leaves.
A dry ravine emerged from under boughs
Into the pasture.

        "That looks like a path.
Is that the way to reach the top from here?—
Not for this morning, but some other time:
I must be getting back to breakfast now."

"I don't advise your trying from this side.
There is no proper path, but those that *have*
Been up, I understand, have climbed from Ladd's.
That's five miles back. You can't mistake the place:
They logged it there last winter some way up.
I'd take you, but I'm bound the other way."

"You've never climbed it?"

        "I've been on the sides
Deer-hunting and trout-fishing. There's a brook
That starts up on it somewhere—I've heard say
Right on the top, tip-top—a curious thing.
But what would interest you about the brook,
It's always cold in summer, warm in winter.
One of the great sights going is to see
It steam in winter like an ox's breath,
Until the bushes all along its banks
Are inch-deep with the frosty spines and bristles—
You know the kind. Then let the sun shine on it!"

"There ought to be a view around the world
From such a mountain—if it isn't wooded
Clear to the top." I saw through leafy screens
Great granite terraces in sun and shadow,
Shelves one could rest a knee on getting up—
With depths behind him sheer a hundred feet;
Or turn and sit on and look out and down,
With little ferns in crevices at his elbow.

"As to that I can't say. But there's the spring,
Right on the summit, almost like a fountain.
That ought to be worth seeing."

                              "If it's there.
You never saw it?"

                        "I guess there's no doubt
About its being there. I never saw it.
It may not be right on the very top:
It wouldn't have to be a long way down
To have some head of water from above,
And a *good distance* down might not be noticed
By anyone who'd come a long way up.
One time I asked a fellow climbing it
To look and tell me later how it was."

"What did he say?"

                        "He said there was a lake
Somewhere in Ireland on a mountain top."

"But a lake's different. What about the spring?"

"He never got up high enough to see.
That's why I don't advise your trying this side.
He tried this side. I've always meant to go
And look myself, but you know how it is:
It doesn't seem so much to climb a mountain
You've worked around the foot of all your life.
What would I do? Go in my overalls,
With a big stick, the same as when the cows
Haven't come down to the bars at milking time?
Or with a shotgun for a stray black bear?
'Twouldn't seem real to climb for climbing it."

"I shouldn't climb it if I didn't want to—
Not for the sake of climbing. What's its name?"

"We call it Hor: I don't know if that's right."

"Can one walk around it? Would it be too far?"

"You can drive round and keep in Lunenburg,
But it's as much as you can ever do,
The boundary lines keep in so close to it.
Hor is the township, and the township's Hor—
And a few houses sprinkled round the foot,
Like boulders broken off the upper cliff,
Rolled out a little farther than the rest."

"Warm in December, cold in June, you say?"

"I don't suppose the water's changed at all.
You and I know enough to know it's warm
Compared with cold, and cold compared with warm.
But all the fun's in how you say a thing."

"You've lived here all your life?"

                              "Ever since Hor
Was no bigger than a——" What, I did not hear.
He drew the oxen toward him with light touches
Of his slim goad on nose and offside flank,
Gave them their marching orders and was moving.

In dwelling on an exchange between two speakers, "The Mountain"
extends the model established by "Mending Wall" and "The Death of
the Hired Man." However, for the first time in the book the conversation
takes place between strangers. Frost's comment that in *North of Boston*
he dropped below even Wordsworth's level of diction (*SL*, 83–84) proves
that Wordsworth's example was prominent in his mind. "The Moun-
tain" is the most Wordsworthian poem in *North of Boston,* not just in
its everyday diction and blank verse, but also in characterization. The
slow-moving farmer who describes the locality is a direct descendant of
Wordsworth's old Cumberland beggar and especially his leech-gatherer,
figures whose intimacy with their environment grants them an intui-
tive wisdom. (Significantly for so watery a poem as Frost's, the leech-
gatherer's voice is "like a stream.") Frost interrogates this tradition even
as he inherits it: "The Mountain" explores the limitations as well as the
depths of the farmer's knowledge, and explores, ultimately, the nature
of knowledge itself.

The mountain's overwhelming physicality "takes all the room."
This seems borne out rhythmically: five of the seven lines containing the
"mountain," including the poem's opening line, have an extra syllable;
and in three of those cases, where the word occurs at the end of a line, its
trochaic beat ensures a feminine ending which necessarily disrupts the
iambic pentameter. (Here and elsewhere in *North of Boston,* and more
strictly in a later poem like "For Once, Then, Something," the meter is
hendecasyllabic, as derived from Frost's study of Catullus.) But for all

its inescapable bulk, the mountain generates errors and uncertainties. It seems "near," and yet the first-person persona is surprised to discover fields and a river "between the town and it." Coming across another town, he first mistakes it for the one he had stayed in, and then learns that it is not a town at all or even a village. What looks to him like a path "is no proper path." The common view that the brook is warm in winter and cold in summer is true only in relative terms. The farmer admits to not knowing whether the mountain is wooded "Clear to the top." There may be a spring on the summit, or a little way down—"I guess there's no doubt," the farmer states, doubtfully. Even the name of the mountain remains mysterious: "We call it Hor: I don't know if that's right." (The name Hor gives the mountain a biblical antiquity and authority because it was on Mount Hor that Aaron, brother of Moses, died.) Fittingly for so unsure a poem, it begins with occlusion (the stars blocked by the mountain), and ends in lacuna, as the reader can only guess at the farmer's joke about how small Hor might have been (a pebble, a boulder?) when he first lived there.

Unlike "The Death of the Hired Man," "The Mountain" has no third-person voice; the descriptive passages are the work of the traveler recording the context in which his conversation with the farmer took place, and therefore they lack any authority to solve the poem's mysteries. One effect is to emphasize differences in the diction of the two men. Although his contribution to the dialogue consists mostly of short questions, the traveler elsewhere indulges in overelaborate rhetorical constructions. Even the opening line—"The mountain held the town as in a shadow"—sounds unnaturally fussy, and it is soon followed by an inversion ("Near me it seemed"), the most rhythmically leaden of clauses ("Behind which I was sheltered from a wind"), and an archaic adverb ("When I walked forth"). At its worst, the traveler's language is so stuffy as to verge on parody: "the town of my sojourn, / Beyond the bridge, was not that of the mountain." Compare the traveler's fustian with the farmer's living tones: " 'We can't in nature grow to many more' "; " 'Right on the top, tip-top' "; " 'One of the great sights going' "; " 'Twouldn't seem real to climb for climbing it' " (a sentence immediately and verbosely translated by the traveler: " 'I shouldn't climb it if I didn't want to—/Not for the sake of climbing' "). Frost explained to Amy Lowell that in *North of Boston* he hadn't "put dialect into the mouths of his people because not one of them, not one, spoke dialect" (*SL,* 220). But there are other ways of marking differences in speech. The farmer's is the colloquial language of a man who believes that " 'all the fun's in how you say a thing' "; the traveler's is finicky, correct, and lifeless.

Appropriately for so puzzled and misconstruing a poem, "The Mountain" itself belongs among the most misconstrued of Frost's works, as apparent in critics' assumption that the "brook" and the "spring" are synonymous (Poirier, 110; Lentricchia, 46). Lentricchia, arguing that "the farmer has never seen the brook," concludes that the farmer enjoys "an anarchic moment of imagination" as he describes in such poetic detail what the brook must look like. But not only has the farmer seen the brook, he has even gone trout-fishing in it. It is the brook's source, rumored to be a spring at or near the mountaintop, which has not been seen by him or by anyone he has spoken to. The mountain never gives up that secret. Although it can be driven round, even a man who has spent his life underneath it has only heard rumors that people have been to the top.

Mountain springs are traditionally associated with poetic inspiration—Mount Helicon held two springs sacred to the Muses. The farmer is unable or unwilling to climb the mountain and check this myth of origins. (The name Hor is itself originating—its biblical namesake is the "mountain of mountains.") It is sufficient, for him, to fish in the brook and to turn it into poetry; and to make jokes to strangers about his own and the mountain's origins. Frost even smuggles his own signature into a description of the brook's glorious powers:

> One of the great sights going is to see
> It steam in winter like an ox's breath,
> Until the bushes all along its banks
> Are inch-deep with the frosty spines and bristles—

This frostiness is more than a tricksy way for Frost to semaphore his presence (as he doesn't *quite* in "Mending Wall") on the slopes of inspiration. Among other things, "The Mountain" here concerns itself with the ancillary business (a business so prominently ancillary as almost to be primary) of creating a parable of its own making. Whereas the spring of "The Pasture" could be cleaned, in "The Mountain" the poet who fishes poetry's brook can only tell stories about the mysterious origins of his power; and although "The Mountain" culminates in "moving" (yet another feminine ending), that movement takes a different direction from the unknown, unknowable source.

A Hundred Collars

Lancaster bore him—such a little town,
Such a great man. It doesn't see him often
Of late years, though he keeps the old home-stead
And sends the children down there with their mother
To run wild in the summer—a little wild.
Sometimes he joins them for a day or two
And sees old friends he somehow can't get near.
They meet him in the general store at night,
Pre-occupied with formidable mail,
Rifling a printed letter as he talks.
They seem afraid. He wouldn't have it so:
Though a great scholar, he's a democrat,
If not at heart, at least on principle.
Lately when coming up to Lancaster
His train being late he missed another train
And had four hours to wait at Woodsville Junction
After eleven o'clock at night. Too tired
To think of sitting such an ordeal out,
He turned to the hotel to find a bed.

"No room," the night clerk said. "Unless——"
Woodsville's a place of shrieks and wandering lamps
And cars that shock and rattle—and *one* hotel.

"You say 'unless.'"

                    "Unless you wouldn't mind
Sharing a room with someone else."

                              "Who is it?"

"A man."

So I should hope. What kind of man?"

"I know him: he's all right. A man's a man.
Separate beds of course you understand."
The night clerk blinked his eyes and dared him on.

"Who's that man sleeping in the office chair?
Has he had the refusal of my chance?"

"He was afraid of being robbed or murdered.
What do you say?"

"I'll have to have a bed."

The night clerk led him up three flights of stairs
And down a narrow passage full of doors,
At the last one of which he knocked and entered.
"Lafe, here's a fellow wants to share your room."

"Show him this way. I'm not afraid of him.
I'm not so drunk I can't take care of myself."

The night clerk clapped a bedstead on the foot.
"This will be yours. Good-night," he said, and went.

"Lafe was the name, I think?"

"Yes, *Lay*fayette.
You got it the first time. And yours?"

"Magoon.

Doctor Magoon."

"A Doctor?"

"Well, a teacher."

"Professor Square-the-circle-till-you're-tired?
Hold on, there's something I don't think of now
That I had on my mind to ask the first
Man that knew anything I happened in with.
I'll ask you later—don't let me forget it."

The Doctor looked at Lafe and looked away.
A man? A brute. Naked above the waist,
He sat there creased and shining in the light,
Fumbling the buttons in a well-starched shirt.
"I'm moving into a size-larger shirt.
I've felt mean lately; mean's no name for it.
I've just found what the matter was to-night:
I've been a-choking like a nursery tree
When it outgrows the wire band of its name tag.
I blamed it on the hot spell we've been having.
'Twas nothing but my foolish hanging back,
Not liking to own up I'd grown a size.
Number eighteen this is. What size do you wear?"

The Doctor caught his throat convulsively.
"Oh—ah—fourteen—fourteen."

"Fourteen! You say so!
I can remember when I wore fourteen.
And come to think I must have back at home
More than a hundred collars, size fourteen.
Too bad to waste them all. You ought to have them.
They're yours and welcome; let me send them to you.
What makes you stand there on one leg like that?

You're not much furtherer than where Kike left you.
You act as if you wished you hadn't come.
Sit down or lie down, friend; you make me nervous."

The Doctor made a subdued dash for it,
And propped himself at bay against a pillow.

"Not that way, with your shoes on Kike's white bed.
You can't rest that way. Let me pull your shoes off."

"Don't touch me, please—I say, don't touch me, please.
I'll not be put to bed by you, my man."

"Just as you say. Have it your own way then.
'My man' is it? You talk like a professor.
Speaking of who's afraid of who, however,
I'm thinking I have more to lose than you
If anything should happen to be wrong.
Who wants to cut your number fourteen throat!
Let's have a show down as an evidence
Of good faith. There is ninety dollars.
Come, if you're not afraid."

               "*I*'m not afraid.
There's five: that's all I carry."

                "I can search you?
Where are you moving over to? Stay still.
You'd better tuck your money under you
And sleep on it the way I always do
When I'm with people I don't trust at night."

"Will you believe me if I put it there
Right on the counterpane—that I do trust you?"

"You'd say so, Mister Man.—I'm a collector.
My ninety isn't mine—you won't think that.
I pick it up a dollar at a time
All round the country for the *Weekly News,*
Published in Bow. You know the *Weekly News?*"

"Known it since I was young."

                              "Then you know me.
Now we are getting on together—talking.
I'm sort of Something for it at the front.
My business is to find what people want:
They pay for it, and so they ought to have it.
Fairbanks, he says to me—he's editor—
Feel out the public sentiment—he says.
A good deal comes on me when all is said.
The only trouble is we disagree
In politics: I'm Vermont Democrat—
You know what that is, sort of double-dyed;
The *News* has always been Republican.
Fairbanks, he says to me, 'Help us this year,'
Meaning by us their ticket. 'No,' I says,
'I can't and won't. You've been in long enough:
It's time you turned around and boosted us.
You'll have to pay me more than ten a week
If I'm expected to elect Bill Taft.
I doubt if I could do it anyway.' "

"You seem to shape the paper's policy."

"You see I'm in with everybody, know 'em all.
I almost know their farms as well as they do."

"You drive around? It must be pleasant work."

"It's business, but I can't say it's not fun.
What I like best's the lay of different farms,
Coming out on them from a stretch of woods,
Or over a hill or round a sudden corner.
I like to find folks getting out in spring,
Raking the dooryard, working near the house.
Later they get out further in the fields.
Everything's shut sometimes except the barn;
The family's all away in some back meadow.
There's a hay load a-coming—when it comes.
And later still they all get driven in:
The fields are stripped to lawn, the garden patches
Stripped to bare ground, the apple trees
To whips and poles. There's nobody about.
The chimney, though, keeps up a good brisk smoking.
And I lie back and ride. I take the reins
Only when someone's coming, and the mare
Stops when she likes: I tell her when to go.
I've spoiled Jemima in more ways than one.
She's got so she turns in at every house
As if she had some sort of curvature,
No matter if I have no errand there.
She thinks I'm sociable. I maybe am.
It's seldom I get down except for meals, though.
Folks entertain me from the kitchen doorstep,
All in a family row down to the youngest."

"One would suppose they might not be as glad
To see you as you are to see them."

                              "Oh,
Because I want their dollar. I don't want
Anything they've not got. I never dun.
I'm there, and they can pay me if they like.

I go nowhere on purpose: I happen by.
Sorry there is no cup to give you a drink.
I drink out of the bottle—not your style.
Mayn't I offer you——?"

          "No, no, no, thank you."

"Just as you say. Here's looking at you then.—
And now I'm leaving you a little while.
You'll rest easier when I'm gone, perhaps—
Lie down—let yourself go and get some sleep.
But first—let's see—what was I going to ask you?
Those collars—who shall I address them to,
Suppose you aren't awake when I come back?"

"Really, friend, I can't let you. You—may need them."

"Not till I shrink, when they'll be out of style."

"But really I—I have so many collars."

"I don't know who I rather would have have them.
They're only turning yellow where they are.
But you're the doctor as the saying is.
I'll put the light out. Don't you wait for me:
I've just begun the night. You get some sleep.
I'll knock so-fashion and peep round the door
When I come back so you'll know who it is.
There's nothing I'm afraid of like scared people.
I don't want you should shoot me in the head.
What am I doing carrying off this bottle?
There now, you get some sleep."

He shut the door.
The Doctor slid a little down the pillow.

Despite Frost's claim in later years that *North of Boston* "was written as scattered poems" (*CPr*, 196), it remained the most coherent of his volumes, more so than the autobiographical narrative of *A Boy's Will*. In at least two important ways, "A Hundred Collars" picks up and develops structures and motifs from earlier poems. Like its predecessors, it consists mostly of dialogue; and it continues an alternating pattern of internal and external space. "The Pasture" had invited the reader to accompany the poet-farmer outside; "Mending Wall" had set about enclosing that outside world; "The Death of the Hired Man" had centered on the return of Silas to the sanctuary of "home"; and despite the natural grandeur of its setting, "The Mountain" had described Hor as "a wall . . . tak[ing] all the room." "A Hundred Collars" returns to internal space—an overfilled hotel in which anyone wanting a bed for the night must share a room with a stranger. The suffocating collars mentioned in the title are an appropriate emblem for the poem's assault on personal space.

Like "The Death of the Hired Man," "A Hundred Collars" opens with a passage in the third person: the poetic voice is separate from the voices of the two protagonists. This does not guarantee impartiality. Already the poem's first two lines establish a preoccupation with outgrowing and constraint: the "great man" has escaped the womb of the "little town" which "bore him." The mockery—"Such a great man"—is barely held in check, and any lingering doubts about the poem's sympathies are dispelled by the report that the children are annually sent down to the "old homestead" with their mother to "run wild" but only "a little wild." Despite having outgrown his diminutive town, this great man is no freer than his children: he can join them sometimes for "a day or two," but even there he is pursued by "formidable mail." He "can't get near" old friends, and frightens them. Any regret about this state of affairs is more intellectual than heartfelt:

> He wouldn't have it so:
> Though a great scholar, he's a democrat,
> If not at heart, at least on principle.

"Though a great scholar, he's a democrat"—there is something viciously comic about that line. So determined is the poetic voice to prejudice the reader against this still-anonymous man that the criticism risks becoming self-defeating. Were "A Hundred Collars" merely another in the tradition of antischolarly poems, it might deserve its neglect. (It is one of the least discussed poems in *North of Boston;* and Yeats's twelve-line poem "The Scholars," published just a few years later, assaults that benighted vocation far more economically.) But Frost's poem fails, finally, to bear out its introduction. The portrayal of the scholar turns out to be more complex and ambivalent than the reader is initially led to expect.

The case for the prosecution (which is what it nearly amounts to) might be further strengthened by details later in the poem. The great man responds to the informality of his roommate's name (Lafe) with the unnecessary formality of his own (Doctor Magoon). And the description of Lafe, although written in the third person, is evidently shaped by Magoon's intolerance: "A man? A brute." Although this internalized hostility comes immediately after Lafe's outspoken mockery of scholars ("'Professor Square-the-circle-till-you're-tired?'"), Magoon's reaction is itself brutal. Lafe, on the other hand, is presented as everything that Magoon is not. Whereas Magoon manages to be a (lowercase) "democrat" only on principle, Lafe describes himself as (uppercase) "'Vermont Democrat . . . sort of double-dyed,'" with no conflict between instincts and convictions; money could never persuade him to support Bill Taft (who was president from 1909 to 1913). Lafe is as loquacious as Magoon is reserved (in *North of Boston,* taciturnity is the greatest crime of all), and his language is alive with colloquialisms ("'They're yours and welcome'"; "'furtherer'"; "'I've been a-choking'"; "'I maybe am'"; "'so-fashion'"). And whereas Magoon struggles to relate to his "old friends," Lafe has the knack of making new friends wherever he goes. "'It's business,'" he reports, "'but I can't say it's not fun.'" That fun makes Lafe a kindred spirit of the farmer in "The Mountain" who found that " 'all the fun's in how you say a thing.' " Magoon conspicuously lacks any sense of fun at all.

None of this challenges Mark Richardson's argument that the poem "presents yet another treatment of the intellectual as an alien in the villages of New England" (Richardson 1997, 77). But if there is an unbridgeable gap, losses are incurred on both sides. Far from being a monster, Magoon wants nothing more than to be treated equally. At reception he sees a man sleeping in an office chair, and enquires whether the stranger " 'had the refusal of my chance?' " It should not be surprising that Magoon seems nervous subsequently: the man had turned down the room because " 'He was afraid of being robbed or murdered.' " Lafe's opening comments are hardly designed to put Magoon at his ease: " 'I'm not afraid of him. / I'm not so drunk I can't take care of myself.' " Knowing that someone has chosen to sleep in an office chair rather than risk sharing a room with this (we are led to assume) fairly drunk stranger—naked from the waist up, ready for a fight if necessary—Magoon has good reason to resist when Lafe suddenly starts to pull his shoes off for him.

For all his self-reported ability to socialize with the subscribers to his newspaper, Lafe seems remarkably unaware of how best to interact with his new acquaintance. It is not so much his jokey insult to Magoon's profession as his attempts to act generously which cause the problems. Lafe wants to pull off Magoon's shoes; invites him to take a swig from his bottle; and first and last offers the eponymous collars. In case Magoon should come across as unduly snobbish for turning down the opportunity to receive a bountiful supply of secondhand collars from a stranger, Lafe's final touch confirms the wisdom of that judgment: " 'They're only turning yellow where they are.' " Magoon is strangled by the thought of those perfectly fitting collars. Lafe's temporary departure provides only a small respite: "The Doctor slid a little down the pillow." That feminine ending (following feminine endings in "Mending Wall," "The Death of the Hired Man," and "The Mountain") draws attention to a closure which is no closure at all. Like his children allowed to run "a little wild," Magoon can never relax into freedom.

Home Burial

He saw her from the bottom of the stairs
Before she saw him. She was starting down,
Looking back over her shoulder at some fear.
She took a doubtful step and then undid it
To raise herself and look again. He spoke
Advancing toward her: "What is it you see
From up there always—for I want to know."
She turned and sank upon her skirts at that,
And her face changed from terrified to dull.
He said to gain time: "What is it you see,"
Mounting until she cowered under him.
"I will find out now—you must tell me, dear."
She, in her place, refused him any help
With the least stiffening of her neck and silence.
She let him look, sure that he wouldn't see,
Blind creature; and a while he didn't see.
But at last he murmured, "Oh," and again, "Oh."

"What is it—what?" she said.

                                    "Just that I see."

"You don't," she challenged. "Tell me what it is."

"The wonder is I didn't see at once.
I never noticed it from here before.
I must be wonted to it—that's the reason.
The little graveyard where my people are!
So small the window frames the whole of it.
Not so much larger than a bedroom, is it?
There are three stones of slate and one of marble,
Broad-shouldered little slabs there in the sunlight

On the sidehill. We haven't to mind *those*.
But I understand: it is not the stones,
But the child's mound——"

"Don't, don't, don't, don't," she cried.

She withdrew shrinking from beneath his arm
That rested on the banister, and slid downstairs;
And turned on him with such a daunting look,
He said twice over before he knew himself:
"Can't a man speak of his own child he's lost?"

"Not you! Oh, where's my hat? Oh, I don't need it!
I must get out of here. I must get air.
I don't know rightly whether any man can."

"Amy! Don't go to someone else this time.
Listen to me. I won't come down the stairs."
He sat and fixed his chin between his fists.
"There's something I should like to ask you, dear."

"You don't know how to ask it."

"Help me, then."
Her fingers moved the latch for all reply.

"My words are nearly always an offense.
I don't know how to speak of anything
So as to please you. But I might be taught
I should suppose. I can't say I see how.
A man must partly give up being a man
With women-folk. We could have some arrangement
By which I'd bind myself to keep hands off
Anything special you're a-mind to name.

Though I don't like such things 'twixt those that love.
Two that don't love can't live together without them.
But two that do can't live together with them."
She moved the latch a little. "Don't—don't go.
Don't carry it to someone else this time.
Tell me about it if it's something human.
Let me into your grief. I'm not so much
Unlike other folks as your standing there
Apart would make me out. Give me my chance.
I do think, though, you overdo it a little.
What was it brought you up to think it the thing
To take your mother-loss of a first child
So inconsolably—in the face of love.
You'd think his memory might be satisfied——"

"There you go sneering now!"

                        "I'm not, I'm not!
You make me angry. I'll come down to you.
God, what a woman! And it's come to this,
A man can't speak of his own child that's dead."

"You can't because you don't know how.
If you had any feelings, you that dug
With your own hand—how could you?—his little grave;
I saw you from that very window there,
Making the gravel leap and leap in air,
Leap up, like that, like that, and land so lightly
And roll back down the mound beside the hole.
I thought, Who is that man? I didn't know you.
And I crept down the stairs and up the stairs
To look again, and still your spade kept lifting.
Then you came in. I heard your rumbling voice
Out in the kitchen, and I don't know why,

But I went near to see with my own eyes.
You could sit there with the stains on your shoes
Of the fresh earth from your own baby's grave
And talk about your everyday concerns.
You had stood the spade up against the wall
Outside there in the entry, for I saw it."

"I shall laugh the worst laugh I ever laughed.
I'm cursed. God, if I don't believe I'm cursed."

"I can repeat the very words you were saying.
'Three foggy mornings and one rainy day
Will rot the best birch fence a man can build.'
Think of it, talk like that at such a time!
What had how long it takes a birch to rot
To do with what was in the darkened parlor.
You *couldn't* care! The nearest friends can go
With anyone to death, comes so far short
They might as well not try to go at all.
No, from the time when one is sick to death,
One is alone, and he dies more alone.
Friends make pretense of following to the grave,
But before one is in it, their minds are turned
And making the best of their way back to life
And living people, and things they understand.
But the world's evil. I won't have grief so
If I can change it. Oh, I won't, I won't!"

"There, you have said it all and you feel better.
You won't go now. You're crying. Close the door.
The heart's gone out of it: why keep it up.
Amy! There's someone coming down the road!"

"You—oh, you think the talk is all. I must go—
Somewhere out of this house. How can I make you——"

"If—you—do!" She was opening the door wider.
"Where do you mean to go? First tell me that.
I'll follow and bring you back by force. I *will!*—"

When Randall Jarrell read "Home Burial" to the Beats as an example
of literary excellence, Allen Ginsberg butted in to denounce the poem:
"Coupla squares yakking!" (Jarrell 1985, 418). The effect is of a cartoon
iconoclasm, like doodling a moustache on the Mona Lisa. What makes
Ginsberg's intervention doubly shocking (or, from certain perspectives,
doubly predictable) is the poem's subject: the breakdown of a marriage
following a child's death. Frost considered the poem "too sad to read
aloud," although he deflected any suggestion that it related to the death
of his own son, Elliott, by insisting that he had been remembering his
sister-in-law's marital difficulties after the death of her child (Thompson
1966, 597–598).

As the reader of *North of Boston* would have come to expect by
now, "Home Burial" is yet another conversation poem. Whereas "The
Death of the Hired Man" had presented a marital idyll thrown into re-
lief—rather than interrupted—by death, here the marriage is disintegrat-
ing due to incompatible ways of mourning the loss of a child. Fittingly,
"Home Burial" is positioned in *North of Boston* so as to break patterns.
The alternation of outside and inside space beginning with "The Pas-
ture" is brought to an end: the suffocating atmosphere of "Home Burial"
follows a different kind of claustrophobia in "A Hundred Collars." Yet
the emotional focus *is* outside the house. The poem stops short with
Amy standing on the threshold, but both she and her husband look
through the window at the family graveyard where their child and with
him their marriage lie buried. The husband already seems to be calling
after Amy at the end, his italicized promise to bring her back ("'I *will!*'")

standing in pointed contrast to the feminine endings of the previous four poems.

Richard Poirier's bravura reading of "Home Burial" has—whether acknowledged or not—so thoroughly influenced Frost criticism as to become the orthodoxy. Poirier notes that the poem's title "means something about the couple as well as about the dead child" (Poirier, 124), with "home" having become "a burial plot for all of them." Home—that is, any sense of home as a place of comfort, security, love, and mutual respect—has been buried, and its occupants with it. The phrase "home burial" fuses (and confuses) inside and outside, invigoration and suffocation, life and death. The graveyard is " 'Not so much larger than a bedroom,' " and if that metaphor recalls the familiar idea of the dead lying at rest in their narrow bed, it also hints at the likelihood that the marital bedroom has become a graveyard. A window " 'frames' " the graveyard, bringing it into the house as the most goading of artworks. What it depicts most painfully is the " 'child's mound,' " which serves as a rebuke to those who—as Amy bitterly puts it—" 'mak[e] the best of their way back to life / And living people.' "

Frost does not allow the reader the easy refuge of taking sides in the conflict between husband and wife. His genius in dialogue and dramatic monologue, Karen L. Kilcup has noted, is to "endow other perspectives with complexity and subjectivity," as demonstrated time and again in *North of Boston* by, for example, "the actualization of the voices of women" (Kilcup, 8). The protagonists of "Home Burial" torture each other, but unintentionally; and each suffers unbearably as a result. Initially, the husband seems to dominate a vulnerable wife. She is "doubtful" and looks back as if "at some fear"; "Advancing toward her," he speaks decisively, and with an aggression which is at least partly sexual, "Mount[s] until she cower[s] under him." His questions (which lack question marks) sound like—and soon become—commands: " 'You must tell me, dear.' " She resists, and it is her perspective which influences the narrative voice when he is called "Blind creature." But his moment of seeing breaks his confidence, and forceful speech becomes murmured repetitive inarticulacy: " 'Oh,' and again, 'Oh.' " In a sudden shift of power, she is now the one who gives orders: " 'Tell me what it is.' "

Those kinds of modulation occur throughout the poem. Roles change as one attacks and then the other; despite being united in grief, husband and wife can never find common cause or common language. After Amy challenges her husband to speak, she stops him with an order which is also a plea for mercy: " 'Don't, don't, don't, don't,' she cried." This may not quite match Lear's fivefold "Never" uttered over his daughter's corpse, but it poignantly conveys the impossibility of reconciliation: the husband must and cannot speak; the wife is desperate to hear and yet cannot listen to him. Neither understands the other. " 'All the fun's in how you say a thing,' " the farmer's lighthearted credo in "The Mountain," here encounters its horrible antitheses: " 'You don't know how to ask it' "; " 'You can't because you don't know how [to speak].' "

Their terminal misunderstanding centers on Amy's recollection of the day her husband dug their child's grave. It is an article of faith for Frost's poetry that labor can be therapeutic, but Amy sees only its callousness; for the man who has just lost a son to act in that way—to act at all—is to betray his lack of feelings. The fact of its being therapeutic becomes part of the problem: the grieving father is already looking to salve his loss. His behavior afterward exacerbates the fault:

> "I can repeat the very words you were saying.
> 'Three foggy mornings and one rainy day
> Will rot the best birch fence a man can build.'
> Think of it, talk like that at such a time!
> What had how long it takes a birch to rot
> To do with what was in the darkened parlor."

The passage is distinctively Frostian, with its tessellation of thirty-eight consecutive monosyllables building to the more formal setting of the "darkened parlor" (a polysyllabic phrase which also stands out by breaking the meter with a characteristic feminine ending). What Amy misses in the extremity of her grief is an appreciation of her husband's more indirect expression of his emotions. *North of Boston* returns many times to walls and fences, as giving identity and individuality to that which they enclose. The something which, in this poem, doesn't love a fence would no more love the coffin wood; and the word "rot," so redolent of decomposition after death ("To lie in cold obstruction, and to rot," as *Measure for Measure* unblinkingly settles it), confirms that the husband is preoccupied with a grief of which he can speak only obliquely. His is the kind of ulteriority extolled by Frost—the ability of poetry to speak of one thing in terms of another. The husband may not even be consciously aware of the full range of his meanings, and he does not elaborate when Amy challenges him. But his reaction to accusations of indifference (" 'I'm cursed' ") indicates his own grievance that his wife should criticize his expression of mourning as a divagation from that instinctive duty.

What most obviously divides husband and wife is not the depth of their grief but their attitude to consolation. Amy sees consolation as betrayal. She does not want to make her " 'way back to life' " because to do so would be to turn away from her dead son and toward " 'evil.' " The charge is directly leveled at Amy that she is wrong " 'To take [her] mother-loss of a first child / So inconsolably—in the face of love.' " Her husband finds consolation not just in labor but in talking, and assumes that talking will offer some respite for Amy, too: " 'There, you have said it all and you feel better.' " Her untempered response—" 'you think the talk is all' "—makes hers the dissenting and disruptive voice in what must be the most talkative of poetry books. Amy rejects her husband's therapy, rejecting at the same time a founding principle of *North of Boston*. She must be at odds even with the poem which creates and depicts her. Frost expressed his pride in having written the husband's " 'If—you—do!,' " claiming that it was an example of the "hearing imagination" (*SL,* 130). It is testament to his genius that in hearing Amy, Frost portrays so sympathetically a character unsympathetic to everything he holds dear.

The Black Cottage

We chanced in passing by that afternoon
To catch it in a sort of special picture
Among tar-banded ancient cherry trees,
Set well back from the road in rank lodged grass,
The little cottage we were speaking of,
A front with just a door between two windows,
Fresh painted by the shower a velvet black.
We paused, the minister and I, to look.
He made as if to hold it at arm's length
Or put the leaves aside that framed it in.
"Pretty," he said. "Come in. No one will care."
The path was a vague parting in the grass
That led us to a weathered window-sill.
We pressed our faces to the pane. "You see," he said,
"Everything's as she left it when she died.
Her sons won't sell the house or the things in it.
They say they mean to come and summer here
Where they were boys. They haven't come this year.
They live so far away—one is out west—
It will be hard for them to keep their word.
Anyway they won't have the place disturbed."
A buttoned hair-cloth lounge spread scrolling arms
Under a crayon portrait on the wall
Done sadly from an old daguerreotype.
"That was the father as he went to war.
She always, when she talked about war,
Sooner or later came and leaned, half knelt
Against the lounge beside it, though I doubt
If such unlifelike lines kept power to stir
Anything in her after all the years.
He fell at Gettysburg or Fredericksburg,
I ought to know—it makes a difference which:

Fredericksburg wasn't Gettysburg, of course.
But what I'm getting to is how forsaken
A little cottage this has always seemed;
Since she went more than ever, but before—
I don't mean altogether by the lives
That had gone out of it, the father first,
Then the two sons, till she was left alone.
(Nothing could draw her after those two sons.
She valued the considerate neglect
She had at some cost taught them after years.)
I mean by the world's having passed it by—
As we almost got by this afternoon.
It always seems to me a sort of mark
To measure how far fifty years have brought us.
Why not sit down if you are in no haste?
These doorsteps seldom have a visitor.
The warping boards pull out their own old nails
With none to tread and put them in their place.
She had her own idea of things, the old lady.
And she liked talk. She had seen Garrison
And Whittier, and had her story of them.
One wasn't long in learning that she thought
Whatever else the Civil War was for
It wasn't just to keep the States together,
Nor just to free the slaves, though it did both.
She wouldn't have believed those ends enough
To have given outright for them all she gave.
Her giving somehow touched the principle
That all men are created free and equal.
And to hear her quaint phrases—so removed
From the world's view to-day of all those things.
That's a hard mystery of Jefferson's.
What did he mean? Of course the easy way
Is to decide it simply isn't true.

It may not be. I heard a fellow say so.
But never mind, the Welshman got it planted
Where it will trouble us a thousand years.
Each age will have to reconsider it.
You couldn't tell her what the West was saying,
And what the South to her serene belief.
She had some art of hearing and yet not
Hearing the latter wisdom of the world.
White was the only race she ever knew.
Black she had scarcely seen, and yellow never.
But how could they be made so very unlike
By the same hand working in the same stuff?
She had supposed the war decided that.
What are you going to do with such a person?
Strange how such innocence gets its own way.
I shouldn't be surprised if in this world
It were the force that would at last prevail.
Do you know but for her there was a time
When to please younger members of the church,
Or rather say non-members in the church,
Whom we all have to think of nowadays,
I would have changed the Creed a very little?
Not that she ever had to ask me not to;
It never got so far as that; but the bare thought
Of her old tremulous bonnet in the pew,
And of her half asleep was too much for me.
Why, I might wake her up and startle her.
It was the words 'descended into Hades'
That seemed too pagan to our liberal youth.
You know they suffered from a general onslaught.
And well, if they weren't true why keep right on
Saying them like the heathen? We could drop them.
Only—there was the bonnet in the pew.
Such a phrase couldn't have meant much to her.

But suppose she had missed it from the Creed
As a child misses the unsaid Good-night,
And falls asleep with heartache—how should *I* feel?
I'm just as glad she made me keep hands off,
For, dear me, why abandon a belief
Merely because it ceases to be true.
Cling to it long enough, and not a doubt
It will turn true again, for so it goes.
Most of the change we think we see in life
Is due to truths being in and out of favor.
As I sit here, and often times, I wish
I could be monarch of a desert land
I could devote and dedicate forever
To the truths we keep coming back and back to.
So desert it would have to be, so walled
By mountain ranges half in summer snow,
No one would covet it or think it worth
The pains of conquering to force change on.
Scattered oases where men dwelt, but mostly
Sand dunes held loosely in tamarisk
Blown over and over themselves in idleness.
Sand grains should sugar in the natal dew
The babe born to the desert, the sand storm
Retard mid-waste my cowering caravans—

There are bees in this wall." He struck the clapboards,
Fierce heads looked out; small bodies pivoted.
We rose to go. Sunset blazed on the windows.

"The Black Cottage," written sometime between 1905 and 1907, seems to have undergone substantial revisions during the seven years in which Frost unsuccessfully sent it to editors. Lawrance Thompson published a very different and much shorter version in *Robert Frost: The Early Years* (Thompson 1966, 592–593). That version is a lyric describing the old widow alone in the cottage as she nears death. There is no direct speech, no minister, and no mention of the Civil War.

The biggest influence is Wordsworth's "The Ruined Cottage," a blank-verse poem in which the poet is told the story of a woman whose husband had enlisted as a soldier and never returned. Its position in *North of Boston* also draws attention to parallels with "Home Burial" as it traces the potential for a house to be both a sanctuary and a prison; but in each case, death has invaded the private sphere. The crucial proximity of the graveyard in "Home Burial" may even be inspired by the earlier version of "The Black Cottage," in which the grave of the fallen husband, "Across the way beside the wood," is visible from the house. Whereas "Home Burial" situated the protagonists inside looking out, here they are outside looking in; and while the graveyard in "Home Burial" had been "frame[d]" by the window, now it is the cottage itself "framed" by leaves which must be pushed aside. The object of scrutiny, in each case, is explicitly presented as an artwork, "a sort of special picture" as the second line of "The Black Cottage" puts it; and the ekphrastic element is further reinforced by the description of the cottage door as "Fresh painted by the shower a velvet black."

This is the first poem in *North of Boston* since "The Pasture" not to use dialogue: the minister speaks without reply from the narrator, whose job is merely to set the scene and record the story. Consequently, the poem seems as much about the minister as it is about the dead woman and the eponymous black cottage. It is fitting for a volume so concerned with thresholds that the minister should tell his tale at a windowsill and then while sitting on the "doorsteps." By mediating the woman's story through this character, Frost adds a level of complication to his narrative which was missing in the earlier version quoted by Thompson. Focused on the life history of the woman, the minister manages to range over matters of family, politics, religion, and history, and is encouraged to offer his own (unintentionally dystopian) vision of a society in which he is "monarch." It is no surprise, then, that Frost should have chosen to make his speaker a minister: although chatty and likable (two qualities often synonymous in *North of Boston*), he speaks with an authority which unexpectedly betrays itself as barren. His professional expertise in last things befits a poem concerned with reading the significance of items left behind after death: the " 'unlifelike lines' " of a crayon portrait "Done sadly from an old daguerreotype" give little impression of the husband, and also raise the question of how much the wife's lineaments can really be detected in the cottage she inhabited for fifty years. The minister's confident understanding of the woman may not be contradicted by an-other speaker, but there are clues even in his own monologue that his assurance is unwarranted.

The minister is not always accurate. He remembers that the hus-band " 'fell at Gettysburg or Fredericksburg, / I ought to know—it makes a difference which.' " In several senses he is right: " 'Fredericksburg wasn't Gettysburg, of course,' " not least because the Union lost the first and won the second of those Civil War battles. But for the purposes of his story it makes no difference which, except that, as Ian Hamilton notes, the refusal to intellectualize or compress creates the impression of an "irresistible" sincerity (Hamilton, 16). That impression tends to disguise the fact that the minister is more unjustifiably assertive of things which do make a difference, surmising (for example) that the portrait of her husband would not have " 'kept power to stir / Anything in her after all the years,' " and that she would have taken offense if the min-ister had " 'changed the Creed a very little.' " Yet this account is all the reader has, and when the minister states that the " 'old lady . . . liked talk' " and " 'had her own ideas of things,' " it is necessary to assume that he has heard her holding forth on countless occasions. Already in the early years of the twentieth century, he represents the woman as a remnant of a bygone age, who had seen the abolitionists Garrison and Whittier (which cannot have been particularly unusual—their dates of death having been 1879 and 1892, respectively) and held the view that her husband's sacrifice "'touched the principle / That all men are created free and equal.'" Modern views on such matters—"'the latter wisdom of the world'"—affected her "'serene belief'" not at all.

But the minister's condescension grates. He patronizes the widow's innocence (as he calls it); and when he imagines how she might have reacted to a revision of the Creed, he compares her to a child who "'misses the unsaid Good-night, / And falls asleep with heartache.'" (Frost's notebooks describe but don't identify the source: "'She would have felt as sad for any omission in the creed as the child who remembers in bed that he has forgotten to kiss his mother good night'" [N, 117].) Even the minister's attempts at sympathy—"'why abandon a belief / Merely because it ceases to be true'"—sound like a roundabout way of bolstering the case against the widow. It is when the minister attempts to portray himself as a fellow old-style believer that the most profound differences emerge. His fantasy of being "'monarch of a desert land'" already betrays Jefferson's self-evident truth that all men are created equal; and his vision is of a society which is no society at all, being shut off from the rest of humankind. Nor is there sustenance: "'Sand grains should sugar in the natal dew / The babe born to the desert.'" That desolate image is countered by a sudden return to the black cottage, supposedly "forsaken" but now discovered to be abrim with life:

> ["]There are bees in this wall." He struck the clapboards,
> Fierce heads looked out; small bodies pivoted.
> We rose to go. Sunset blazed on the windows.

The word "windows" provides the characteristic feminine ending, but the imagery resists the rhythm's dying fall. Had those bees turned out to be wasps, the threat would have been still greater; but bees, no matter how "fierce," augur a rich harvest of honey. The cottage continues to nourish life, and sunset provokes a new intensity rather than a dying of the light. This may be an end, the poem seems to suggest, but it is also a glorious illumination—associated with the old woman's legacy—which will sustain the future.

Blueberries

"You ought to have seen what I saw on my way
To the village, through Mortenson's pasture to-day:
Blueberries as big as the end of your thumb,
Real sky-blue, and heavy, and ready to drum
In the cavernous pail of the first one to come!
And all ripe together, not some of them green
And some of them ripe! You ought to have seen!"

"I don't know what part of the pasture you mean."

"You know where they cut off the woods—let me see—
It was two years ago—or no!—can it be
No longer than that?—and the following fall
The fire ran and burned it all up but the wall."

"Why, there hasn't been time for the bushes to grow.
That's always the way with the blueberries, though:
There may not have been the ghost of a sign
Of them anywhere under the shade of the pine,
But get the pine out of the way, you may burn
The pasture all over until not a fern
Or grass-blade is left, not to mention a stick,
And presto, they're up all around you as thick
And hard to explain as a conjuror's trick."

"It must be on charcoal they fatten their fruit.
I taste in them sometimes the flavor of soot.
And after all really they're ebony skinned:
The blue's but a mist from the breath of the wind,
A tarnish that goes at a touch of the hand,
And less than the tan with which pickers are tanned."

"Does Mortenson know what he has, do you think?"

"He may and not care and so leave the chewink
To gather them for him—you know what he is.
He won't make the fact that they're rightfully his
An excuse for keeping us other folk out."

"I wonder you didn't see Loren about."

"The best of it was that I did. Do you know,
I was just getting through what the field had to show
And over the wall and into the road,
When who should come by, with a democrat-load
Of all the young chattering Lorens alive,
But Loren, the fatherly, out for a drive."

"He saw you, then? What did he do? Did he frown?"

"He just kept nodding his head up and down.
You know how politely he always goes by.
But he thought a big thought—I could tell by his eye—
Which being expressed, might be this in effect:
'I have left those there berries, I shrewdly suspect,
To ripen too long. I am greatly to blame.'"

"He's a thriftier person than some I could name."

"He seems to be thrifty; and hasn't he need,
With the mouths of all those young Lorens to feed?
He has brought them all up on wild berries, they say,
Like birds. They store a great many away.
They eat them the year round, and those they don't eat
They sell in the store and buy shoes for their feet."

"Who cares what they say? It's a nice way to live,
Just taking what Nature is willing to give,
Not forcing her hand with harrow and plow."

"I wish you had seen his perpetual bow—
And the air of the youngsters! Not one of them turned,
And they looked so solemn-absurdly concerned."

"I wish I knew half what the flock of them know
Of where all the berries and other things grow,
Cranberries in bogs and raspberries on top
Of the boulder-strewn mountain, and when they will crop.
I met them one day and each had a flower
Stuck into his berries as fresh as a shower;
Some strange kind—they told me it hadn't a name."

"I've told you how once not long after we came,
I almost provoked poor Loren to mirth
By going to him of all people on earth
To ask if he knew any fruit to be had
For the picking. The rascal, he said he'd be glad
To tell if he knew. But the year had been bad.
There *had* been some berries—but those were all gone.
He didn't say where they had been. He went on:
'I'm sure—I'm sure'—as polite as could be.
He spoke to his wife in the door, 'Let me see,
Mame, *we* don't know any good berrying place?'
It was all he could do to keep a straight face."

"If he thinks all the fruit that grows wild is for him,
He'll find he's mistaken. See here, for a whim,
We'll pick in the Mortensons' pasture this year.
We'll go in the morning, that is, if it's clear,
And the sun shines out warm: the vines must be wet.

It's so long since I picked I almost forget
How we used to pick berries: we took one look round,
Then sank out of sight like trolls underground,
And saw nothing more of each other, or heard,
Unless when you said I was keeping a bird
Away from its nest, and I said it was you.
'Well, one of us is.' For complaining it flew
Around and around us. And then for a while
We picked, till I feared you had wandered a mile,
And I thought I had lost you. I lifted a shout
Too loud for the distance you were, it turned out,
For when you made answer, your voice was as low
As talking—you stood up beside me, you know."

"We shan't have the place to ourselves to enjoy—
Not likely, when all the young Lorens deploy.
They'll be there to-morrow, or even to-night.
They won't be too friendly—they may be polite—
To people they look on as having no right
To pick where they're picking. But we won't complain.
You ought to have seen how it looked in the rain,
The fruit mixed with water in layers of leaves,
Like two kinds of jewels, a vision for thieves."

"Blueberries" is an anomaly. Not quite the only poem in *North of Boston*
to rhyme—"Good Hours" and "After Apple-Picking" share that distinc-
tion—it nevertheless stands apart because it marries rhyme with dia-
logue. For a poet so keen to capture and record the rhythms of speech,
the decision to rhyme is a curious one. Blank verse, Frost's preferred
medium for anglicizing the dactylic hexameter of Virgil (*CPP&P*, 849),
is not much more precisely representative of everyday speech; and Frost
may have decided against heroic couplets as bringing him too close to

one of his masters, Robert Browning. But by coupling his rhymes with an anapestic rhythm far more inflexible than *North of Boston*'s iambic pentameter ever sounds, Frost blazons the artificiality of the poem's conversation. The self-corrections and interjections of speech seem done primarily for the sake of rhyme: " 'You know where they cut off the woods—let me see—/ It was two years ago—or no!—can it be / No longer than that?—.' "

Few critics have made the effort to see past the formal characteristics of "Blueberries"—the poem remains almost entirely neglected. It does little with the volume's presiding symbols of house and threshold, and it loses all dramatic tension by exporting its sense of dialogic competitiveness: the speakers, so often presented as rivals throughout *North of Boston,* here find themselves united against a foe which readers encounter only by report. Even conceding the argument of Patrick Kavanagh's "Epic," in which Homer encourages the latter-day poet to write of neighborly disputes ("I made the Iliad from such / A local row"), any reader might find the local row of which Frost writes in "Blueberries" unworthy of attention. The blueberries themselves seem strangely changeable: although they are first described as " 'Real sky-blue,' " before long the same speaker confesses that " 'after all really they're ebony skinned: / The blue's but a mist from the breath of the wind.' "

The poem turns on claims of ownership similar to those in "Rose Pogonias": to whom do wild fruits belong, and who is entitled to pick them? The Lorens act proprietorially, but even through the lens of their wryly disapproving rivals there is a perceived merit to their lifestyle: " 'It's a nice way to live, / Just taking what Nature is willing to give, / Not forcing her hand with harrow and plow.' " Loren is " 'a thriftier person than some I could name' "; such coyness does nothing to prevent the implication that numbered among those less thrifty souls is Mortenson, the farmer in whose field the blueberries grow. Mortenson may know what he has " 'and not care' "—" 'you know what he is.' " The tone verges on disapproval: " 'rightfully' " the blueberries are his, but he seems more blameworthy than those who would enjoy nature's harvest rather than allow it to be squandered. Only taking what nature gives, the Lorens are also contrasted with the mischievous speakers, who plan " 'for a whim' "—that is, in order to spite the Lorens—to pick the blueberries. The speakers want to assert their right, but at the end of the poem they tacitly acknowledge their criminality: the fruit in the rain was " 'a vision for thieves.' " Those issues of need, entitlement, and selfishness will be more powerfully explored elsewhere in Frost's work. The best that can be said for "Blueberries" is that it prepares for a later and greater poem like "Two Tramps in Mud Time."

A Servant to Servants

I didn't make you know how glad I was
To have you come and camp here on our land.
I promised myself to get down some day
And see the way you lived, but I don't know!
With a houseful of hungry men to feed
I guess you'd find . . . It seems to me
I can't express my feelings any more
Than I can raise my voice or want to lift
My hand (oh, I can lift it when I have to).
Did ever you feel so? I hope you never.
It's got so I don't even know for sure
Whether I *am* glad, sorry, or anything.
There's nothing but a voice-like left inside
That seems to tell me how I ought to feel,
And would feel if I wasn't all gone wrong.
You take the lake. I look and look at it.
I see it's a fair, pretty sheet of water.
I stand and make myself repeat out loud
The advantages it has, so long and narrow,
Like a deep piece of some old running river
Cut short off at both ends. It lies five miles
Straight away through the mountain notch
From the sink window where I wash the plates,
And all our storms come up toward the house,
Drawing the slow waves whiter and whiter and whiter.
It took my mind off doughnuts and soda biscuit
To step outdoors and take the water dazzle
A sunny morning, or take the rising wind
About my face and body and through my wrapper,
When a storm threatened from the Dragon's Den,
And a cold chill shivered across the lake.
I see it's a fair, pretty sheet of water,

Our Willoughby! How did you hear of it?
I expect, though, everyone's heard of it.
In a book about ferns? Listen to that!
You let things more like feathers regulate
Your going and coming. And you like it here?
I can see how you might. But I don't know!
It would be different if more people came,
For then there would be business. As it is,
The cottages Len built, sometimes we rent them,
Sometimes we don't. We've a good piece of shore
That ought to be worth something, and may yet.
But I don't count on it as much as Len.
He looks on the bright side of everything,
Including me. He thinks I'll be all right
With doctoring. But it's not medicine—
Lowe is the only doctor's dared to say so—
It's rest I want—there, I have said it out—
From cooking meals for hungry hired men
And washing dishes after them—from doing
Things over and over that just won't stay done.
By good rights I ought not to have so much
Put on me, but there seems no other way.
Len says one steady pull more ought to do it.
He says the best way out is always through.
And I agree to that, or in so far
As that I can see no way out but through—
Leastways for me—and then they'll be convinced.
It's not that Len don't want the best for me.
It was his plan our moving over in
Beside the lake from where that day I showed you
We used to live—ten miles from anywhere.
We didn't change without some sacrifice,
But Len went at it to make up the loss.
His work's a man's, of course, from sun to sun,

But he works when he works as hard as I do—
Though there's small profit in comparisons.
(Women and men will make them all the same.)
But work ain't all. Len undertakes too much.
He's into everything in town. This year
It's highways, and he's got too many men
Around him to look after that make waste.
They take advantage of him shamefully,
And proud, too, of themselves for doing so.
We have four here to board, great good-for-nothings,
Sprawling about the kitchen with their talk
While I fry their bacon. Much they care!
No more put out in what they do or say
Than if I wasn't in the room at all.
Coming and going all the time, they are:
I don't learn what their names are, let alone
Their characters, or whether they are safe
To have inside the house with doors unlocked.
I'm not afraid of them, though, if they're not
Afraid of me. There's two can play at that.
I have my fancies: it runs in the family.
My father's brother wasn't right. They kept him
Locked up for years back there at the old farm.
I've been away once—yes, I've been away.
The State Asylum. I was prejudiced;
I wouldn't have sent anyone of mine there;
You know the old idea—the only asylum
Was the poorhouse, and those who could afford,
Rather than send their folks to such a place,
Kept them at home; and it does seem more human.
But it's not so: the place is the asylum.
There they have every means proper to do with,
And you aren't darkening other people's lives—
Worse than no good to them, and they no good

To you in your condition; you can't know
Affection or the want of it in that state.
I've heard too much of the old-fashioned way.
My father's brother, he went mad quite young.
Some thought he had been bitten by a dog,
Because his violence took on the form
Of carrying his pillow in his teeth;
But it's more likely he was crossed in love,
Or so the story goes. It was some girl.
Anyway all he talked about was love.
They soon saw he would do someone a mischief
If he wa'n't kept strict watch of, and it ended
In father's building him a sort of cage,
Or room within a room, of hickory poles,
Like stanchions in the barn, from floor to ceiling,—
A narrow passage all the way around.
Anything they put in for furniture
He'd tear to pieces, even a bed to lie on.
So they made the place comfortable with straw,
Like a beast's stall, to ease their consciences.
Of course they had to feed him without dishes.
They tried to keep him clothed, but he paraded
With his clothes on his arm—all of his clothes.
Cruel—it sounds. I s'pose they did the best
They knew. And just when he was at the height,
Father and mother married, and mother came,
A bride, to help take care of such a creature,
And accommodate her young life to his.
That was what marrying father meant to her.
She had to lie and hear love things made dreadful
By his shouts in the night. He'd shout and shout
Until the strength was shouted out of him,
And his voice died down slowly from exhaustion.
He'd pull his bars apart like bow and bow-string,

And let them go and make them twang until
His hands had worn them smooth as any ox-bow.
And then he'd crow as if he thought that child's play—
The only fun he had. I've heard them say, though,
They found a way to put a stop to it.
He was before my time—I never saw him;
But the pen stayed exactly as it was
There in the upper chamber in the ell,
A sort of catch-all full of attic clutter.
I often think of the smooth hickory bars.
It got so I would say—you know, half fooling—
"It's time I took my turn upstairs in jail"—
Just as you will till it becomes a habit.
No wonder I was glad to get away.
Mind you, I waited till Len said the word.
I didn't want the blame if things went wrong.
I was glad though, no end, when we moved out,
And I looked to be happy, and I was,
As I said, for a while—but I don't know!
Somehow the change wore out like a prescription.
And there's more to it than just window-views
And living by a lake. I'm past such help—
Unless Len took the notion, which he won't,
And I won't ask him—it's not sure enough.
I s'pose I've got to go the road I'm going:
Other folks have to, and why shouldn't I?
I almost think if I could do like you,
Drop everything and live out on the ground—
But it might be, come night, I shouldn't like it,
Or a long rain. I should soon get enough,
And be glad of a good roof overhead.
I've lain awake thinking of you, I'll warrant,
More than you have yourself, some of these nights.
The wonder was the tents weren't snatched away

From over you as you lay in your beds.
I haven't courage for a risk like that.
Bless you, of course you're keeping me from work,
But the thing of it is, I need to *be* kept.
There's work enough to do—there's always that;
But behind's behind. The worst that you can do
Is set me back a little more behind.
I shan't catch up in this world, anyway.
I'd *rather* you'd not go unless you must.

Several of the poems in *North of Boston* are dialogues in which conversation becomes so one-sided as to verge on soliloquy. "The Mountain" and "The Code" are driven by a garrulous speaker who is in turn spurred on to new speculations by a near-silent interlocutor. "A Servant to Servants" takes the further step of dispensing altogether with the interlocutor, and adopts a technique learned from Robert Browning of assimilating the subsidiary character's infrequent comments into the onrush of the woman's own monologue:

> How did you hear of it?
> I expect, though, everyone's heard of it.
> In a book about ferns? Listen to that!
> You let things more like feathers regulate
> Your going and coming. And you like it here?
> I can see how you might.

That passage is as close as we ever come to hearing directly from the botanizing visitors. Their interest in feathery ferns befits an identity so intangible as to barely register (as well as establishing one of Frost's most characteristic dichotomies, between those tied to the necessities of labor and those free to indulge in less practical kinds of endeavor). By comparison, Browning's silent characters assert their forceful presence. The eponymous hero of "Mr. Sludge, 'The Medium'" can hardly speak his monologue for being throttled by the exposer of his fraud: "Aie—aie—aie!/Please, sir! your thumbs are through my windpipe, sir!/Ch—ch!" Frost's speaker seems more lonely and isolated, talking of intimate things to an audience which minimally interacts, and which seems at the end to be making polite excuses to leave only to be held back by the desperate woman: "I'd *rather* you'd not go unless you must." Rarely have italics been more poignantly deployed, as they set the frantic emphasis of the speaking voice against the phrase's polite formulation.

The poem's title alludes to Genesis, in which Noah curses his youngest son Ham (and, consequently, Ham's descendants, the people of Canaan) for having seen him naked: "Cursed be Canaan; a servant of servants shall he be unto his brethren" (Genesis 9:25). Frost's speaker literally acts as a servant to servants, cooking for the hired men who take advantage of her and her husband, Len. But the biblical allusion goes deeper. Ham's great crime was not only seeing his father's nakedness but reporting it to his brothers Shem and Japheth; they reacted by covering their father with a garment while "their faces were backward." "A Servant to Servants" is concerned with nakedness, exposure, and coverings, and with curses passed down through generations (the curse being madness). Take, for example, the woman's concern for the botanists who lack "a good roof overhead." Noah's tent in which he lies drunken and exposed is here transformed into their tents, feared to be inadequate and insufficient in a storm: "The wonder was the tents weren't snatched away/From over you as you lay in your beds." And the uncle who had been locked in a purpose-built cage—not so much the madwoman in the attic as the madman in the barn—parades his nakedness with "his clothes on his arm" despite the best efforts of others "to keep him clothed."

Her uncle's fate has shadowed the woman as a threat but perhaps, at times, as a possible refuge: those "half fooling" comments about taking her turn "upstairs in jail" convey a strange sense of longing even though she reports herself as having been "glad to get away." But her chosen destiny seems no more preferable: it has merely locked her in a different kind of cage. Hollowed out by overwork, she despairs that the sanctuary of the home has been invaded by the "great good-for-nothings" who carelessly exploit her hospitality. She admits to a lack of affect—"There's nothing but a voice-like left inside / That seems to tell me how I ought to feel." That detachment from her own emotions symptomizes utter defeat. Her innermost identity has been whittled down to an adjective: "a voice-like." Meanwhile, her husband hides behind aphorisms like the neighbor in "Mending Wall"; it is ironic that his offering, "the best way out is always through," has developed a life outside the poem as a piece of homely wisdom, when here it sounds more like a substitute for necessary action. She may claim that she "can't express [her] feelings"—a claim which her monologue erodes or at least complicates; but that accusation seems more appropriately aimed at Len, whose other piece of reported speech ("one more steady pull ought to do it") is an exercise in fatuity.

Often described as a study of a woman on the edge of madness, "A Servant to Servants" portrays a character too self-knowing in her diagnoses for that assessment to ring quite true. She may be exhausted and enervated, but she is also extraordinarily articulate; only once in her monologue (at line six) does she break off and have to start again. It would not be at all surprising, she broadly suggests, if she did go mad, given her mental history and her current circumstances; yet the fact that she states that case, rather than showing it through incoherence or sudden shifts of register, goes some way toward contradicting it. More evident is her isolation, and in that respect she joins a cast of characters—the doctor of "A Hundred Collars," the widow of "The Black Cottage," the husband and wife of "Home Burial"—who are lonely or cannot engage with those around them. Love and marriage are represented as joylessly destructive: there is the uncle's madness after being "crossed in love"; the mother who must "accommodate her young life" to the blighted fate of her brother-in-law ("That was what marrying father meant to her") and who must lie in the marital bed hearing "love things made dreadful" by his shouts; and the speaker herself, who (if her hints are to be trusted) lives alongside her husband, but not *with* him in any but the most meaningless way. She says she wants rest, but her reaction at the end of the poem suggests that she is even more needful of human companionship. (That need makes Frost's use of monologue all the more bitterly ironic.) It may be a sign of the emptiness of her marriage that her audience's attention, muted and sporadic though its responses may be, provides more solace than her husband. Her monologue is no talking cure; by now, it is too late for any talk of cures. But it does at least do what Frost argued that all poems should: offer a momentary stay against confusion.

After Apple-Picking

My long two-pointed ladder's sticking through a tree
Toward heaven still,
And there's a barrel that I didn't fill
Beside it, and there may be two or three
Apples I didn't pick upon some bough.
But I am done with apple-picking now.
Essence of winter sleep is on the night,
The scent of apples: I am drowsing off.
I cannot rub the strangeness from my sight
I got from looking through a pane of glass
I skimmed this morning from the drinking trough
And held against the world of hoary grass.
It melted, and I let it fall and break.
But I was well
Upon my way to sleep before it fell,
And I could tell
What form my dreaming was about to take.
Magnified apples appear and disappear,
Stem end and blossom end,
And every fleck of russet showing clear.
My instep arch not only keeps the ache,
It keeps the pressure of a ladder-round.
I feel the ladder sway as the boughs bend.
And I keep hearing from the cellar bin
The rumbling sound
Of load on load of apples coming in.
For I have had too much
Of apple-picking: I am overtired
Of the great harvest I myself desired.
There were ten thousand thousand fruit to touch,
Cherish in hand, lift down, and not let fall.

For all
That struck the earth,
No matter if not bruised or spiked with stubble,
Went surely to the cider-apple heap
As of no worth.
One can see what will trouble
This sleep of mine, whatever sleep it is.
Were he not gone,
The woodchuck could say whether it's like his
Long sleep, as I describe its coming on,
Or just some human sleep.

Nothing in *North of Boston,* or in Frost's earlier work, prepares the reader for the surprise of "After Apple-Picking." So often memorized and anthologized, it has helped fulfill its author's ambition to "lodge a few poems where they will be hard to get rid of" (*CPP&P,* 744). Frost himself recognized its strange separateness: "But one poem in the book [*North of Boston*] will intone and that is 'After Apple-Picking.' The rest talk" (*SL,* 129–130). The difference is partly generic, as the lyric voice is allowed rare and full expression amid the dialogues and dramatic monologues which otherwise dominate the volume. There is also a freedom from blank verse: Frost temporarily puts to one side his ambition to record the rhythms of natural speech.

Although "After Apple-Picking" is not the only poem in *North of Boston* to rhyme, its metrical irregularities set it conspicuously apart. The meter remains predominantly iambic throughout, but this poem of blurred distinctions is suitably fluid in both rhyme and line length. Rhymes can be adjacent or separated by as many as seven lines; lines range from two syllables to twelve. Reuben Brower's detailed analysis maps the ways in which the poem "comes to the reader through sentences filled with incantatory repetitions and rhymes and in waves of sound linked by likeness of pattern" (Brower, 24), and he demonstrates that these repetitions and rhymes are never allowed to settle into anything approaching a *predictable* pattern.

Although such formal experiments make the poem seem like a wild holiday from *North of Boston*'s usual practices, it is not entirely oblivious to its position within larger structures. *North of Boston* begins in the "spring mending-time" of "Mending Wall," and ends with the "frozen swamp" of "The Wood-Pile" and the "winter evening walk" of "Good Hours." The autumnal mood of "After Apple-Picking" fits this chronology of seasonal change. It appears just more than halfway through the volume, immediately after the blueberries' summer harvest and the windy nights which so worried the speaker of "A Servant to Servants," but preceding the dark advance of cloud in "The Code" and the constant rainfall reported in "The Generations of Men."

"After Apple-Picking" is, therefore, concerned with climatic transitions from summer to fall and from fall to winter. It is also concerned with other kinds of transition, such as the shifts from past to present and from the physical labor of waking hours to the promise of sleep. These transitions are never simple: far from bringing rest, sleep may turn out to be "trouble[d]" by the daytime's activities; so blurred have boundaries become between sleep and wake that it is impossible to distinguish them. The great poet of sleep (and of autumn), John Keats, had wondered in "Ode to a Nightingale" whether he had just experienced "a vision, or a waking dream," and concluded in further uncertainty: "do I wake or sleep?" Keats gives voice to a question which Frost's persona might equally ask himself.

As if to illustrate the point, for all its dreamy peculiarities of focus "After Apple-Picking" is intensely physical, retaining and reliving the ache on the instep arch. Ironically, the poem's feast of the senses ("the scent of apples," "looking through a pane of glass," "hearing . . . The rumbling sound," "ten thousand thousand fruit to touch") omits the one sense which ought to be pleasured by the apple harvest: taste. After apple picking should come apple eating, but that seems to be the last thing on the protagonist's mind. The experience of picking is its own mixed blessing, as it can lead to an unpalatable surfeit: "I am overtired / Of the great harvest I myself desired." "Overtired" evokes boredom as well as exhaustion, implying that the persona has not been careful in what he wished for. "I am done with apple-picking now"—an expression tonally distinct from merely reporting that the apple picking is done—conveys something less than enthusiasm for the business undertaken. The promise of "heaven" in the poem's opening lines has remained unfulfilled: the only legacy of the apple picking is a troubled and aching sleep.

The word "sleep" occurs seven times, and its fourfold repetition in the last five lines bolsters the authority of the poem's final word:

> One can see what will trouble
> This sleep of mine, whatever sleep it is.
> Were he not gone,
> The woodchuck could say whether it's like his
> Long sleep, as I describe its coming on,
> Or just some human sleep.

Commentators have referred to this "long sleep" as the big sleep, the sleep of death, but it is explicitly hibernation as experienced by the woodchuck—hence the contrast with "just some human sleep." John Hollander has shown how the line break in Frost's couplet "But I was well / Upon my way to sleep before it fell" insists on the desirability of this impending state: to be on the way to sleep is to be "well" (Hollander 1975, 109). In waking, the protagonist had experienced a "strangeness" of "sight" after looking through ice; sleep seems just as strange and potentially unhuman, with its obsessive dream of "Magnified apples" and "every fleck of russet showing clear." Unsure whether he is already sleeping or about to sleep, and with (bizarrely, as if *Alice*-like dream logic has taken over) just the absent woodchuck able to clarify the nature of his sleep, the protagonist has moved from the vertical aspirations of the opening lines to the imminent prospect of a respite which is, if not necessarily recuperative, at least safely earthbound.

The Code

There were three in the meadow by the brook
Gathering up windrows, piling cocks of hay,
With an eye always lifted toward the west
Where an irregular sun-bordered cloud
Darkly advanced with a perpetual dagger
Flickering across its bosom. Suddenly
One helper, thrusting pitchfork in the ground,
Marched himself off the field and home. One stayed.
The town-bred farmer failed to understand.

"What is there wrong?"

                              "Something you just now said."

"What did I say?"

                        "About our taking pains."

"To cock the hay?—because it's going to shower?
I said that more than half an hour ago.
I said it to myself as much as you."

"You didn't know. But James is one big fool.
He thought you meant to find fault with his work.
That's what the average farmer would have meant.
James would take time, of course, to chew it over
Before he acted: he's just got round to act."

"He is a fool if that's the way he takes me."

"Don't let it bother you. You've found out something.
The hand that knows his business won't be told

To do work better or faster—those two things.
I'm as particular as any one:
Most likely I'd have served you just the same.
But I know you don't understand our ways.
You were just talking what was in your mind,
What was in all our minds, and you weren't hinting.
Tell you a story of what happened once:
I was up here in Salem at a man's
Named Sanders with a gang of four or five
Doing the haying. No one liked the boss.
He was one of the kind sports call a spider,
All wiry arms and legs that spread out wavy
From a humped body nigh as big's a biscuit.
But work! that man could work, especially
If by so doing he could get more work
Out of his hired help. I'm not denying
He was hard on himself. I couldn't find
That he kept any hours—not for himself.
Daylight and lantern-light were one to him:
I've heard him pounding in the barn all night.
But what he liked was someone to encourage.
Them that he couldn't lead he'd get behind
And drive, the way you can, you know, in mowing—
Keep at their heels and threaten to mow their legs off.
I'd seen about enough of his bulling tricks
(We call that bulling). I'd been watching him.
So when he paired off with me in the hayfield
To load the load, thinks I, Look out for trouble.
I built the load and topped it off; old Sanders
Combed it down with a rake and says, 'O.K.'
Everything went well till we reached the barn
With a big catch to empty in a bay.
You understand that meant the easy job
For the man up on top of throwing *down*

The hay and rolling it off wholesale,
Where on a mow it would have been slow lifting.
You wouldn't think a fellow'd need much urging
Under these circumstances, would you now?
But the old fool seizes his fork in both hands,
And looking up bewhiskered out of the pit,
Shouts like an army captain, 'Let her come!'
Thinks I, D'ye mean it? 'What was that you said?'
I asked out loud, so's there'd be no mistake,
'Did you say, Let her come?' 'Yes, let her come.'
He said it over, but he said it softer.
Never you say a thing like that to a man,
Not if he values what he is. God, I'd as soon
Murdered him as left out his middle name.
I'd built the load and knew right where to find it.
Two or three forkfuls I picked lightly round for
Like meditating, and then I just dug in
And dumped the rackful on him in ten lots.
I looked over the side once in the dust
And caught sight of him treading-water-like,
Keeping his head above. 'Damn ye,' I says,
'That gets ye!' He squeaked like a squeezed rat.
That was the last I saw or heard of him.
I cleaned the rack and drove out to cool off.
As I sat mopping hayseed from my neck,
And sort of waiting to be asked about it,
One of the boys sings out, 'Where's the old man?'
'I left him in the barn under the hay.
If ye want him, ye can go and dig him out.'
They realized from the way I swobbed my neck
More than was needed something must be up.
They headed for the barn; I stayed where I was.
They told me afterward. First they forked hay,
A lot of it, out into the barn floor.

Nothing! They listened for him. Not a rustle.
I guess they thought I'd spiked him in the temple
Before I buried him, or I couldn't have managed.
They excavated more. 'Go keep his wife
Out of the barn.' Someone looked in a window,
And curse me if he wasn't in the kitchen
Slumped way down in a chair, with both his feet
Stuck in the oven, the hottest day that summer.
He looked so clean disgusted from behind
There was no one that dared to stir him up,
Or let him know that he was being looked at.
Apparently I hadn't buried him
(I may have knocked him down); but my just trying
To bury him had hurt his dignity.
He had gone to the house so's not to meet me.
He kept away from us all afternoon.
We tended to his hay. We saw him out
After a while picking peas in his garden:
He couldn't keep away from doing something."

"Weren't you relieved to find he wasn't dead?"

"No! and yet I don't know—it's hard to say.
I went about to kill him fair enough."

"You took an awkward way. Did he discharge you?"

"Discharge me? No! He knew I did just right."

"After Apple-Picking" had marked a brief departure, but "The Code"
returns to *North of Boston*'s familiar territory of (characteristically
lopsided) dialogue in blank verse, even down to the hendecasyllabic

Frostian line: "Darkly advanced with a perpetual dagger"; "'Don't let it bother you. You've found out something'"; "'Nothing! They listened for him. Not a rustle.'" Each opening with a trochaic foot, these examples bring together Frost's two most common strategies for varying the iambic meter. Giving an account of *North of Boston*'s versification in 1914, he explained that "there are the very regular preestablished accent and measure of blank verse; and there are the very irregular accent and measure of speaking intonation. I am never more pleased than when I can get these into strained relation" (*CPP&P*, 680); or as he put it more aphoristically elsewhere, "Poetry plays the rhythms of dramatic speech on the grid of meter" (*CPP&P*, 809). In this respect, Frost is the twentieth century's most profound heir to Shakespeare: the tension between blank verse and the speaking voice is as much the poem's drama as the events which the poem happens to describe.

Like "The Mountain" and "Home Burial," "The Code" begins by setting the scene before any dialogue takes place. The opening passage establishes a clear stylistic distinction between the narrator's overblown metaphor ("a perpetual dagger / Flickering across its bosom") and the more homely vocabulary of the farmhand whose metaphors allude to biscuits, spiders, and rats. On the rare occasion when the farmhand does employ an obscure word ("bulling"), he stops to explain it before proceeding with his story. Yet that generous accommodation is part of a more sinister strategy. The farmhand comes across as a sympathetic figure, who takes the farmer and the reader into his confidence; and yet he tells a story of attempted murder, weakly justified by a sense of dislike for his victim and a callously literal interpretation of an unfortunate comment. Frost's challenge is to avoid prompting the reader to any moral judgment against his behavior.

Frost originally published the poem under the title "The Code—Heroics," which made the farmhand easier to denounce. "Heroics" claims too much, seems too obviously ironic. By removing the clue, Frost also removes any sign of dissent. Even the narrator implies approval of the farmhand's actions. The farmhand tells his tale, after all, to a "town-bred farmer," and the narrator's barb immediately marks the farmer as an alien and an interloper who can never hope to share or break the "code." When Lionel Trilling, speaking at the dinner to celebrate Frost's eighty-fifth birthday, felt himself to be incongruous as "a man of the city" (Trilling, 155), he might have been reacting to the kind of prejudice capable of turning the adjective "town-bred" into an insult. James, the offended farmhand, is dismissed as " 'one big fool' " for marching home without a word, but the extent of his foolishness is measured by his failure to take into account the farmer's own foolishness. The farmhand who stays does so only because he makes allowance for the town-bred farmer's ignorance: " 'But I know you don't understand our ways.' " To criticize those ways is to condemn oneself to exclusion from the natural life of the land.

In "The Code" as in "Home Burial," the way that a thing is said can have disastrous consequences. Tell men *what* to do, but not *when* or how quickly. The farmer's innocent remark, made as much to himself as to his fellow workers, prompts one of them to leave; but it transpires that the farmer has got away lightly, because he is then told a tale in which just such a mis-saying is nearly punished by death. Stung by Amy Lowell's claim that his poetry lacked a sense of humor, Frost argued that "seven out of fifteen of the poems in N. of Boston are almost humorous—four are almost jokes: The Mountain, A Hundred Collars, The Code, The Generations of Men" (*LU*, 40). Attempted murder is a curious kind of joke, not even "almost" a joke unless it be like the laugh of the Miller, in a later poem, "The Vanishing Red," after he has cold-bloodedly killed "the last Red Man / In Acton." Admittedly, there is a certain cartoony panache in the description of the farmhand's victim " 'treading-water-like, / Keeping his head above,' " but that comes with a vengeful outburst which is both reportage and a continuing sense of sadistic enjoyment at the memory of the incident: " ' "Damn ye," I says, / "That gets ye!" He squeaked like a squeezed rat.' " If comedy is at work here, it exists only in the farmhand's retelling, and its effect is to exacerbate the brutality of a man who will murder without compunction in order to prove to himself that he " 'values what he is.' "

Despite all the pressures on him to consent, the farmer does muster some opposition: "'You took an awkward way.'" That phrase remembers the farmhand's accusation that the farmer fails to "'understand our ways'"; the ways of the farmhand will not be followed by the farmer, who remains critically distant. As the misunderstood "boss" who has just heard of another boss's fortunate escape, he has good reason to feel vulnerable. And yet "awkward" is the most delicate of euphemisms, enacting an unwillingness to deplore too openly what he has just heard. Even the farmer's limited dissent is overruled when Frost gives the authority of the final line to the farmhand, who reports his victim's acquiescence: "'He knew I did just right.'" If the victim accepts the rightness of his fate, then how is the town-bred farmer to object? Trilling caused controversy when he called Frost a "terrifying poet" who had conceived a "terrifying universe"; he alluded to two poems, "Design" and "Neither Out Far Nor In Deep," which linger on a cosmic viciousness and a cosmic emptiness, respectively. "The Code" may have little to say about the universe, but in its more intimate earthly way it is at least as terrifying. It tempts the reader with the all-too-human inclination to overlook the murderous failings of those whose approval we seek.

The Generations of Men

A governor it was proclaimed this time,
When all who would come seeking in New Hampshire
Ancestral memories might come together.
And those of the name Stark gathered in Bow,
A rock-strewn town where farming has fallen off,
And sprout-lands flourish where the axe has gone.
Someone had literally run to earth
In an old cellar hole in a by-road
The origin of all the family there.
Thence they were sprung, so numerous a tribe
That now not all the houses left in town
Made shift to shelter them without the help
Of here and there a tent in grove and orchard.
They were at Bow, but that was not enough:
Nothing would do but they must fix a day
To stand together on the crater's verge
That turned them on the world, and try to fathom
The past and get some strangeness out of it.
But rain spoiled all. The day began uncertain,
With clouds low trailing and moments of rain that misted.
The young folk held some hope out to each other
Till well toward noon when the storm settled down
With a swish in the grass. "What if the others
Are there," they said. "It isn't going to rain."
Only one from a farm not far away
Strolled thither, not expecting he would find
Anyone else, but out of idleness.
One, and one other, yes, for there were two.
The second round the curving hillside road
Was a girl; and she halted some way off
To reconnoitre, and then made up her mind

At least to pass by and see who he was,
And perhaps to hear some word about the weather.
This was some Stark she didn't know. He nodded.
"No fête to-day," he said.

                    "It looks that way."
She swept the heavens, turning on her heel.
"I only idled down."

              "I idled down."

Provision there had been for just such meeting
Of stranger cousins, in a family tree
Drawn on a sort of passport with the branch
Of the one bearing it done in detail—
Some zealous one's laborious device.
She made a sudden movement toward her bodice,
As one who clasps her heart. They laughed together.
"Stark?" he inquired. "No matter for the proof."

"Yes, Stark. And you?"

                    "I'm Stark." He drew his passport.

"You know we might not be and still be cousins:
The town is full of Chases, Lowes, and Baileys,
All claiming some priority in Starkness.
My mother was a Lane, yet might have married
Anyone upon earth and still her children
Would have been Starks, and doubtless here to-day."

"You riddle with your genealogy
Like a Viola. I don't follow you."

"I only mean my mother was a Stark
Several times over, and by marrying father
No more than brought us back into the name."

"One ought not to be thrown into confusion
By a plain statement of relationship,
But I own what you say makes my head spin.
You take my card—you seem so good at such things—
And see if you can reckon our cousinship.
Why not take seats here on the cellar wall
And dangle feet among the raspberry vines?"

"Under the shelter of the family tree."

"Just so—that ought to be enough protection."

"Not from the rain. I think it's going to rain."

"It's raining."

              "No, it's misting; let's be fair.
Does the rain seem to you to cool the eyes?"

The situation was like this: the road
Bowed outward on the mountain half-way up,
And disappeared and ended not far off.
No one went home that way. The only house
Beyond where they were was a shattered seedpod.
And below roared a brook hidden in trees,
The sound of which was silence for the place.
This he sat listening to till she gave judgment.

"On father's side, it seems, we're—let me see——"

"Don't be too technical.—You have three cards."

"Four cards, one yours, three mine, one for each branch
Of the Stark family I'm a member of."

"D'you know a person so related to herself
Is supposed to be mad."

        "I may be mad."

"You look so, sitting out here in the rain
Studying genealogy with me
You never saw before. What will we come to
With all this pride of ancestry, we Yankees?
I think we're all mad. Tell me why we're here
Drawn into town about this cellar hole
Like wild geese on a lake before a storm?
What do we see in such a hole, I wonder."

"The Indians had a myth of Chicamoztoc,
Which means The Seven Caves that We Came out of.
This is the pit from which we Starks were digged."

"You must be learned. That's what you see in it?"

"And what do you see?"

        "Yes, what *do* I see?
First let me look. I see raspberry vines——"

"Oh, if you're going to use your eyes, just hear
What *I* see. It's a little, little boy,
As pale and dim as a match flame in the sun;

He's groping in the cellar after jam,
He thinks it's dark and it's flooded with daylight."

"He's nothing. Listen. When I lean like this
I can make out old Grandsir Stark distinctly,—
With his pipe in his mouth and his brown jug—
Bless you, it isn't Grandsir Stark, it's Granny,
But the pipe's there and smoking and the jug.
She's after cider, the old girl, she's thirsty;
Here's hoping she gets her drink and gets out safely."

"Tell me about her. Does she look like me?"

"She should, shouldn't she, you're so many times
Over descended from her. I believe
She does look like you. Stay the way you are.
The nose is just the same, and so's the chin—
Making allowance, making due allowance."

"You poor, dear, great, great, great, great Granny!"

"See that you get her greatness right. Don't stint her."

"Yes, it's important, though you think it isn't.
I won't be teased. But see how wet I am."

"Yes, you must go; we can't stay here for ever.
But wait until I give you a hand up.
A bead of silver water more or less
Strung on your hair won't hurt your summer looks.
I wanted to try something with the noise
That the brook raises in the empty valley.
We have seen visions—now consult the voices.
Something I must have learned riding in trains

When I was young. I used the roar
To set the voices speaking out of it,
Speaking or singing, and the band-music playing.
Perhaps you have the art of what I mean.
I've never listened in among the sounds
That a brook makes in such a wild descent.
It ought to give a purer oracle."

"It's as you throw a picture on a screen:
The meaning of it all is out of you;
The voices give you what you wish to hear."

"Strangely, it's anything they wish to give."

"Then I don't know. It must be strange enough.
I wonder if it's not your make-believe.
What do you think you're like to hear to-day?"

"From the sense of our having been together—
But why take time for what I'm like to hear?
I'll tell you what the voices really say.
You will do very well right where you are
A little longer. I mustn't feel too hurried,
Or I can't give myself to hear the voices."

"Is this some trance you are withdrawing into?"

"You must be very still; you mustn't talk."

"I'll hardly breathe."

       "The voices seem to say——"

"I'm waiting."

"Don't! The voices seem to say:
Call her Nausicaa, the unafraid
Of an acquaintance made adventurously."

"I let you say that—on consideration."

"I don't see very well how you can help it.
You want the truth. I speak but by the voices.
You see they know I haven't had your name,
Though what a name should matter between us——"

"I shall suspect——"

"Be good. The voices say:
Call her Nausicaa, and take a timber
That you shall find lies in the cellar charred
Among the raspberries, and hew and shape it
For a door-sill or other corner piece
In a new cottage on the ancient spot.
The life is not yet all gone out of it.
And come and make your summer dwelling here,
And perhaps she will come, still unafraid,
And sit before you in the open door
With flowers in her lap until they fade,
But not come in across the sacred sill——"

"I wonder where your oracle is tending.
You can see that there's something wrong with it,
Or it would speak in dialect. Whose voice
Does it purport to speak in? Not old Grandsir's
Nor Granny's, surely. Call up one of them.
They have best right to be heard in this place."

"You seem so partial to our great-grandmother
(Nine times removed. Correct me if I err.)
You will be likely to regard as sacred
Anything she may say. But let me warn you,
Folks in her day were given to plain speaking.
You think you'd best tempt her at such a time?"

"It rests with us always to cut her off."

"Well then, it's Granny speaking: 'I dunnow!
Mebbe I'm wrong to take it as I do.
There ain't no names quite like the old ones though,
Nor never will be to my way of thinking.
One mustn't bear too hard on the new comers,
But there's a dite too many of them for comfort.
I should feel easier if I could see
More of the salt wherewith they're to be salted.
Son, you do as you're told! You take the timber—
It's as sound as the day when it was cut—
And begin over——' There, she'd better stop.
You can see what is troubling Granny, though.
But don't you think we sometimes make too much
Of the old stock? What counts is the ideals,
And those will bear some keeping still about."

"I can see we are going to be good friends."

"I like your 'going to be.' You said just now
It's going to rain."

                    "I know, and it was raining.
I let you say all that. But I must go now."

"You let me say it? on consideration?
How shall we say good-bye in such a case?"

"How shall we?"

        "Will you leave the way to me?"

"No, I don't trust your eyes. You've said enough.
Now give me your hand up.—Pick me that flower."

"Where shall we meet again?"

            "Nowhere but here
Once more before we meet elsewhere."

               "In rain?"

"It ought to be in rain. Sometime in rain.
In rain to-morrow, shall we, if it rains?
But if we must, in sunshine." So she went.

Initially called "The Cellar Hole" and described by Frost as a "love affair" (*SL*, 89), "The Generations of Men" moves *de bas en haut* in its retitling, from the murky subterranean world to the rhetorical afflatus of a phrase occurring eight times in Genesis: "These are the generations." Concerned with beginnings like the "zealous" recorder of the Starks' family tree, Genesis can follow pedigrees backward and forward through many generations. But while Genesis traces the origins of life back to God's design, and the origins of humanity back to the Garden of Eden, the cellar hole serves as a countervailing symbol which replaces light with darkness, clarity with mystery, the heavenly with the chthonic. To discuss "The Generations of Men" in these terms is to risk unduly burdening what is superficially one of the more frivolous poems in *North of Boston*. Yet the poem's effectiveness derives from that ability to address such themes with the lightest of touches.

Frost's own doubts about "The Generations of Men" (*SL*, 89) have been shared by several critics unpersuaded of the poem's worth. Richard Poirier, for example, finds in the poem an obnoxious gentility which would appeal only to "the prosperous academic weekenders" who had "notoriously laid claim to southern New Hampshire" (Poirier, 108–109). It is true that the conversation between the young man and young woman is especially genteel—more than any other dialogue in *North of Boston*—but this seems the appropriate mode for the first meeting of decorous strangers who (the poem broadly hints) are interested in and attracted to each other. The title's portentousness is fittingly matched by the opening lines, with their churchy if not outright biblical resonance: "A governor it was proclaimed this time, / When all who would come seeking in New Hampshire," and so on. The language is essentially comic, opening a gap between what is described and the style of the description; but through this comedy the issues of love and ancestry are introduced.

Admittedly, the two young people place great (if, as it transpires, justified) confidence in each other's learning. " 'You riddle with your genealogy / Like a Viola,' " he tells her, referring to Viola disguised as a boy while she hints at her true identity in *Twelfth Night:* "My father had a daughter loved a man. . . . I am all the daughters of my father's house." The response of the young woman trumps such learning with the Indian myth of Chicamoztoc, " 'Which means The Seven Caves that We Came out of.' " Later, under cover of the "voices," he risks a compliment by calling her Nausicaä, the princess renowned for her beauty who never declares her love for Odysseus. Immediately recognizing the implications of his reference, the young woman allows it but with a gentle warning: " 'I let you say that—on consideration.' "

The to-and-fro of cultural allusion points to shared sympathies. Of all *North of Boston*'s blank-verse dialogues, this is the most balanced. The speakers enjoy such a degree of sympathy that the absence of textual markers can sometimes make it hard to follow which one is talking. They contribute equally, they question and tease each other, they joke and talk in earnest, they keep the rhythms of their conversation alive by veering from quickfire to longer and more considered responses—a verbal equivalent of body-language mirroring—and as their natural reserve is relaxed they begin to play games of the imagination together. This may make the poem seem vulnerable to Frost's own observation that "Writing is unboring to the extent that it is dramatic" (*CPr*, 202). But initial differences and tensions do emerge in the game playing. The young man is at first hesitant when asked what he sees. Only after being prompted by his companion's example does he lose his inhibitions and reveal his humorous vision of Granny Stark, their common ancestor. (Whereas the family trees of Genesis obliterate the female as men beget men, and the obsession with the patronymic—Stark—threatens a similar blindness, the visions of Granny Stark and Nausicaä reestablish the female at the center of generation.) In keeping with Frost's own tendency to "cultivate . . . the hearing imagination rather than the seeing imagination" (*SL*, 130), the young man then consults the "purer oracle" of the "voices" speaking out of a brook which, like the brook in "The Mountain," hints at inspired origins. For all their make-believe, both he and she realize that " 'The voices give you what you wish to hear.' " But the pretense of external inspiration grants them in their utterances a liberty which can also *take liberties*—hence the risky allusion to Nausicaä.

Frank Lentricchia argues that the poem's protagonists "redeem the past by asserting in the face of its crumbling remains the will to renewal" (Lentricchia, 51). This chimes with the young man's fantasy of restoration, in which a charred timber from the cellar hole becomes a doorsill " 'In a new cottage on the ancient spot.' " The thresholds of houses, like the houses themselves, are recurring symbols throughout *North of Boston*, and here the sill becomes "sacred" as the woman is imagined—in a vision which, although erotic, is less erotic than romantic—sitting in the open door " 'With flowers in her lap until they fade.' " (Compare the marital idyll of "The Death of the Hired Man," in which moonlight pours onto Mary's lap.) When she asks him, " 'Pick me that flower,' " she accepts the identification and promises that the sacred threshold may eventually be crossed.

Theirs, then, is a kind of flirtation, albeit neither coy nor salacious. They may not know each other's names, and yet their family histories are so intimately related that they need no introductions: "'Though what a name should matter between us—.'" Having already alluded to *Twelfth Night*, the young man must here have in mind *Romeo and Juliet*, in which young lovers refuse to accept the barriers which names can erect: "That which we call a rose / By any other name would smell as sweet." This is his second romantic identification, although (unlike the stories of Nausicaä and Odysseus, and Romeo and Juliet) there is no sign that his love will be star-crossed. The young man plans to make some sort of declaration at parting, but he is stopped in a way which can only encourage his hopes:

> "I don't trust your eyes. You've said enough.
> Now give me your hand up.—Pick me that flower."

The prohibition in the first line is immediately softened by the invitation in the second. Although the poem remains too delicate to allow certainty, it ends with the suggestion that the past may have brought about the future: the "'family tree'" under which they shelter is still bearing fruit. The search for origins has augured the origin of a new relationship, as the generations of men not only go backward from the couple but also, potentially, forward out of their shared future together.

The Housekeeper

I let myself in at the kitchen door.

"It's you," *she said.* "I can't get up. Forgive me
Not answering your knock. I can no more
Let people in than I can keep them out.
I'm getting too old for my size, I tell them.
My fingers are about all I've the use of
So's to take any comfort. I can sew:
I help out with this beadwork what I can."

"That's a smart pair of pumps you're beading there.
Who are they for?"

           "You mean?—oh, for some miss.
I can't keep track of other people's daughters.
Lord, if I were to dream of everyone
Whose shoes I primped to dance in!"

                    "And where's John?"

"Haven't you seen him? Strange what set you off
To come to his house when he's gone to yours.
You can't have passed each other. I know what:
He must have changed his mind and gone to Garland's.
He won't be long in that case. You can wait.
Though what good you can be, or anyone—
It's gone so far. You've heard? Estelle's run off."

"Yes, what's it all about? When did she go?"

"Two weeks since."

"She's in earnest, it appears."

"I'm sure she won't come back. She's hiding somewhere.
I don't know where myself. John thinks I do.
He thinks I only have to say the word,
And she'll come back. But, bless you, I'm her mother—
I can't talk to her, and, Lord, if I could!"

"It will go hard with John. What will he do?
He can't find anyone to take her place."

"Oh, if you ask me that, what *will* he do?
He gets some sort of bakeshop meals together,
With me to sit and tell him everything,
What's wanted and how much and where it is.
But when I'm gone—of course I can't stay here:
Estelle's to take me when she's settled down.
He and I only hinder one another.
I tell them they can't get me through the door, though:
I've been built in here like a big church organ.
We've been here fifteen years."

                    "That's a long time
To live together and then pull apart.
How do you see him living when you're gone?
Two of you out will leave an empty house."

"I don't just see him living many years,
Left here with nothing but the furniture.
I hate to think of the old place when we're gone,
With the brook going by below the yard,
And no one here but hens blowing about.
If he could sell the place, but then, he can't:
No one will ever live on it again.

It's too run down. This is the last of it.
What I think he will do, is let things smash.
He'll sort of swear the time away. He's awful!
I never saw a man let family troubles
Make so much difference in his man's affairs.
He's just dropped everything. He's like a child.
I blame his being brought up by his mother.
He's got hay down that's been rained on three times.
He hoed a little yesterday for me:
I thought the growing things would do him good.
Something went wrong. I saw him throw the hoe
Sky-high with both hands. I can see it now—
Come here—I'll show you—in that apple tree.
That's no way for a man to do at his age:
He's fifty-five, you know, if he's a day."

"Aren't you afraid of him? What's that gun for?"

"Oh, that's been there for hawks since chicken-time.
John Hall touch me! Not if he knows his friends.
I'll say that for him, John's no threatener
Like some men folk. No one's afraid of him;
All is, he's made up his mind not to stand
What he has got to stand."

                              "Where is Estelle?
Couldn't one talk to her? What does she say?
You say you don't know where she is."

                              "Nor want to!
She thinks if it was bad to live with him,
It must be right to leave him."

　　　　　　　　"Which is wrong!"

"Yes, but he should have married her."

　　　　　　　　　　　　"I know."

"The strain's been too much for her all these years:
I can't explain it any other way.
It's different with a man, at least with John:
He knows he's kinder than the run of men.
Better than married ought to be as good
As married—that's what he has always said.
I know the way he's felt—but all the same!"

"I wonder why he doesn't marry her
And end it."

　　　　　　Too late now: she wouldn't have him.
He's given her time to think of something else.
That's his mistake. The dear knows my interest
Has been to keep the thing from breaking up.
This is a good home: I don't ask for better.
But when I've said, 'Why shouldn't they be married,'
He'd say, 'Why should they?' no more words than that."

"And after all why should they? John's been fair
I take it. What was his was always hers.
There was no quarrel about property."

"Reason enough, there was no property.
A friend or two as good as own the farm,
Such as it is. It isn't worth the mortgage."

"I mean Estelle has always held the purse."

"The rights of that are harder to get at.
I guess Estelle and I have filled the purse.
'Twas we let him have money, not he us.
John's a bad farmer. I'm not blaming him.
Take it year in, year out, he doesn't make much.
We came here for a home for me, you know,
Estelle to do the housework for the board
Of both of us. But look how it turns out:
She seems to have the housework, and besides
Half of the outdoor work, though as for that,
He'd say she does it more because she likes it.
You see our pretty things are all outdoors.
Our hens and cows and pigs are always better
Than folks like us have any business with.
Farmers around twice as well off as we
Haven't as good. They don't go with the farm.
One thing you can't help liking about John,
He's fond of nice things—too fond, some would say.
But Estelle don't complain: she's like him there.
She wants our hens to be the best there are.
You never saw this room before a show,
Full of lank, shivery, half-drowned birds
In separate coops, having their plumage done.
The smell of the wet feathers in the heat!
You spoke of John's not being safe to stay with.
You don't know what a gentle lot we are:
We wouldn't hurt a hen! You ought to see us
Moving a flock of hens from place to place.
We're not allowed to take them upside down,
All we can hold together by the legs.
Two at a time's the rule, one on each arm,
No matter how far and how many times
We have to go."

"You mean that's John's idea."

"And we live up to it; or I don't know
What childishness he wouldn't give way to.
He manages to keep the upper hand
On his own farm. He's boss. But as to hens:
We fence our flowers in and the hens range.
Nothing's too good for them. We say it pays.
John likes to tell the offers he has had,
Twenty for this cock, twenty-five for that.
He never takes the money. If they're worth
That much to sell, they're worth as much to keep.
Bless you, it's all expense, though. Reach me down
The little tin box on the cupboard shelf,
The upper shelf, the tin box. That's the one.
I'll show you. Here you are."

        "What's this?"

                "A bill—

For fifty dollars for one Langshang cock—
Receipted. And the cock is in the yard."

"Not in a glass case, then?"

          "He'd need a tall one:
He can eat off a barrel from the ground.
He's been in a glass case, as you may say,
The Crystal Palace, London. He's imported.
John bought him, and we paid the bill with beads—
Wampum, I call it. Mind, we don't complain.
But you see, don't you, we take care of him."

"And like it, too. It makes it all the worse."

"It seems as if. And that's not all: he's helpless
In ways that I can hardly tell you of.
Sometimes he gets possessed to keep accounts
To see where all the money goes so fast.
You know how men will be ridiculous.
But it's just fun the way he gets bedeviled—
If he's untidy now, what will he be——?"

"It makes it all the worse. You must be blind."

"Estelle's the one. You needn't talk to me."

"Can't you and I get to the root of it?
What's the real trouble? What will satisfy her?"

"It's as I say: she's turned from him, that's all."

"But why, when she's well off? Is it the neighbors,
Being cut off from friends?"

                                   "We have our friends.
That isn't it. Folks aren't afraid of us."

"She's let it worry her. You stood the strain,
And you're her mother."

                                   "But I didn't always.
I didn't relish it along at first.
But I got wonted to it. And besides—
John said I was too old to have grandchildren.
But what's the use of talking when it's done?
She won't come back—it's worse than that—she can't."

"Why do you speak like that? What do you know?
What do you mean?—she's done harm to herself?"

"I mean she's married—married someone else."

"Oho, oho!"

"You don't believe me."

"Yes, I do,
Only too well. I knew there must be something!
So that was what was back. She's bad, that's all!"

"Bad to get married when she had the chance?"

"Nonsense! See what's she done! But who, who——"

"Who'd marry her straight out of such a mess?
Say it right out—no matter for her mother.
The man was found. I'd better name no names.
John himself won't imagine who he is."

"Then it's all up. I think I'll get away.
You'll be expecting John. I pity Estelle;
I suppose she deserves some pity, too.
You ought to have the kitchen to yourself
To break it to him. You may have the job."

"You needn't think you're going to get away.
John's almost here. I've had my eye on someone
Coming down Ryan's Hill. I thought 'twas him.
Here he is now. This box! Put it away.
And this bill."

"What's the hurry? He'll unhitch."

"No, he won't, either. He'll just drop the reins
And turn Doll out to pasture, rig and all.
She won't get far before the wheels hang up
On something—there's no harm. See, there he is!
My, but he looks as if he must have heard!"

John threw the door wide but he didn't enter.
"How are you, neighbor? Just the man I'm after.
Isn't it Hell," *he said.* "I want to know.
Come out here if you want to hear me talk.
I'll talk to you, old woman, afterward.
I've got some news that maybe isn't news.
What are they trying to do to me, these two?"

"Do go along with him and stop his shouting."
She raised her voice against the closing door:
"Who wants to hear your news, you—dreadful fool?"

Marriage and the home are fundamental to the concerns of *North of Boston*. Poems like "Home Burial" and "A Servant to Servants" prove that the conjunction does not always result in happiness; but there are also more positive examples, such as the young man's fantasy of rebuilding a house over the cellar hole in "The Generations of Men," which serves as a barely coded invitation to the woman he has just met, and "The Black Cottage," which asserts the value of marriage by showing what has been lost in the abandoned museum of a once-happy marital home. "The Housekeeper," written in 1905 or 1906 with claims to be *North of Boston*'s earliest poem, relates oddly to these poems of marital harmony and disharmony, because it focuses on a marriage which is not quite a marriage, in a home which has never quite been a home. The old woman argues differently: " 'This is a good home: I don't ask for better.' " To which the reader, recalling "The Death of the Hired Man," is entitled to respond: it all depends on what you mean by home. The woman has come to the house only as part of an economic arrangement on which the poem's title continues to insist: her daughter, Estelle, acted as a housekeeper, and by leaving the house she has acknowledged (or insisted) that she remained a housekeeper throughout. She may have exchanged one man for another, but her decision has been prompted by the desire to exchange a job for a marriage, and a house for a home. Although John's helpless despair is described, the impossibility of replacing Estelle focuses on her qualities as housekeeper more than as a wife. That economic emphasis suits a poem which, as Guy Rotella argues, brings together "matters of vocation, competing valences of ownership and self-possession, the relative claims of charity and independence, the worth and value of work, and the relation between labor and gender" (Rotella, 256).

Rejecting his original title, "Slack Ties"—with its conspicuous authorial steer—in favor of the more neutral tones of "The Housekeeper," Frost draws attention to those issues of work and property ownership which recur throughout *North of Boston*. Keeping house is crucially different from keeping (or owning) *the* house, and on that distinction the one who keeps house chooses to abandon it. Frost signals his preoccupation with thresholds in the poem's opening line: "*I let myself in at the kitchen door.*" But the guest's freedom of access is denied to others: Estelle has crossed a threshold and won't (even worse: *can't*) come back; her mother is waiting to join her, despite having been " 'built in here like a big church organ' "; and John on his return "*threw the door wide but he didn't enter.*" The farmer prefers to talk outside, and closes the door on the old woman as she hurls insults from inside. The poem is framed by a door opening and a door closing. It is the inability of the characters to cross thresholds together—both figuratively and literally—which fractures the family unit beyond repair.

"The Housekeeper" may belong with Frost's other one-sided dialogues (again in blank verse, and again allowing an extra syllable for feminine endings), but even with his relatively few lines the poem's first-person protagonist is more distinctive than his counterparts in "The Mountain" and "The Black Cottage." There is a suspicion that he has been trying to avoid John, as the old woman implies: " 'Strange what set you off / To come to his house when he's gone to yours.' " And that suspicion seems borne out at the poem's end, when he intends to " 'get away' " before John's return. His visit also seems to have been prompted by nosiness (he squeezes twenty-one questions into the conversation) and by some undefined desire to be of assistance: " 'Can't you and I get to the root of it?' " Yet for all the old woman's attempts to convince him otherwise, he never budges from his belief that Estelle is at fault: his bemusement at her behavior becomes outright condemnation (" 'She's bad, that's all!' ") when he discovers that she has married someone else. As the poem develops, his contributions grow longer, and his accusations draw out more information from the mother who would vindicate her daughter. What starts as a pattern of short enquiry followed by long explanation becomes—if never quite a quickfire dialogue—a brisker and more equal exchange of views:

> "I mean she's married—married someone else."
>
> "Oho, oho!"
>
>   "You don't believe me."
>
>   "Yes, I do,
> Only too well."

Does " 'I do' " mockingly echo the marriage service? After all, the passage raises questions of tone. Frost's claim that he liked to "drag and break the intonation across the meter as waves first comb and then break stumbling on the shingle" (*SL*, 128) is here fulfilled, as the swift interchanges of the speakers, with all their subtleties of emphasis, still make up a regular iambic line. In wondering aloud whether he has doubted her truthfulness, the old woman pretends to misunderstand his reaction even though she must in reality understand him " 'Only too well.' " His subverbal response to her revelatory news combines discovery with superiority: " 'Oho, oho!' " unmasks a cheat. And she, by forcing him to elaborate (" 'You don't believe me' "), gives herself the opportunity to fight back against that accusing tone. The exchange represents Frostian drama at its most nuanced, as the speakers express polarized views barely within the etiquettes of polite conversation.

This being a poem about, inter alia, the breakup of a relationship, "The Housekeeper" tempts readers to take sides. Estelle is elsewhere; John returns at the end of the poem, but we hear only his anger and never his version of events. In their absence, the old woman is an unreliable and biased narrator, quite capable of hiding the truth to protect her daughter: she claims not to know where Estelle has gone, but later admits to knowing whom she has married. She never convinces her visitor, who musters only a grudging sympathy for Estelle: " 'I pity Estelle; / I suppose she deserves some pity, too.' " And the case she makes against John is too flimsy to justify Estelle's betrayal. He is portrayed as less than a man, having become " 'like a child' " and allowed family troubles to affect his " 'man's affairs.' " " 'No one's afraid of him,' " so even the fact that " 'John's no threatener / Like some men folk' " counts against him; and again, because " 'he's kinder than the run of men,' " his kindness becomes less a virtue than another aspersion on his masculinity. John is a bad farmer (as another slack tie clearly indicates—his not bothering to unhitch his horse), " 'fond of nice things,' " and in case that hint of effeminacy is missed, the old woman continues: " 'too fond, some would say.' " He is gentle with his hens, taking a childish pride in showing them. But these stories of John's kindness and helpless impracticality do nothing to excuse Estelle's abandonment, and only serve to make it " 'all the worse' "—a judgment emphatically repeated and never gainsaid despite all her mother's special pleading. The old woman's seeming efforts to be nonpartisan are revealed as a sham in her parting insult to John: " 'Who wants to hear your news, you—dreadful fool?' " John may well be foolish, but as Frost argues in his essay on Emerson, "The one inalienable right is to go to destruction in your own way." The same essay may have something to say about Estelle's behavior: "Loyalty is that for the lack of which your gang will shoot you without benefit of trial by jury. And serves you right" (*CPr*, 203–204).

The Fear

A lantern light from deeper in the barn
Shone on a man and woman in the door
And threw their lurching shadows on a house
Near by, all dark in every glossy window.
A horse's hoof pawed once the hollow floor,
And the back of the gig they stood beside
Moved in a little. The man grasped a wheel,
The woman spoke out sharply, "Whoa, stand still!
I saw it just as plain as a white plate,"
She said, "as the light on the dashboard ran
Along the bushes at the roadside—a man's face.
You *must* have seen it too."

                              "I didn't see it.
Are you sure——"

                    "Yes, I'm sure!"

                              "—it was a face?"

"Joel, I'll have to look. I can't go in,
I can't, and leave a thing like that unsettled.
Doors locked and curtains drawn will make no difference.
I always have felt strange when we came home
To the dark house after so long an absence,
And the key rattled loudly into place
Seemed to warn someone to be getting out
At one door as we entered at another.
What if I'm right, and someone all the time—
Don't hold my arm!"

            "I say it's someone passing."

"You speak as if this were a traveled road.
You forget where we are. What is beyond
That he'd be going to or coming from
At such an hour of night, and on foot too.
What was he standing still for in the bushes?"

"It's not so very late—it's only dark.
There's more in it than you're inclined to say.
Did he look like——?"

                    "He looked like anyone.
I'll never rest to-night until I know.
Give me the lantern."

                    "You don't want the lantern."

She pushed past him and got it for herself.

"You're not to come," she said. "This is my business.
If the time's come to face it, I'm the one
To put it the right way. He'd never dare—
Listen! He kicked a stone. Hear that, hear that!
He's coming towards us. Joel, *go* in—please.
Hark!—I don't hear him now. But please go in."

"In the first place you can't make me believe it's——"

"It is—or someone else he's sent to watch.
And now's the time to have it out with him
While we know definitely where he is.
Let him get off and he'll be everywhere
Around us, looking out of trees and bushes

Till I shan't dare to set a foot outdoors.
And I can't stand it. Joel, let me go!"

"But it's nonsense to think he'd care enough."

"You mean you couldn't understand his caring.
Oh, but you see he hadn't had enough—
Joel, I won't—I won't—I promise you.
We mustn't say hard things. You mustn't either."

"I'll be the one, if anybody goes!
But you give him the advantage with this light.
What couldn't he do to us standing here!
And if to see was what he wanted, why
He has seen all there was to see and gone."

He appeared to forget to keep his hold,
But advanced with her as she crossed the grass.

"What do you want?" she cried to all the dark.
She stretched up tall to overlook the light
That hung in both hands hot against her skirt.

"There's no one; so you're wrong," he said.

                              "There is.—
What do you want?" she cried, and then herself
Was startled when an answer really came.

"Nothing." It came from well along the road.

She reached a hand to Joel for support:
The smell of scorching woolen made her faint.
"What are you doing round this house at night?"

"Nothing." A pause: there seemed no more to say.

And then the voice again: "You seem afraid.
I saw by the way you whipped up the horse.
I'll just come forward in the lantern light
And let you see."

            "Yes, do.—Joel, go back!"

She stood her ground against the noisy steps
That came on, but her body rocked a little.

"You see," the voice said.

                  "Oh." She looked and looked.

"You don't see—I've a child here by the hand."

"What's a child doing at this time of night——?"

"Out walking. Every child should have the memory
Of at least one long-after-bedtime walk.
What, son?"

         "Then I should think you'd try to find
Somewhere to walk——"

             "The highway as it happens—
We're stopping for a fortnight down at Dean's."

"But if that's all—Joel—you realize—
You won't think anything. You understand?
You understand that we have to be careful.
This is a very, very lonely place.

Joel!" She spoke as if she couldn't turn.
The swinging lantern lengthened to the ground,
It touched, it struck, it clattered and went out.

In a letter from England on 7 August 1913, Frost told John T. Bartlett: "I have written [a poem] today that I may call The Lantern if Mrs. Frost doesn't dissuade me: she doesn't think [the title] a fit" (*SL*, 89). The poem was already titled "The Fear" when first published in December 1913. Lawrance Thompson in his biography relates that Frost, during a nocturnal walk with his son Carol while on holiday in 1907, had been challenged by a woman carrying a lantern (Thompson 1966, 344). When he explained his circumstances, she apologized, and he later discovered that the woman had abandoned her marriage for another man and lived in fear that her husband would find her.

That information connects "The Fear" with its predecessor, "The Housekeeper." Both poems explore the consequences of a woman's abandonment of a relationship: in "The Housekeeper," Estelle has secretly married someone else; "The Fear," a kind of sequel, explores the woman's anxiety that the partner she has left behind will hunt her down and confront her. Yet this reading, encouraged though it may be by Frost's ordering of his poems, makes overexplicit what are present only as hints and clues in "The Fear." The story of betrayal is interrupted at each possible moment of revelation. "'Did he look like——?,'" Joel asks, but the woman impatiently intervenes and names go unnamed: "'He looked like anyone.'" Again, Joel tells her, "'you can't make me believe it's——,'" and again, he is stopped in his tracks: "'It is—or someone else he's sent to watch.'" The woman says that it is her "business," and her reaction to Joel's incredulity comes close to detailing her troubled history:

"But it's nonsense to think he'd care enough."

"You mean you couldn't understand his caring.

Oh, but you see he hadn't had enough—"

This illuminates her previous relationship, and hints at strains in her current. If Joel cannot understand his rival's depth of feeling about the woman he has lost, the clear insinuation—almost an accusation—is that he himself cares less than he ought.

Dedicating *North of Boston* to his wife, Frost called it "this book of people." He might almost as well have called it a book of houses. "The Fear," as Richard Poirier has noted, begins cinematically in a play of light and shadow (Poirier, 119), as the lantern which illuminates the opening scene (and which, by being suddenly extinguished, will bring the poem to a close) throws the "lurching shadows" of a man and a woman onto a house. Identities are enigmatic at this stage, but the ironic implication of "lurching" must be that the woman who fears being stalked is herself, with her husband, a stalker, or at least an outsider with little right of belonging. Consequently, the house provides no sanctuary from her fear. Although she worries that she may end up too scared " 'to set a foot outdoors,' " her fear has contaminated internal space as well, so that she imagines the rattle of her key warning an intruder to escape " 'At one door as we entered at another.' " (A similar fear is expressed in "The Hill Wife" from *Mountain Interval.*) The devastating corollary of such an invasion may be mental and marital disintegration. When suffering has crossed the threshold into the private domain, as it has in "Home Burial" and "A Servant to Servants," *North of Boston* can provide no balm.

The formal strategies and preoccupations of "The Fear"—the blank-verse dialogue with an extra syllable for feminine endings, the conversational interruptions and omissions, the symbol of the house, the tense relationship, the isolated and vulnerable woman—are absolutely characteristic, as is the everyday diction: Frost expressed special pride in that plainest and prosiest of lines, "She pushed past him and got it for herself" (*SL,* 83–84, 130). But what makes the poem so memorably great is an unexpected twist in its telling. Joel's skepticism is shared by the reader as he asks his agitated partner whether she is "sure" that she saw something; and although he seems slightly spooked by her panicky insistence, and anxiously quick to declare her wrong, the suspicion remains that her guilty conscience is making her frightened of shadows. Her fear does turn out to be groundless, but not in the way expected. While the poem could end powerfully but more conventionally with her crying "'What do you want?' . . . to all the dark" (just as a later poem, "The Most of It," has its protagonist vainly seeking a human answer to his call), Frost courts bathos by providing a response at the point when even she, for all her previous certainty, is startled to be given an answer.

The emergence of father and son from the shadows immediately dispels a disquieting atmosphere and replaces it with the mundane explanations of rational discourse. Diogenes had scoured the streets of Athens with his lamp, in search of one honest man. Accordingly, as the pair step forward in the lantern light with nothing to hide, they present themselves as honest and not shadowy. The lantern may have (apparently unbeknownst to her) scorched the woman's woolen skirt, but its scrutiny can do them no harm. Even so, there is one more surprise. Far from having her mind put at rest by their innocent account, the woman reacts with still more fearful intensity. Joel's understanding had been questioned once before, when he doubted whether his rival would "'care enough'" to track the couple down; now, having been proven right or at least not wrong, he is still told to "'understand that we have to be careful.'" Joel understands her only too well, and whether through exasperation or embarrassment, he seems to have vanished at precisely the moment when she emphasizes how "'very, very lonely'" the place is. Dropping the lantern, she is left defenseless and alone, in the dark, with nothing for company but her fear.

The Self-Seeker

"Willis, I didn't want you here to-day:
The lawyer's coming for the company.
I'm going to sell my soul, or, rather, feet.
Five hundred dollars for the pair, you know."

"With you the feet have nearly been the soul;
And if you're going to sell them to the devil,
I want to see you do it. When's he coming?"

"I half suspect you knew, and came on purpose
To try to help me drive a better bargain."

"Well, if it's true! Yours are no common feet.
The lawyer don't know what it is he's buying:
So many miles you might have walked you won't walk.
You haven't run your forty orchids down.
What does he think?—How *are* the blessed feet?
The doctor's sure you're going to walk again?"

"He thinks I'll hobble. It's both legs and feet."

"They must be terrible—I mean to look at."

"I haven't dared to look at them uncovered.
Through the bed blankets I remind myself
Of a starfish laid out with rigid points."

"The wonder is it hadn't been your head."

"It's hard to tell you how I managed it.
When I saw the shaft had me by the coat,
I didn't try too long to pull away,

Or fumble for my knife to cut away,
I just embraced the shaft and rode it out—
Till Weiss shut off the water in the wheel-pit.
That's how I think I didn't lose my head.
But my legs got their knocks against the ceiling."

"Awful. Why didn't they throw off the belt
Instead of going clear down in the wheel-pit?"

"They say some time was wasted on the belt—
Old streak of leather—doesn't love me much
Because I make him spit fire at my knuckles,
The way Ben Franklin used to make the kite-string.
That must be it. Some days he won't stay on.
That day a woman couldn't coax him off.
He's on his rounds now with his tail in his mouth
Snatched right and left across the silver pulleys.
Everything goes the same without me there.
You can hear the small buzz saws whine, the big saw
Caterwaul to the hills around the village
As they both bite the wood. It's all our music.
One ought as a good villager to like it.
No doubt it has a sort of prosperous sound,
And it's our life."

                    "Yes, when it's not our death."

"You make that sound as if it wasn't so
With everything. What we live by we die by.
I wonder where my lawyer is. His train's in.
I want this over with; I'm hot and tired."

"You're getting ready to do something foolish."

"Watch for him, will you, Will? You let him in.
I'd rather Mrs. Corbin didn't know;
I've boarded here so long, she thinks she owns me.
You're bad enough to manage without her."

"And I'm going to be worse instead of better.
You've got to tell me how far this is gone:
Have you agreed to any price?"

                                    "Five hundred.
Five hundred—five—five! One, two, three, four, five.
You needn't look at me."

                        "I don't believe you."

"I told you, Willis, when you first came in.
Don't you be hard on me. I have to take
What I can get. You see they have the feet,
Which gives them the advantage in the trade.
I can't get back the feet in any case."

"But your flowers, man, you're selling out your flowers."

"Yes, that's one way to put it—all the flowers
Of every kind everywhere in this region
For the next forty summers—call it forty.
But I'm not selling those, I'm giving them,
They never earned me so much as one cent:
Money can't pay me for the loss of them.
No, the five hundred was the sum they named
To pay the doctor's bill and tide me over.
It's that or fight, and I don't want to fight—
I just want to get settled in my life,
Such as it's going to be, and know the worst,

Or best—it may not be so bad. The firm
Promise me all the shooks I want to nail."

"But what about your flora of the valley?"

"You have me there. But that—you didn't think
That was worth money to me? Still I own
It goes against me not to finish it
For the friends it might bring me. By the way,
I had a letter from Burroughs—did I tell you?—
About my *Cyprepedium reginæ;*
He says it's not reported so far north.
There! there's the bell. He's rung. But you go down
And bring him up, and don't let Mrs. Corbin.—
Oh, well, we'll soon be through with it. I'm tired."

Willis brought up besides the Boston lawyer
A little barefoot girl who in the noise
Of heavy footsteps in the old frame house,
And baritone importance of the lawyer,
Stood for a while unnoticed with her hands
Shyly behind her.

                    "Well, and how is Mister——"

The lawyer was already in his satchel
As if for papers that might bear the name
He hadn't at command. "You must excuse me,
I dropped in at the mill and was detained."

"Looking round, I suppose," said Willis.

                                        "Yes,
Well, yes."

"Hear anything that might prove useful?"

The Broken One saw Anne. "Why, here is Anne.
What do you want, dear? Come, stand by the bed;
Tell me what is it?" Anne just wagged her dress
With both hands held behind her. "Guess," she said.

"Oh, guess which hand? My, my! Once on a time
I knew a lovely way to tell for certain
By looking in the ears. But I forget it.
Er, let me see. I think I'll take the right.
That's sure to be right even if it's wrong.
Come, hold it out. Don't change.—A Ram's Horn orchid!
A Ram's Horn! What would I have got, I wonder,
If I had chosen left. Hold out the left.
Another Ram's Horn! Where did you find those,
Under what beech tree, on what woodchuck's knoll?"

Anne looked at the large lawyer at her side,
And thought she wouldn't venture on so much.

"Were there no others?"

                              "There were four or five.
I knew you wouldn't let me pick them all."

"I wouldn't—so I wouldn't. You're the girl!
You see Anne has her lesson learned by heart."

"I wanted there should be some there next year."

"Of course you did. You left the rest for seed,
And for the backwoods woodchuck. You're the girl!
A Ram's Horn orchid seedpod for a woodchuck

Sounds something like. Better than farmer's beans
To a discriminating appetite,
Though the Ram's Horn is seldom to be had
In bushel lots—doesn't come on the market.
But, Anne, I'm troubled; have you told me all?
You're hiding something. That's as bad as lying.
You ask this lawyer man. And it's not safe
With a lawyer at hand to find you out.
Nothing is hidden from some people, Anne.
You don't tell me that where you found a Ram's Horn
You didn't find a Yellow Lady's Slipper.
What did I tell you? What? I'd blush, I would.
Don't you defend yourself. If it was there,
Where is it now, the Yellow Lady's Slipper?"

"Well, wait—it's common—it's too *common*."

                                        "Common?
The Purple Lady's Slipper's commoner."

"I didn't bring a Purple Lady's Slipper
To *You*—to you I mean—they're both too common."

The lawyer gave a laugh among his papers
As if with some idea that she had scored.

"I've broken Anne of gathering bouquets.
It's not fair to the child. It can't be helped though:
Pressed into service means pressed out of shape.
Somehow I'll make it right with her—she'll see.
She's going to do my scouting in the field,
Over stone walls and all along a wood
And by a river bank for water flowers,
The floating Heart, with small leaf like a heart,

161   *The Self-Seeker*

And at the *sinus* under water a fist
Of little fingers all kept down but one,
And that thrust up to blossom in the sun
As if to say, 'You! You're the Heart's desire.'
Anne has a way with flowers to take the place
Of that she's lost: she goes down on one knee
And lifts their faces by the chin to hers
And says their names, and leaves them where they are."

The lawyer wore a watch the case of which
Was cunningly devised to make a noise
Like a small pistol when he snapped it shut
At such a time as this. He snapped it now.

"Well, Anne, go, dearie. Our affair will wait.
The lawyer man is thinking of his train.
He wants to give me lots and lots of money
Before he goes, because I hurt myself,
And it may take him I don't know how long.
But put our flowers in water first. Will, help her:
The pitcher's too full for her. There's no cup?
Just hook them on the inside of the pitcher.
Now run.—Get out your documents! You see
I have to keep on the good side of Anne.
I'm a great boy to think of number one.
And you can't blame me in the place I'm in.
Who will take care of my necessities
Unless I do?"

                    "A pretty interlude,"
The lawyer said. "I'm sorry, but my train—
Luckily terms are all agreed upon.
You only have to sign your name. Right—there."

"You, Will, stop making faces. Come round here
Where you can't make them. What is it you want?
I'll put you out with Anne. Be good or go."

"You don't mean you will sign that thing unread?"

"Make yourself useful then, and read it for me.
Isn't it something I have seen before?"

"You'll find it is. Let your friend look at it."

"Yes, but all that takes time, and I'm as much
In haste to get it over with as you.
But read it, read it. That's right, draw the curtain:
Half the time I don't know what's troubling me.—
What do you say, Will? Don't you be a fool,
You! crumpling folks's legal documents.
Out with it if you've any real objection."

"Five hundred dollars!"

                    "What would you think right?"

"A thousand wouldn't be a cent too much;
You know it, Mr. Lawyer. The sin is
Accepting anything before he knows
Whether he's ever going to walk again.
It smells to me like a dishonest trick."

"I think—I think—from what I heard today—
And saw myself—he would be ill-advised——"

"What did you hear, for instance?" Willis said.

"Now the place where the accident occurred—"

The Broken One was twisted in his bed.
"This is between you two apparently.
Where I come in is what I want to know.
You stand up to it like a pair of cocks.
Go outdoors if you want to fight. Spare me.
When you come back, I'll have the papers signed.
Will pencil do? Then, please, your fountain pen.
One of you hold my head up from the pillow."

Willis flung off the bed. "I wash my hands—
I'm no match—no, and I don't pretend to be——"

The lawyer gravely capped his fountain pen.
"You're doing the wise thing: you won't regret it.
We're very sorry for you."

                    Willis sneered:
"Who's *we?*—some stockholders in Boston?
I'll go outdoors, by gad, and won't come back."

"Willis, bring Anne back with you when you come.
Yes. Thanks for caring. Don't mind Will: he's savage.
He thinks you ought to pay me for my flowers.
You don't know what I mean about the flowers.
Don't stop to try to now. You'll miss your train.
Good-bye." He flung his arms around his face.

The last of the dialogue poems in *North of Boston*, "The Self-Seeker" offers no metrical departure from its predecessors. On display are the consciously plain style of Frost's blank verse (" 'Five hundred—five—five! One, two, three, four, five' "); the conversational back-and-forth between a brief interrogator and a much more expansive speaker; and the careful attention to intoned nuances of meaning, especially where that meaning is not fully articulated. " 'I think—I think—from what I heard today—/ And saw myself—he would be ill-advised——,' " the lawyer manages to stutter, and Willis at a moment of high emotion seems hardly more fluent: " 'I wash my hands—/ I'm no match—no, and I don't pretend to be——.' " Words fail them, but meaning is conveyed by their inarticulacy.

Like "The Death of the Hired Man," "The Self-Seeker" explores the worth of things it is impossible to price. The lawyer, at one extreme, understands the cost of everything and the value of nothing: he is interested not in justice, nor quality of life, and still less in someone's future as an amateur botanist, but only in securing the best deal for the company. At the other extreme stands Willis, who believes that his friend should be compensated financially for intangibles to which moneymen are blind. The unnamed victim takes the pragmatic view, valuing his botany but appreciating that others would not. His epistrophic repetition in dismissing the lawyer combines resignation with pity and a mild contempt: " 'He thinks you ought to pay me for my flowers. / You don't know what I mean about the flowers.' " There is no rebuke or attempt to persuade: the lawyer is taken to be not so much mean-spirited as simply incapable of appreciation. " 'I'm going to sell my soul, or, rather, feet,' " the invalid jokes, because the lawyer is certainly no Mephistopheles. (Despite having himself witnessed an injured friend's negotiations with an ungenerous insurance representative, Frost evidently realized that his original title, "The Wrong," was itself wrong.) In this one crucial respect, the lawyer is more reminiscent of the speaker in "A Servant to Servants," who expresses her amazement that her visitors have come to camp on her land because of its ferns: " 'You let things more like feathers regulate / Your going and coming.' "

Blandford Parker has proposed a rule of thumb for Frost's work: "The meditative poems have all the pleasures of the parable, while the narrative poems, however complicated, aim at moral transparency" (Parker, 182). Readers might justifiably cavil at the suggestion of "moral transparency"; even so, one reason why "The Self-Seeker" deserves sustained attention is that, despite its conventional and characteristic strategies, it flouts the rule in another way, by embodying what Parker considers to be the pleasures of the meditative poems. Its competing attitudes to the " 'flora of the valley' " allow Frost to talk parabolically about the value and purpose of art in a world driven by the unsympathetic demands of labor and commerce. The concern is written through Frost's verse, from early poems like "Mowing" and "The Tuft of Flowers" (both of which find in the beauty of flowers-as-art a solace from the demands of work) to the attempt to unite vocation and avocation in "Two Tramps in Mud Time." Such poems show how work and play, so often the contrary pulls of the pastoral tradition, meet in art and can be reconciled by it.

"The Self-Seeker" dramatizes the inappropriateness of assessing art's monetary value. In a later poem, "Christmas Trees," Frost alludes aphoristically to "The trial by market everything must come to." Yet according to that test the flowers of the region are shown to be worthless, having " 'never earned' " their loving student " 'so much as one cent.' " Expectations for his botanical work-in-progress had been no higher: " 'you didn't think / That was worth money to me?,' " he asks Willis. But while seeming to repudiate his botanical ambitions, the invalid distracts himself by proudly reporting the reaction of an expert to his discovery of *Cyprepedium reginæ* " 'so far north.' " Not worth money, perhaps, and therefore useless in helping to " 'pay the doctor's bill' "; but botany also embodies other (less practical though no less important) values to do with selfhood and quality of life. So tightly is his avocation bound up with his sense of identity that the flower seeker becomes the "self-seeker" of the poem's title. Money can pay for the loss of his legs, not of his flowers; but the prime reason why his fate seems so tormenting is that it entails losing the flowers which have become part of his identity. That Frost, classicist and botanist, should have chosen Harold Wilson's Latin and the self-seeker's orchid hunting as the volume's examples of economically useless endeavor indicates his own sympathies. The financial haggling, about which the "Broken One" seems rightly impatient, is beside the point. His flowers are worth nothing and everything; without them he must seek a new identity, and no amount of money can compensate for what he has lost or buy him a replacement.

"The Self-Seeker" gives voice to Frost's career-long fascination with the art of labor and the labor of art. The invalid's botany may have served as (and symbolized) an artistic avocation, but even the factory produces a strange kind of "music." Frost himself makes a discordant music out of workplace fatalities in later poems like "'Out, Out—'" and "The Vanishing Red," and the philosophy of "The Self-Seeker"—"'What we live by we die by'"—is pronounced with an assurance which seems authorial. The victim describes his accident with gusto, personifying as irascible the belt which "'doesn't love me much,'" and taking more than cold comfort from the fact that he saved his head even while losing his legs. The iambic confidence of his quick thinking ("'I just embraced the shaft and rode it out'") contrasts with a horrible anapestic awkwardness as the injury is nevertheless inflicted: "'But my legs got their knocks against the ceiling.'" All the same, that life can be compensated for, and not just by money. The company has promised him "'all the shooks [he] want[s] to nail,'" so that even without the use of his legs there can be continuity of labor. The little girl, Anne, may be able to do his "'scouting in the field,'" but for all his pride in her, that is a much less personally satisfying kind of continuity. After a long demonstration of poise and self-control, his strange gesture of despair at the poem's end—"He flung his arms around his face"—seems mostly a reaction to the loss of his irreplaceable flowers.

The Wood-Pile

Out walking in the frozen swamp one gray day
I paused and said, "I will turn back from here.
No, I will go on farther—and we shall see."
The hard snow held me, save where now and then
One foot went down. The view was all in lines
Straight up and down of tall slim trees
Too much alike to mark or name a place by
So as to say for certain I was here
Or somewhere else: I was just far from home.
A small bird flew before me. He was careful
To put a tree between us when he lighted,
And say no word to tell me who he was
Who was so foolish as to think what *he* thought.
He thought that I was after him for a feather—
The white one in his tail; like one who takes
Everything said as personal to himself.
One flight out sideways would have undeceived him.
And then there was a pile of wood for which
I forgot him and let his little fear
Carry him off the way I might have gone,
Without so much as wishing him good-night.
He went behind it to make his last stand.
It was a cord of maple, cut and split
And piled—and measured, four by four by eight.
And not another like it could I see.
No runner tracks in this year's snow looped near it.
And it was older sure than this year's cutting,
Or even last year's or the year's before.
The wood was gray and the bark warping off it
And the pile somewhat sunken. Clematis
Had wound strings round and round it like a bundle.

What held it though on one side was a tree
Still growing, and on one a stake and prop,
These latter about to fall. I thought that only
Someone who lived in turning to fresh tasks
Could so forget his handiwork on which
He spent himself, the labor of his axe,
And leave it there far from a useful fireplace
To warm the frozen swamp as best it could
With the slow smokeless burning of decay.

Despite marking a final move away from the dialogue poems which domi-
nate *North of Boston,* "The Wood-Pile" does pursue a subject explored
by its immediate predecessor, "The Self-Seeker": the value of work. The
unexpected discovery of the woodpile provokes questions about work's
necessity and pleasure, leaving the poet to make sense of (or impose sense
on) this forgotten remnant of human effort.

In another respect, "The Wood-Pile" makes "The Self-Seeker"
seem out of place. With its spring-flowering orchids prominently dis-
played, "The Self-Seeker" is a jarring exception to the pattern of climatic
change developed through the volume. The wintery bleakness of "The
Wood-Pile" rejoins and brings full circle the seasonal journey begun in
the opening lines of "Mending Wall." (The italics of *North of Boston*'s
first and last poems, "The Pasture" and "Good Hours," set them apart
as foreword and afterword to the main body of the text.) Appropriately,
the volume begins with spring's memory of winter (in "Mending Wall"),
and ends in the midst of the following winter ("The Wood-Pile"), as the
temperatures responsible for the "frozen-ground-swell" return in the
"frozen swamp." Reaching across the length of the volume, "Mending
Wall" and "The Wood-Pile" make strange companions. Both are con-
templative lyrics, and both situate the work of man in an unforgiving
natural environment where it seems exposed and isolated. But nature
in "Mending Wall" disrupts the best efforts of neighbors to maintain

their boundary and requires annual upkeep. Notwithstanding the precarious support of the "stake and prop, / These latter about to fall," the woodpile stubbornly persists as a sign of long-past human enterprise ("it was older sure than this year's cutting, / Or even last year's or the year's before") in an otherwise nonhuman—rather than dehumanized—landscape.

Beginning with "Into My Own," the first poem of his first collection, Frost's poetry is full of wilderness journeys either real or imagined. The desire to escape networks of personal and social relations inspires "The Wood-Pile," too: there is no wall and no neighbor with whom it will be necessary to engage. Save for that neglected woodpile, the wilderness lacks human markers. It may be "just far from home," but "home" is a word interrogated often enough in *North of Boston* to alert readers to its complexities. Here, "home" relates to the domain of the species as well as the individual: the swamp seems to lie well beyond the proper orbit of humankind. And yet the woodpile constitutes a marker of colonization as plain as any flag, serving to remind the poem's would-be pioneer as he " 'go[es] on farther' " into trackless snow that the human sphere is impossible to evade. Far out in the swamp, the "small bird" still knows enough about humanity to keep its distance.

The walk into the wilderness in Frost's poetry merges the human desire to go beyond itself with the inability to satisfy that desire. As David Bromwich has observed in an essay on Ted Hughes: "Looked at in the terms that poetry demands . . . nature ceases to be the object required by nature poetry" (Bromwich 2001, 164). There is no pure perception of nature; nature perceived by the human is nature transfigured or tainted by the human. Nature ceases to be nature in the attempt to understand it. The problem for the protagonist of "The Wood-Pile" is that, as he heads into the heart of nature, he can leave human society behind but he must bring himself. He recognizes as much even as he projects himself into the mind of a bird presumed to be saying "no word to tell me who he was / Who was so foolish as to think what *he* thought." (Condemning this passage as "picture-book anthropomorphism," Ian Hamilton both misses and proves Frost's point about the impossibility of translating from species to species [Hamilton, 17].) Frost's phrasing may be complex and ambiguous enough to create multilayered ironies, but underpinning them is a knowledge that the avian will always "fl[y] before" and escape human understanding no matter how assertive the anthropomorphic gesture of possession. Metaphor being one such gesture, the final irony comes in a comparison which encapsulates denial and transference: the bird is "like one who takes / Everything said as personal to himself." Reluctant to accept that he can never hope to escape the self by means of the self's immersion in the natural world, the human traps the bird in a mental cage identical to his own.

Having given so much sustained attention to the bird, the poem's protagonist is at last distracted by "a pile of wood." It is easy to understand why a product of human labor—even one so unpromisingly mundane—should seem like a more amenable object for contemplation. Initially, the approach is factual, and recalls Frost's boast about *North of Boston*'s sub-Wordsworthian diction (*SL,* 83–84). In "The Thorn," Wordsworth recorded the dimensions of a "little muddy pond" he had been inspecting: "I've measured it from side to side: / 'Tis three feet long, and two feet wide." Frost's "cord of maple" is "measured, four by four by eight." Wordsworth chose to revise his lines' glorious bathos out of existence in subsequent editions; but Frost's measurements seem entirely appropriate both to his plain unrhymed idiom and to the frugality of a landscape consisting of "lines / Straight up and down."

After describing so meticulously the woodpile's graying color, its warping bark, and the work of the clematis which binds it, Frost's protagonist turns his attention to the human mystery. The speaking voice of "The Tuft of Flowers" had claimed a companion in absentia, as the laborer who had spared the flowers from his scythe becomes a spirit akin to those who toil subsequently. But "The Wood-Pile" cannot quite manage the same alliance, and this time the work of the predecessor causes puzzlement: thoughts and intentions are more confidently ascribed to the bird than to a fellow human. The consequent failure of sympathy lapses into disapproval:

> I thought that only
> Someone who lived in turning to fresh tasks
> Could so forget his handiwork on which
> He spent himself, the labor of his axe,
> And leave it there far from a useful fireplace
> To warm the frozen swamp as best it could
> With the slow smokeless burning of decay.

This tone of accusation is strange, given the protagonist's determination to escape the world of fireplaces and his own forgetfulness. The absent laborer who "Could so forget his handiwork" sounds very much like the protagonist who also "turn[s] to fresh tasks" when he dismisses the bird with the abrupt phrase "I forgot him." Fittingly for someone who takes everything as personal to himself while denying doing so, he interprets the woodpile solely according to his own mental predilections. The heavy gravitas of the poem's final line, with the long assonantal vowels in "slow" and "smokeless" echoing the "frozen swamp," conveys the futility which the woodpile is taken to represent. Certainly, it is no match for the tuft of flowers as a symbol of companionship. But at the risk of making an almost unremittingly bleak poem sound uplifting, it may be worth acknowledging that the woodpile is not wasted among the wastes: the result of someone's pains, it exemplifies a lingering (if meager) human warmth amid the natural world's desolate expanses.

Good Hours

I had for my winter evening walk—
No one at all with whom to talk,
But I had the cottages in a row
Up to their shining eyes in snow.

And I thought I had the folk within:
I had the sound of a violin;
I had a glimpse through curtain laces
Of youthful forms and youthful faces.

I had such company outward bound.
I went till there were no cottages found.
I turned and repented, but coming back
I saw no window but that was black.

Over the snow my creaking feet
Disturbed the slumbering village street
Like profanation, by your leave,
At ten o'clock of a winter eve.

Set apart from the rest of the book typographically (it was printed in italics), "Good Hours" was not listed in *North of Boston*'s table of contents. Befitting its curious status, this little poem has always risked being overlooked. "Good Hours" is both part of *North of Boston* and an adjunct to it, and Poirier's description of it as "unassuming" (Poirier, 90) seems irrefutable. Frost never saw fit to include it in any later selection of his work. Compare that with the fate of the other obviously minor-key poem in *North of Boston*, "The Pasture," which later became the foreword for successive collected editions. Unloved and unnoticed, "Good Hours" has lingered in the margins of Frost's canon.

The scholar who has done most to rescue the poem from its spectral position is Mark Richardson, who makes the bold claim that in anatomizing the relationship between poet and villagers, "Good Hours" "functions as a kind of synecdoche for *North of Boston* and therefore makes an appropriate end piece" (Richardson 1997, 72). Recalling Frost's description of the volume as "this book of people," Richardson inspects some of the ways in which "Good Hours" both justifies and qualifies that claim. Justifies, in that Frost has for company "the folk within" as his persona takes his evening walk; but qualifies, too, because the poem ends with the walker shut out from the sleeping community, alone and isolated in the cold night. Richardson's careful reading does much to illuminate some of the ways in which "Good Hours" commentates on the volume to which it hesitatingly belongs. There is also a more immediately obvious connection, only partially concealed by the blank page and the italic font: formally very different from "The Wood-Pile," "Good Hours" nevertheless continues to explore similar themes in a similar setting. The speaker of "The Wood-Pile," out walking in the frozen swamp, had "paused and said, 'I will turn back from here. / No, I will go on farther—and we shall see.'" That moment of indecision is repeated in the equally severe climatic conditions of "Good Hours," but with the opposite outcome: "I went till there were no cottages found. / I turned and repented." "The Wood-Pile" had been concerned with the desire and inability to escape human influence by walking on into the wilderness; the speaker of "Good Hours" does return to human society only to find himself debarred from it. In those complementary destinies, Frost conveys the poet's curse: he neither belongs nor is special because he does not belong. Finding no kinship in his community, he journeys beyond it only to discover a path already worn by predecessors. (It is no coincidence that the first poem of Frost's next book, *Mountain Interval*, is "The Road Not Taken.") He is the would-be companion kept at one remove by vocation, and the would-be pioneer taunted by precedence.

"Good Hours" addresses such loneliness in the most discreet of ways. The poem's title promises nothing of the *poète maudit*, because although the expression "to keep good hours" is defined (in *Webster's*

Dictionary, 1913) as "to be customarily early in returning home or in retiring to rest," initially it appears to relate more to the poet's pleasant evening stroll than to the admirably regular bedtime habits of his community. The full-rhymed, mostly end-stopped, octosyllabic couplets also seem suitably untroubled; the insistent anaphoric repetition of "I had" conveys not just ownership but the sense of an artist having successfully captured a likeness; and that decorous archaism—"by your leave"—little doubts the poet's modesty, as he risks in the word "profanation" a Latinate polysyllable and immediately apologizes to the reader for having done so. Yet "by your leave" smacks too much of fine writing to be taken as sincere; it counts against Frost's own claim to be interested in "the talk of everyday life" rather than the "literary, sophisticated, artificial, elegant language that belongs to books" (*CPP&P,* 694). The phrase is animated by tonal uncertainty. Is the reader being mocked, or at least treated like those early-to-bed villagers who offer the poet no companionship? " 'You come too,' " Frost had invited us at the start of his journey through *North of Boston;* in "Good Hours" he checks whether we have accompanied him to the end, and (just as important) whether we understood what we saw and heard along the way.

The community fails to appreciate its poet (who is usually presented in *North of Boston* as less rooted, and less knowledgeable about the locale, than his neighbors), but there is at least some anxiety that the misunderstanding may be mutual. The repetition of "I had" comes with a confidence which breaks in the fifth line: "I thought I had the folk within" allows for the possibility of error. Having "the cottages in a row" is one thing; having "the sound of a violin" and a "glimpse" of those nebulous "youthful forms and youthful faces" is another; but having "the folk within," with all that the phrase implies of insight into other people's lives, seems nowhere supported by evidence. The last use of "I had," in the ninth line, is already ironic: "I had such company outward bound" only emphasizes the poet's loneliness as he spies on a vivacity which he can never hope to share. On his return, even that vicarious enjoyment is denied him by forbiddingly "black" windows. If the villagers keep good hours, he clearly does not.

The protagonist of "The Wood-Pile" had noticed that "The hard snow held me, save where now and then / One foot went down." Frost later revised "went down" to "went through," prompting Timothy Steele to make the ingenious suggestion that the line break mimics what is described: "Just as the snow-crust cannot hold the speaker's weight, the line-end cannot contain the clause, which breaks through the measure to the next verse" (Steele, 136). This gains credence from a similar moment in the final stanza of "Good Hours":

> Over the snow my creaking feet
> Disturbed the slumbering village street
> Like profanation, by your leave,
> At ten o'clock of a winter eve.

The poet's "creaking feet" are his own poetic measures, here modestly described and reduced to a disturbance of the peace. Worse than that, they are "Like profanation," developing the hint of religious sin in the previous stanza ("I turned and repented"). That which is profane, etymologically, stands in front of or outside the temple; it is unholy and not admitted to join the initiates inside. And so *North of Boston*, this magnificent book of people, ends in failure with the poet excluded from those about whom he writes. No matter how passionate his attempts at understanding, he must remain an outsider condemned only to enjoy brief and tantalizing glimpses of their lives.

MOUNTAIN INTERVAL

EAGER TO CAPITALIZE on the success of *North of Boston,* Holt wanted the next volume as soon as possible. Frost was able to oblige. He had returned from his two and a half years in England in February 1915 with something approaching two-thirds of a finished manuscript, and the poems which he wrote in the following months brought it to completion. So *Mountain Interval* was published in the United States in late 1916. But sales proved disappointing, despite favorable reviews, and Frost vowed that he would never be rushed again.

Compared with its predecessors, *Mountain Interval* seems less like a coherent volume than a hodgepodge of the poems Frost had to hand. That view is supported by Lawrance Thompson's account that the poems had been written "over a period of approximately twenty years." Twelve were drafted before 1911 (and had therefore been available for *A Boy's Will* if Frost had wanted to use them); seven more were written in England, and thirteen in the prolific months after arriving back in the States (Thompson 1970, 541–542). Looking back over his work many years later, Frost considered that several poems had appeared in the wrong book: he felt, for example, that "An Old Man's Winter Night" and "Snow" properly belonged in an expanded *North of Boston,* which he made some efforts to publish in the 1950s (*CPr,* 344).

Even the title seems to hint at lowered sights. Frost wanted what he called "its double meaning"—"a New England dialect term for land in a valley," and a break or pause (Thompson 1970, 539; Parini, 278). (Dedicating the volume to his wife, he listed three "intervals" where they had lived.) A book which advertises itself as an "interval" makes modest claims, while implicitly praising the lofty heights which surround it.

None of this should disguise the importance of *Mountain Interval*, described by Paul Muldoon as the finest book of poems of the past century. It includes two poems—"The Road Not Taken" and "Birches"— which no anthology of modern poetry can do without. Others, like "An Old Man's Winter Night," "Putting in the Seed," "The Bonfire," " 'Out, Out—' " and "The Vanishing Red," also belong among Frost's best. *Mountain Interval* may be no more than the sum of its parts, but it is not entirely undesigned. Frost has again italicized the first and last poems, both of which describe journeys taken or imagined. And in the portrayal of "home," a consistent change is discernible. Whereas *North of Boston* situated poet and protagonists at one remove from their landscapes, the speakers of *Mountain Interval* share an authoritative sense of belonging. Small wonder that the most prominent exception to this rule, "An Old Man's Winter Night," should have seemed to its author like an escapee from the earlier volume.

The Road Not Taken

Two roads diverged in a yellow wood,
And sorry I could not travel both
And be one traveler, long I stood
And looked down one as far as I could
To where it bent in the undergrowth;

Then took the other, as just as fair,
And having perhaps the better claim,
Because it was grassy and wanted wear;
Though as for that the passing there
Had worn them really about the same,

And both that morning equally lay
In leaves no step had trodden black.
Oh, I kept the first for another day!
Yet knowing how way leads on to way,
I doubted if I should ever come back.

I shall be telling this with a sigh
Somewhere ages and ages hence:
Two roads diverged in a wood, and I—
I took the one less traveled by,
And that has made all the difference.

"The Road Not Taken," printed in italic at the start of *Mountain Interval,* has probably caused more confusion, despite or because of its apparent simplicity, than any other of Frost's poems. Some of the author's comments about its making and meaning have been usefully preserved by Lawrance Thompson (Thompson 1970, 545–548). What they reveal is a poet frustrated by readers who, interpreting the poem as the expression of a timeless human truth, have failed to notice the author's distanced and ironic portrayal of his speaker. A dramatic monologue, Frost seems to protest, has been misread as a lyric.

That misreading, if such it is, began in April or May 1915, when Frost sent a version of the newly finished poem, then titled "Two Roads," to his closest friend, the English poet Edward Thomas. Thomas's perplexity throughout the ensuing correspondence marks the most awkward episode in an otherwise remarkably untroubled and mutually enriching relationship. Perhaps hearing a distant echo of the opening of Dante's *Divine Comedy* (with its reference to journeys, paths, and forests), Thomas read the poem as autobiographical, and solicitously expressed the hope that Frost had not made a decision he had regretted lately. (He may have been thinking of Frost's decision to return to the States from England several months previously.) By way of reply, Frost explained that his friend "had failed to see that the sigh [in "The Road Not Taken"] was a mock sigh, hypo-critical for the fun of the thing. I don't suppose I was ever sorry for anything I ever did except by assumption to see how it would feel" (Spencer, 70). Frost had been seeing how it would feel to be Thomas, who would often sigh during their walks together and wish that they had taken a different and better direction. Playfully mocking a facet of his friend's personality, Frost found it disconcerting to be attributed with it himself by his friend; and no matter how many times he explained his intention to audiences subsequently, even going so far as to call "The Road Not Taken" a war poem about Thomas, the sigh is still usually interpreted—as Thomas interpreted it—as sincere. The poem often taken to be most representatively Frostian is, Frost insists, a teasing portrayal of the manner of Edward Thomas.

Acknowledging in later life that his poems had sometimes meant more, or other, than he had intended, Frost nevertheless remained firm in his attitude that the speaker of "The Road Not Taken" should not be viewed entirely seriously. Several textual clues support his insistence. For example, having decided between roads, the speaker tries to persuade himself that the road chosen had a "better claim, / Because it was grassy and wanted wear." That desire to be characterized as someone who deviates from the beaten track, who refuses to follow the herd, is immediately exposed by stubborn facts: the roads are worn "really about the same" (an equivocation which joins company with "as just as fair" and "perhaps the better"), and both are covered in untrodden leaves. The final stanza, supported by the title's regretful focus, leaves little doubt that the speaker panders to his own sense of melancholia. He mournfully remembers a decision taken in the past, while acting out in the present the very grief which he imagines himself inevitably repeating like some cursed Ancient Mariner in the future:

> I shall be telling this with a sigh
> Somewhere ages and ages hence:
> Two roads diverged in a wood, and I—
> I took the one less traveled by,
> And that has made all the difference.

From the repetition of the first-person pronoun, to the inflationary phrase "ages and ages hence" with its hint of childish or childlike self-indulgence, to the rhyme "sigh"/"I," revealing a melancholic identity, to the formal rhythms of the final line, the anticipation of remembrance has become high-flown and ostentatiously performative. This is a poem which eschews any opportunity for elision: "could not," "I should," "I shall," and "that has" together prove that Frost is making no attempt to capture the rhythms of speech. It is fitting, then, that the poem's final word, "difference," should be stretched beyond natural pronunciation into three syllables through the rhyme with "hence" and the need for a stress on the last syllable. (Contrast, in the opening stanza, the rhyme "both"/"undergrowth," which more appropriately sustains the rhythms of pronunciation.) Particular to the point of stuffiness, the language of "The Road Not Taken" has many of the qualities of fine writing which Frost affected to loathe.

Whether these factors should be sufficient to alert the more attentive readers to Frost's intended ironies is questionable. "There's a hint intended there," Frost said of "The Road Not Taken," and he firmly imposed the responsibility for taking it on his audience: "But you ought to know that yourself . . . I can't mark [the hints]—there's no way of marking them" (Thompson 1970, 547). The speaker of "The Road Not Taken" claims to know the "difference" between his options; but as Frost's audience has mostly ignored or failed to share that knowledge, the poem constitutes something of a crisis in his poetics. Its popularity becomes an affront, attracting admiration for the very characteristics which the poet had tried to mock. The strain inherent in Frost's ambition to write for general and learned audiences alike was already clear in another of his italicized introductory poems, "The Pasture"; but the reception of "The Road Not Taken" fully exposes the contradictions. Frost believed that readers had ignored the poem's signposts and chosen the wrong and more commonly trodden road.

Christmas Trees

(A Christmas Circular Letter)

The city had withdrawn into itself
And left at last the country to the country;
When between whirls of snow not come to lie
And whirls of foliage not yet laid, there drove
A stranger to our yard, who looked the city,
Yet did in country fashion in that there
He sat and waited till he drew us out
A-buttoning coats to ask him who he was.
He proved to be the city come again
To look for something it had left behind
And could not do without and keep its Christmas.
He asked if I would sell my Christmas trees;
My woods—the young fir balsams like a place
Where houses all are churches and have spires.
I hadn't thought of them as Christmas Trees.
I doubt if I was tempted for a moment
To sell them off their feet to go in cars
And leave the slope behind the house all bare,
Where the sun shines now no warmer than the moon.
I'd hate to have them know it if I was.
Yet more I'd hate to hold my trees except
As others hold theirs or refuse for them,
Beyond the time of profitable growth,
The trial by market everything must come to.
I dallied so much with the thought of selling.
Then whether from mistaken courtesy
And fear of seeming short of speech, or whether
From hope of hearing good of what was mine,
I said, "There aren't enough to be worth while."

"I could soon tell how many they would cut,
You let me look them over."

                            "You could look.
But don't expect I'm going to let you have them."
Pasture they spring in, some in clumps too close
That lop each other of boughs, but not a few
Quite solitary and having equal boughs
All round and round. The latter he nodded "Yes" to,
Or paused to say beneath some lovelier one,
With a buyer's moderation, "That would do."
I thought so too, but wasn't there to say so.
We climbed the pasture on the south, crossed over,
And came down on the north.

                         He said, "A thousand."

"A thousand Christmas trees!—at what apiece?"

He felt some need of softening that to me:
"A thousand trees would come to thirty dollars."

Then I was certain I had never meant
To let him have them. Never show surprise!
But thirty dollars seemed so small beside
The extent of pasture I should strip, three cents
(For that was all they figured out apiece)
Three cents so small beside the dollar friends
I should be writing to within the hour
Would pay in cities for good trees like those,
Regular vestry-trees whole Sunday Schools
Could hang enough on to pick off enough.

A thousand Christmas trees I didn't know I had!

Worth three cents more to give away than sell,
As may be shown by a simple calculation.
Too bad I couldn't lay one in a letter.
I can't help wishing I could send you one,
In wishing you herewith a Merry Christmas.

"Christmas Trees" was written on Christmas Eve 1915, for use on the Frost family's handmade Christmas card. Begun, then, as an occasional poem, it is comic in a fashion not previously encountered in Frost's work. Although the poet may express regret at not being able to give them away, his title ensures that every reader becomes a recipient of one of his "Christmas Trees." The lighthearted pun comes with serious purpose. "Too bad I couldn't lay one in a letter," Frost complains, but to describe a tree is to make a gift of it to the reader. When Frost mentions "The trial by market everything must come to," he brings together trees and poems alike in that capacious "everything." The poem which begins as a Christmas circular letter for private appreciation must finally take its chances with the paying public at large.

The close relationship between trees and poems brings to mind the organic analogies in Frost's earlier work, especially the poem-as-flower and flower-as-poem tropes of works like "The Tuft of Flowers" and "The Self-Seeker." The comparison allows Frost to create parables about the value and values of poetry. Mark Richardson has drawn attention to Frost's claim in a letter of 1915 that "a book ought to sell. Nothing is quite honest that is not commercial" (*LU*, 8–9). "Christmas Trees" adds a caveat to such hard-nosed capitalism: nothing is quite honest that is *only* commercial. Christmas is, after all, a time of giving as well as a time of selling. Like the invalid of "The Self-Seeker" whose botanizing is too important to be costed, Frost's speaker holds his trees "Beyond the time of profitable growth" while denying that he would ever do such a thing. The poem is a master class of equivocation and prevarication, as the landowner refuses to admit even to himself his own mixed motives; and although the prospect of such tiny financial returns prompts his final refusal, that is reported with a dry humor ("Then I was certain I had never meant / To let him have them") which leaves unspoken the question of how much, if anything, *would* have been enough. After all, despite the material connection between trees and paper, there is one way in which the analogy fails to hold. Sell your poems and you have lost nothing; sell your trees and you are left with "the slope behind the house all bare."

The negotiations between Frost's persona and the "stranger" from the city hint at a new attitude to "home"—the word which had echoed through the previous volume so loudly and often. *North of Boston* had been preoccupied with exploring outsiderdom and (relatedly) the inability to feel secure at home. By setting up a dichotomy between country and city, "Christmas Trees" shares nothing of that anxiety. Early in the poem, the persona emphasizes his sense of belonging with recurrent possessives: "our yard," "my Christmas trees," "My woods." He *is* the country, as much as his antagonist *is* "the city come again" to denude even more of the country's glories and sell them on at vast profit. His sure-footed refusal to sell, despite all temptation, resists the blandishments of an urban marketplace which thrives by profiteering at the country's expense. Here is a character embedded in his locality, who knows the codes and the etiquettes, who is at home in the ways of the countryside, and who will not be bamboozled by the city's slick money-driven operations. It marks a new assurance in Frost's voice when he speaks in propria persona. The Frostian visitor of *North of Boston,* amid strange surroundings outside his natural milieu, has now given way to the landowner whose property provides the inspiration for so many poems in *Mountain Interval* and beyond.

An Old Man's Winter Night

All out of doors looked darkly in at him
Through the thin frost, almost in separate stars,
That gathers on the pane in empty rooms.
What kept his eyes from giving back the gaze
Was the lamp tilted near them in his hand.
What kept him from remembering what it was
That brought him to that creaking room was age.
He stood with barrels round him—at a loss.
And having scared the cellar under him
In clomping there, he scared it once again
In clomping off;—and scared the outer night,
Which has its sounds, familiar, like the roar
Of trees and crack of branches, common things,
But nothing so like beating on a box.
A light he was to no one but himself
Where now he sat, concerned with he knew what,
A quiet light, and then not even that.
He consigned to the moon, such as she was,
So late-arising, to the broken moon
As better than the sun in any case
For such a charge, his snow upon the roof,
His icicles along the wall to keep;
And slept. The log that shifted with a jolt
Once in the stove, disturbed him and he shifted,
And eased his heavy breathing, but still slept.
One aged man—one man—can't fill a house,
A farm, a countryside, or if he can,
It's thus he does it of a winter night.

Frost rated "An Old Man's Winter Night" highly, telling Sidney Cox that the poem was "probably the best thing in [*Mountain Interval*]" (*SL*, 208). It takes as its unadvertised point of departure a poem by Coleridge, even the title of which must have encouraged Frost's engagement. "Frost at Midnight," like Frost's own poem, is a nocturnal meditation in blank verse, focusing on a man's winter solitude as he is warmed by a fire. Both poems make reference to "sleep" ("slept" appears twice in Frost's poem), "snow," "stars," "icicles," "frost," the "moon" (or uppercase "Moon"), the "sun," "tree[s]," and "branch[es]"; and the "quiet Moon" which ends Coleridge's poem prompts another transferred epithet—"quiet light"—in Frost's. A "film" fluttering on the grate in one poem becomes, in the other, a log shifting in the stove.

However, these parallels only lay bare the bleak differences of Frost's vision. His poem is a rejoinder to Coleridge, negating the grounds for hope which the earlier poem had discovered through its "Abstruser musings." Coleridge addresses his child:

> Dear Babe, that sleepest cradled by my side,
> Whose gentle breathings, heard in this deep calm,
> Fill up the interspersed vacancies
> And momentary pauses of the thought!

The passage offers to answer the dread famously induced in Blaise Pascal by "the eternal silence of these infinite spaces"; and Coleridge goes on to find solace in the thought of "The lovely shapes and sounds intelligible / Of that eternal language, which thy God / Utters." But Frost remains closer to Pascal. As the infant's "gentle breathings" in Coleridge's poem are transformed by Frost into an old man's "heavy breathing," the filling of space with anything meaningful becomes a forlorn prospect:

> The log that shifted with a jolt
> Once in the stove, disturbed him and he shifted,

And eased his heavy breathing, but still slept.
One aged man—one man—can't fill a house,
A farm, a countryside, or if he can,
It's thus he does it of a winter night.

Frost later revised the phrase "can't fill a house" to "can't keep a house," claiming that " 'Fill' is awful" (*SL*, 237). The poem's repetition of "keep" implies that the aged man can keep his house only in the same way that, four lines earlier, the moon can "keep" icicles. Even so, Frost's second thoughts ought to be resisted. Frost's "fill" derisively echoes Coleridge's more positive use of the verb. To change "fill" to "keep" is to diminish and domesticate a terror which "fill" had made horribly universal: although "All out of doors looked darkly in at him," the gaze switches at the poem's end as emptiness spreads outward to "fill" first house then farm then countryside. What had been a local and enclosed isolation suddenly seems like an inevitable part of the human condition, contaminating the landscape around. This is no Walden. Any faith in the healing power of the natural world, or a radical correspondence of visible things and human thoughts, is horribly mocked.

"Frost at Midnight" draws comfort from a natural world which is the product of God's wisdom; and comfort, too, from Coleridge's hope for the next generation, represented by the baby who will grow up to be shaped and sustained by his experiences of that world. Frost strips away those consolations. "An Old Man's Winter Night" detects no sign of a benign deity. The aged man is bereft of family and friends ("A light he was to no one but himself"); and far from providing solace, the natural surroundings seem threateningly voyeuristic, as the play on "darkly" in the opening line hints at sinister intent. Such communication as there is comes down to "the roar / Of trees and crack of branches" and, reciprocating the din, the old man's "clomping" which "scare[s] the outer night." A noise "like beating on a box" suggests a hollow futility which belies the "lovely shapes and sounds intelligible" of "Frost at Midnight." Only once is the possibility of benign interaction between mankind and nature broached, in a passage which stands apart for the high pitch of its rhetoric:

He consigned to the moon, such as she was,
So late-arising, to the broken moon
As better than the sun in any case
For such a charge, his snow upon the roof,
His icicles along the wall to keep;
And slept.

While seeming to swoon into the language of high Romanticism, this takes the ultimate revenge by showing it up as nonsensical. Coleridge had brought icicles and the moon into close proximity, ending with the lucent tranquility of icicles "Quietly shining to the quiet Moon." Frost's old man consigns the icicles (and the snow) to the care of the moon only to demonstrate the meaninglessness of positing any relation between them. There is the wry observation that the moon is less ill-equipped for the "charge" than the sun; but even so, that great symbol now appears "late-arising" (as if irresponsibly unpunctual) and "broken." Shelley compared the moon to a "dying lady . . . led by the insane / And feeble wanderings of her fading brain"; and it is tempting to think of Frost's moon as symbolic of the broken old man. But this is a poem which fails to find even that bleak correspondence between the deteriorating individual and the world beyond. Nature neither speaks to nor salves his existence; no matter how great the ulterior powers of poetry, this time the old man's isolation remains absolute.

In the Home Stretch

She stood against the kitchen sink, and looked
Over the sink out through a dusty window
At weeds the water from the sink made tall.
She wore her cape; her hat was in her hand.
Behind her was confusion in the room,
Of chairs turned upside down to sit like people
In other chairs, and something, come to look,
For every room a house has—parlor, bedroom,
And dining-room—thrown pell-mell in the kitchen.
And now and then a smudged, infernal face
Looked in a door behind her and addressed
Her back. She always answered without turning.

"Where will I put this walnut bureau, lady?"

"Put it on top of something that's on top
Of something else," she laughed. "Oh, put it where
You can to-night, and go. It's almost dark;
You must be getting started back to town."
Another blackened face thrust in and looked
And smiled, and when she did not turn, spoke gently,
"What are you seeing out the window, *lady?*"

"Never was I beladied so before.
Would evidence of having been called lady
More than so many times make me a lady
In common law, I wonder."

                              "But I ask,
What are you seeing out the window, lady?"

"What I'll be seeing more of in the years
To come as here I stand and go the round
Of many plates with towels many times."

"And what is that? You only put me off."

"Rank weeds that love the water from the dish-pan
More than some women like the dish-pan, Joe;
A little stretch of mowing-field for you;
Not much of that until I come to woods
That end all. And it's scarce enough to call
A view."

            "And yet you think you like it, dear?"

"That's what you're so concerned to know! You hope
I like it. Bang goes something big away
Off there upstairs. The very tread of men
As great as those is shattering to the frame
Of such a little house. Once left alone,
You and I, dear, will go with softer steps
Up and down stairs and through the rooms, and none
But sudden winds that snatch them from our hands
Will ever slam the doors."

                    "I think you see
More than you like to own to out that window."

"No; for beside the things I tell you of,
I only see the years. They come and go
In alternation with the weeds, the field,
The wood."

"What kind of years?"

                              "Why, latter years—
Different from early years."

                         "I see them, too.
You didn't count them?"

                         "No, the further off
So ran together that I didn't try to.
It can scarce be that they would be in number
We'd care to know, for we are not young now.
And bang goes something else away off there.
It sounds as if it were the men went down,
And every crash meant one less to return
To lighted city streets we, too, have known,
But now are giving up for country darkness."

"Come from that window where you see too much for me,
And take a livelier view of things from here.
They're going. Watch this husky swarming up
Over the wheel into the sky-high seat,
Lighting his pipe now, squinting down his nose
At the flame burning downward as he sucks it."

"See how it makes his nose-side bright, a proof
How dark it's getting. Can you tell what time
It is by that? Or by the moon? The new moon!
What shoulder did I see her over? Neither.
A wire she is of silver, as new as we
To everything. Her light won't last us long.
It's something, though, to know we're going to have her
Night after night and stronger every night
To see us through our first two weeks. But, Joe,

The stove! Before they go! Knock on the window;
Ask them to help you get it on its feet.
We stand here dreaming. Hurry! Call them back!"

"They're not gone yet."

                "We've got to have the stove,
Whatever else we want for. And a light.
Have we a piece of candle if the lamp
And oil are buried out of reach?"
                          Again
The house was full of tramping, and the dark,
Door-filling men burst in and seized the stove.
A cannon-mouth-like hole was in the wall,
To which they set it true by eye; and then
Came up the jointed stovepipe in their hands,
So much too light and airy for their strength
It almost seemed to come ballooning up,
Slipping from clumsy clutches toward the ceiling.
"A fit!" said one, and banged a stovepipe shoulder.
"It's good luck when you move in to begin
With good luck with your stovepipe. Never mind,
It's not so bad in the country, settled down,
When people 're getting on in life. You'll like it."

Joe said: "You big boys ought to find a farm,
And make good farmers, and leave other fellows
The city work to do. There's not enough
For everybody as it is in there."

"God!" one said wildly, and, when no one spoke:
"Say that to Jimmy here. He needs a farm."
But Jimmy only made his jaw recede
Fool-like, and rolled his eyes as if to say

He saw himself a farmer. Then there was a French boy
Who said with seriousness that made them laugh,
"Ma friend, you ain't know what it is you're ask."
He doffed his cap and held it with both hands
Across his chest to make as 'twere a bow:
"We're giving you our chances on de farm."
And then they all turned to with deafening boots
And put each other bodily out of the house.

"Goodby to them! We puzzle them. They think—
I don't know what they think we see in what
They leave us to: that pasture slope that seems
The back some farm presents us; and your woods
To northward from your window at the sink,
Waiting to steal a step on us whenever
We drop our eyes or turn to other things,
As in the game 'Ten-step' the children play."

"Good boys they seemed, and let them love the city.
All they could say was 'God!' when you proposed
Their coming out and making useful farmers."

"Did they make something lonesome go through you?
It would take more than them to sicken you—
Us of the bargain. But they left us so
As to our fate, like fools past reasoning with.
They almost shook *me*."

                    "It's all so much
What we have always wanted, I confess
Its seeming bad for a moment makes it seem
Even worse still, and so on down, down, down.
It's nothing; it's their leaving us at dusk.
I never bore it well when people went.

The first night after guests have gone, the house
Seems haunted or exposed. I always take
A personal interest in the locking up
At bedtime; but the strangeness soon wears off."
He fetched a dingy lantern from behind
A door. "There's that we didn't lose! And these!"—
Some matches he unpocketed. "For food—
The meals we've had no one can take from us.
I wish that everything on earth were just
As certain as the meals we've had. I wish
The meals we haven't had were, anyway.
What have you you know where to lay your hands on?"

"The bread we bought in passing at the store.
There's butter somewhere, too."

                                "Let's rend the bread.
I'll light the fire for company for you;
You'll not have any other company
Till Ed begins to get out on a Sunday
To look us over and give us his idea
Of what wants pruning, shingling, breaking up.
He'll know what he would do if he were we,
And all at once. He'll plan for us and plan
To help us, but he'll take it out in planning.
Well, you can set the table with the loaf.
Let's see you find your loaf. I'll light the fire.
I like chairs occupying other chairs
Not offering a lady——"

                                "There again, Joe!
You're tired."

        "I'm drunk-nonsensical tired out;
Don't mind a word I say. It's a day's work
To empty one house of all household goods
And fill another with 'em fifteen miles away,
Although you do no more than dump them down."

"Dumped down in paradise we are and happy."

"It's all so much what I have always wanted,
I can't believe it's what you wanted, too."

"Shouldn't you like to know?"

                    "I'd like to know
If it is what you wanted, then how much
You wanted it for me."

               "A troubled conscience!
You don't want me to tell if *I* don't know."

"I don't want to find out what can't be known.
But who first said the word to come?"

                  "My dear,
It's who first thought the thought. You're searching, Joe,
For things that don't exist; I mean beginnings.
Ends and beginnings—there are no such things.
There are only middles."

          "What is this?"

                 "This life?
Our sitting here by lantern-light together
Amid the wreckage of a former home?

You won't deny the lantern isn't new.
The stove is not, and you are not to me,
Nor I to you."

        "Perhaps you never were?"

"It would take me forever to recite
All that's not new in where we find ourselves.
New is a word for fools in towns who think
Style upon style in dress and thought at last
Must get somewhere. I've heard you say as much.
No, this is no beginning."

          "Then an end?"

"End is a gloomy word."

          "Is it too late
To drag you out for just a good-night call
On the old peach trees on the knoll to grope
By starlight in the grass for a last peach
The neighbors may not have taken as their right
When the house wasn't lived in? I've been looking:
I doubt if they have left us many grapes.
Before we set ourselves to right the house,
The first thing in the morning, out we go,
To go the round of apple, cherry, peach,
Pine, alder, pasture, mowing, well, and brook.
All of a farm it is."

        "I know this much:
I'm going to put you in your bed, if first
I have to make you build it. Come, the light."

When there was no more lantern in the kitchen,
The fire got out through crannies in the stove
And danced in yellow wrigglers on the ceiling,
As much at home as if they'd always danced there.

There are formal and thematic reasons why "In the Home Stretch,"
although too prolix to count among Frost's very best work, would not
look out of place amid the many poems in *North of Boston* preoccupied
with the meaning of home. A dialogue in blank verse, the poem seems
like a throwback to the practices of that earlier volume. But in other less
obvious ways, "In the Home Stretch" also relates closely to the opening
poems in *Mountain Interval*—the tension between town and country
represented by the two bargainers in "Christmas Trees," for example, or
the still greater tension between the house dweller and his environment
in "An Old Man's Winter Night." That solitary old man, frightening the
night as he clomped from room to room, no longer had the wherewithal
to make his house a home; he lived in but was not a part of it. A similar
"tramping" echoes through "In the Home Stretch" as the removal men
shift furniture into position, prompting the wife to remark that "'The
very tread of men / As great as those is shattering to the frame / Of such
a little house.'" As if to reassure the house, she tells her husband that
their own passage will be with "'softer steps,'" and that only "'sudden
winds'" will "'slam the doors.'" The separate attitudes of the old man
and the woman to similar noises place the two poems at opposite poles:
although each is concerned with the relationship between a house and
its occupants, one describes a bare subsistence in a hostile environment,
the other a delighted confidence that paradise has been regained.

The woman's emotional bond with the house—a bond so conspicu-
ously lacking in "An Old Man's Winter Night"—creates the promise of
future well-being. Whereas "All out of doors" had looked threateningly
in at the old man, "In the Home Stretch" begins with the woman looking
out the kitchen window at her land and using her imagination to appreci-

ate its seasonal cycles. The ritual installation of a stove, which seems to serve as a covenant between the house and its inhabitants (like the obviously eucharistic "rend[ing]" of the bread), is emblematic of a successful transition, as a home is made not just amid but *out of* " 'the wreckage of a former home.' " The poem's final lines confirm the accuracy of the many earlier auguries. The fire escapes "through crannies in the stove" to set "yellow wrigglers on the ceiling," but these are enlivening patterns, not the beginnings of a disastrous conflagration. The "wrigglers" seem "As much at home as if they'd always danced there"—an image colored by the couple's own joyous sense of belonging.

"In the Home Stretch" stresses its suspicion of a word which was never among Frost's favorites: "new." The new, for Frost, usually carries an air of newfangledness. "It may come to the notice of posterity," he begins an introduction to Robinson's *King Jasper*, "that this, our age, ran wild in the quest of new ways to be new." Robinson enjoys Frost's praise for having "stayed content with the old-fashioned way to be new" (*CPP&P*, 741). That praise intimates a credo which, "In the Home Stretch" makes clear, applies as much to life as to art. The moon may be "new" but, as a consequence, " 'Her light won't last us long.' " The only consolation is that over the next fortnight the light will grow stronger as the moon grows older. The couple have left behind the " 'lighted city streets' " in favor of " 'country darkness' "; all the same, the moon promises gradual enlightenment. Initially, the woman considers the moon to be " 'as new as we / To everything,' " but later she radically revises that estimation:

> "It would take me forever to recite
> All that's not new in where we find ourselves.
> New is a word for fools in towns who think
> Style upon style in dress and thought at last
> Must get somewhere. I've heard you say as much.
> No, this is no beginning."

The association of the town with the new and the country with the old and traditional (not to mention the paradisal or Edenic) is itself anything but new. Frost's allegiance to rural values, and his willingness to pick a fight with what he perceives as the fatuity of the urban lifestyle, are still more apparent here than they had been in "Christmas Trees." Although the removal men are " 'Good boys' " who " 'love the city,' " that preference, coupled with their own disparaging comments about the country, makes them seem immature. They are " 'dark, / Door-filling men' " with " 'deafening boots' "; one has a " 'smudged, infernal face' " (whereas Joe's face is only "blackened"); and their "Fool-like" japes mark them out as lacking the wisdom of those who have chosen to escape to paradise. And paradise it is: " 'apple, cherry, peach, / Pine, alder, pasture, mowing, well, and brook.' " More than a mere inventory, the list becomes a catalogue aria, celebrating the familiar features which Frost's audience encounters as he guides us through his poetic landscapes.

Meeting and Passing

As I went down the hill along the wall
There was a gate I had leaned at for the view
And had just turned from when I first saw you
As you came up the hill. We met. But all
We did that day was mingle great and small
Footprints in summer dust as if we drew
The figure of our being less than two
But more than one as yet. Your parasol

Pointed the decimal off with one deep thrust.
And all the time we talked you seemed to see
Something down there to smile at in the dust.
(Oh, it was without prejudice to me!)
Afterward I went past what you had passed
Before we met and you what I had passed.

~✦~

The sonnet form is represented in all but one of Frost's poetry volumes. (*North of Boston,* dominated by eclogues at the lyric's expense, provides the exception.) In Frost's hands, the sonnet's most immediately noticeable characteristic is its diversity, and not just because of a range of subject matters: the four sonnets of *Mountain Interval* have four different rhyme schemes. Frost wrote of Shakespeare's Sonnet 29, "When in disgrace with fortune and men's eyes," that its author "was no doubt bent on the sonnet in the first place from habit, and what's the use in pretending he was a freer agent than he had any ambition to be" (*CPr,* 149–150). Frost's own experiments with a variety of rhyming patterns are one way of asserting freedom of choice within a fixed form.

The mongrel scheme of "Meeting and Passing," with its Italian octave of *abbaabba* followed by a Shakespearean quatrain and rhyming couplet (*cdcdee*), had been adopted once before by Frost, in "A Dream

Pang" from *A Boy's Will*. Traditionally, a change in rhyme scheme might be expected to mark the sonnet's *volta*, or turn; and like that earlier poem, "Meeting and Passing" seems to mark one such change with a stanza break after line 8. Yet the drama of "Meeting and Passing" comes from the inability to choreograph the couple's movements within the larger formal choreographies of the sonnet. Despite being intricately connected through the rhyme scheme, the octave in which the speaker seeks unity must twice contend with the stubborn refusal announced by a "But" which insists on division: "We met" *but* all we mingled were footprints; we were "less than two" *but* more than one. These signs of resistance find embodiment in the parasol, which, thrust swordlike by the woman, enjambs across the stanza break (no natural *volta* here) to emphasize the ill-fittedness of the couple's relationship to the sonnet's patterning. Whereas full rhymes had thrown their disharmony into relief, the mismatch of "parasol" with "small" introduces a discordant note in keeping with the couple's failures to rhyme with each other.

In his brief discussion of Sonnet 29, Frost claims that Shakespeare "gets through in twelve lines and doesn't quite know what to do with the last two" (*CPr*, 150). The worry as to "whether [the sonneteer] will outlast or last out the fourteen lines" is considered by Frost to be an occupational hazard. "Meeting and Passing" seems more in danger of outlasting than failing to last out its proper span. The "meeting" promised by the title ends after twelve lines, so that "passing" needs to be compressed into a final couplet. As if struggling to fit everything in, Frost could hardly make his diction less ornamental:

Afterward I went past what you had passed
Before we met and you what I had passed.

The sonnet form promises a self-conscious performance, aware of its status as written artifice. But even while taking it up, Frost utters his *non serviam*, his rejection of any kind of afflatus. His limited lexicon befits a poet tempted by the "anti-vocabularian" impulse (*CPr*, 201), as the high proportion of monosyllables in his work demonstrates. "Meeting and

Passing" manages perfectly well with monosyllables in its opening lines and its final couplet (and "Afterward" and "Before" are of sturdy Old English stock). The complex Latinate or semi-Latinate polysyllables— "parasol," "decimal," "prejudice"—belong to the unsatisfactory meeting; at its conclusion, life returns to a state of simplicity. There has been no world-changing revelation. The legalistic phrase "without prejudice" implies that nothing should be read into the woman's gestures, and that the meeting will be allowed no bearing on future events.

The final couplet's plain diction makes an epigram at odds with its own form, rejecting the fluent and the memorable in favor of basic reportage. That ostentatious lack of ostentation is matched by the identity rhyme "passed" / "passed," the drudgery of which becomes further enhanced by the repetition with "past." At last, the couple duplicate each other, like the rhyme itself; walking away, they even see things from each other's perspective. The poem which had tried so hard for the unity of mutual understanding seems finally to have delivered it. As Randall Jarrell maintains, the couplet expresses "the transfiguring, almost inexpressible reaching-out of the self to what has become closer and more personal than the self" (Jarrell 1952, 553). Yet Jarrell misses that the moment can be read as devastatingly ironic: when together, they seem gauche, and only while apart do the couple share experiences and exhibit kinship. Repetition may avoid the divisiveness of being "more than one," but only at the cost of providing the most frustrating kind of union.

Hyla Brook

By June our brook's run out of song and speed.
Sought for much after that, it will be found
Either to have gone groping underground
(And taken with it all the Hyla breed
That shouted in the mist a month ago,
Like ghost of sleigh-bells in a ghost of snow)—
Or flourished and come up in jewel-weed,
Weak foliage that is blown upon and bent
Even against the way its waters went.
Its bed is left a faded paper sheet
Of dead leaves stuck together by the heat—
A brook to none but who remember long.
This as it will be seen is other far
Than with brooks taken otherwise in song.
We love the things we love for what they are.

After "Meeting and Passing," "Hyla Brook" looks like another sonnet, and begins suitably with an *abba* rhyme. It also sounds like a sonnet, exploring a theme much beloved of sonneteers: the power of art to protect and preserve from the ravages of time. But the poem about a brook that "runs out of song and speed" embodies a different destiny, by outrunning the fourteen lines with one extra. Perhaps it is an example of a "sonnet that went agley" (as Frost, with a nod to his Scottish ancestry, once put it), of a change from "one form to another after starting" (*CPr*, 150). If so, "Hyla Brook" exploits its near miss by taking itself "otherwhere in song" than where the reader initially expects. Although bound by rhyme, the aphoristic fifteenth line is a fine excess at once concluding, summarizing, and revising what has gone before.

Such formal awareness befits a poem overtly conscious of those other songs "taken otherwhere." "Hyla Brook" freely advertises its own literary status, and in doing so it parallels another of Frost's literary brooks, in "The Mountain," with its unseen but rumored source. Commentators have not been slow to take up the challenge of locating the sources of "Hyla Brook," or at least identifying those brooks which Frost has in mind as having been taken otherwise. "Otherwhere," a word so rare and so arch (not to say archaic), itself provides their first clue. Most immediately associated with Tennyson, it occurs in his work probably more often than any other major poet's; and although his commonly anthologized poem "The Brook" never uses it, that poem's refrain seems to ghost Frost's text. Tennyson's brook babbles of how "men may come and men may go, / But I go on for ever." Frost's poem begins as if in response: "By June *our* brook's run out of song and speed" (my italics). Whereas, in Tennyson's poem, human life is fleeting and the brook eternal, Frost's winterbourne relies on the persistence of human memory; out of season, it is "A brook to none but who remember long." The poem's, and brook's, decline from "song" to the "faded paper sheet" marks a fall from the vivacity of the audible to its dull translation into the printed word. For a writer who placed such emphasis on the accents of living speech, a printed poem might well risk seeming dried up—Frost's own bleak version of Shelley's fading coals of inspiration. Only those capable of remembering, and hearing accents in the voiceless tracks left behind, can continue to "love" the brook after it has disappeared. Art and memory are brought into harmony through the rhyme of "long" and "song." As Frost once told a younger poet, "Only poetry comes close to catching the fast flowing world and holding it" (Parini, 317).

Frost's brook can also be traced back to a classical tradition in which springs, considered holy, are linked to artistic creativity through their association with the Muses. Although that debt seems more generic than specific, Helen Bacon has drawn particular attention to Horace's "O Fons Bandusiae" (*Odes* III, 13), a hymn of praise to a life-giving fountain which will become famous ("nobilium") as a consequence of the poet's art (Bacon, 87). But while the blazing dogstar's cruel hour cannot touch Horace's fountain ("Te flagrantis atrox hora Caniculae / nescit tangere"), which continues to provide refreshment to weary animals, Frost's brook does run dry. From this seeming impoverishment, "Hyla Brook" draws a defiant strength. Robert Faggen in his book on Frost and Darwin (Faggen 1997, 280) spots one further allusion, to Darwin's *The Voyage of the Beagle:*

> Nature, in these climes, chooses her vocalists from more humble performers than in Europe. A small frog, of the genus Hyla, sits on a blade of grass about an inch from the surface of the water, and sends forth a pleasing chirp: when several are together they sing in harmony on different notes.

Those brooks taken otherwhere have something in common: they are European brooks. Frost's is not only American, it is his own property. As he tells one correspondent, the poem is "about the brook on my old farm. It always dried up in summer. The Hyla is a small frog that shouts like jingling bells in the marshes in spring" (*SL*, 171). Even the jewel-weed turns out to be merely "Weak foliage" rather than anything precious. But these discouragements allow Frost's brook to compete with its predecessors: it is authentic and unique, its very humility lending it to a kind of poetry celebrating unidealized truths.

Reuben Brower hears irony in the poem's final line—"We love the things we love for what they are"—because in summer the brook is loved despite *not* being a brook. However, the brook is not loved as a word or a label; it is loved for all its peculiarities and its seasonal transformations. Frost's "We" does not seem to accommodate the singers of other brooks' praises so much as the readers who will share his allegiance to imperfect reality. His poetry will valorize the modest and the local, and will refuse hyperbole as it shows its commitment through memory to the valued springs of its inspiration.

The Oven Bird

There is a singer everyone has heard,
Loud, a mid-summer and a mid-wood bird,
Who makes the solid tree-trunks sound again.
He says that leaves are old and that for flowers
Mid-summer is to spring as one to ten.
He says the early petal-fall is past
When pear and cherry bloom went down in showers
On sunny days a moment overcast;
And comes that other fall we name the fall.
He says the highway dust is over all.
The bird would cease and be as other birds
But that he knows in singing not to sing.
The question that he frames in all but words
Is what to make of a diminished thing.

"The Oven Bird," an irregular sonnet dismissed by Frost himself as a
"not over important poem" (*SL*, 208), continues a tendency established
by "Meeting and Passing" and "Hyla Brook" to keep its sights lowered;
it dwells on the unbeautiful, the unexalted, the desiccated. The reference
to "highway dust" echoes the "summer dust" of "Meeting and Passing"
and the dried-out riverbed in "Hyla Brook"; and just as "Hyla Brook"
had evoked a Horatian and a Tennysonian grandeur only to point up
the contrast, so "The Oven Bird" cannot aspire to the flights of fancy
of Keats's nightingale or Shelley's skylark, or even, for that matter, the
joy illimited of Hardy's darkling thrush. The ovenbird, like the frogs of
"Hyla Brook," is a New World creature, providing an opportunity for
the American poet to stake out a distinctive territory which, no matter
how modest in certain respects, takes pride in its independence from
European examples. (Whitman had done the same in his great elegy for
Lincoln, replacing those Romantic staples of skylark and nightingale

with the American mockingbird.) "These poems are revolutionary," Edward Thomas had written about *North of Boston*, "because they lack the exaggeration of rhetoric" (Parini, 151). Frost's quiet revolution continues in *Mountain Interval*, in which he loves the things he loves because of their familiarity to him outside the domain of literature. The ovenbird and Hyla Brook are *his* things, not a predecessor's, and consequently they lend themselves to an art which (reversing the ovenbird's tendency to hector) knows in not singing how to sing.

Yet Frost is nothing if not pragmatic in his dealings with European literature. Whitman presented his metrical experiments as part of a campaign to cut the shackles of that encumbrance. For Frost, originality stems not from rejection of the past but from deploying its resources in unforeseen ways. The ovenbird may be American, but the sonnet form and the iambic pentameter which accommodate it are not. And the contrarian instinct of "The Oven Bird" (like "Hyla Brook" and the savage rewriting of Coleridge in "An Old Man's Winter Night") requires a knowledge of tradition if only to emphasize how Frost succeeds by doing otherwise. As Richard Poirier has argued, there is often in Frost's work a tension between a vernacular talking voice and a literary voice "taken from the poetry of the past" (Poirier, 20). So Tennyson's brook may go on forever, but *our* brook runs out of song and speed. And whereas the ovenbird's chief antagonist, Hardy's thrush, had produced its "ecstatic sound" in deepest winter, surrounded by seasonal decay, the "mid-summer" ovenbird refuses to rejoice, detecting only symptoms of decline at the zenith of the year.

The ovenbird's reproach to the summer comes with a self-proclaimed authority: its song is traditionally transcribed as a loud and insistent *teacher-teacher-teacher*. Frost's poem knows as much but never spells it out. The ovenbird "says" (three times), and "frames" a question, and values volume over musicality: he "knows in singing not to sing." What he teaches is a miserabilist's denial of seasonal splendor, as he mourns the passing of a spring in which other birds sang but not he. Now that they are silent, he alone "makes the solid tree-trunks sound again," complaining of decline and looking forward to further decline in "that other fall we name the fall." This dwelling on the negative leads to the teacher's final and seemingly rhetorical question, which does not wait for answer:

> The question that he frames in all but words
> Is what to make of a diminished thing.

Presumably with this conclusion in mind, Frost described "The Oven Bird" as having "a little sententious tag" (*SL,* 208). But the work deserves to be defended against its disparaging author, who has again built better than he knew: any sententiousness belongs to the ovenbird, not the poem.

John Hollander has pointed out the double meaning in the last line: "what to make of" holds together matters of *construing* (how to interpret) and *constructing* (what to build from) (Hollander 1997b, 41). Accordingly, an attentive pupil may find an answer to a question which the teacher had thought unanswerable. Rhetorical questions always risk rebounding on their source, and in this case the "diminished thing" can as easily be the ovenbird itself—diminished by its own teachings— as it can be the summer. To the question of what to construct from a diminished thing, Frost's answer is: a poem. The ovenbird's question unwittingly completes the sonnet, as art's formal perfection belies the supposed imperfections of the season.

Birches

When I see birches bend to left and right
Across the lines of straighter darker trees,
I like to think some boy's been swinging them.
But swinging doesn't bend them down to stay.
Ice-storms do that. Often you must have seen them
Loaded with ice a sunny winter morning
After a rain. They click upon themselves
As the breeze rises, and turn many-colored
As the stir cracks and crazes their enamel.
Soon the sun's warmth makes them shed crystal shells
Shattering and avalanching on the snow-crust—
Such heaps of broken glass to sweep away
You'd think the inner dome of heaven had fallen.
They are dragged to the withered bracken by the load,
And they seem not to break; though once they are bowed
So low for long, they never right themselves:
You may see their trunks arching in the woods
Years afterwards, trailing their leaves on the ground
Like girls on hands and knees that throw their hair
Before them over their heads to dry in the sun.
But I was going to say when Truth broke in
With all her matter-of-fact about the ice-storm
(Now am I free to be poetical?)
I should prefer to have some boy bend them
As he went out and in to fetch the cows—
Some boy too far from town to learn baseball,
Whose only play was what he found himself,
Summer or winter, and could play alone.
One by one he subdued his father's trees
By riding them down over and over again
Until he took the stiffness out of them,
And not one but hung limp, not one was left

For him to conquer. He learned all there was
To learn about not launching out too soon
And so not carrying the tree away
Clear to the ground. He always kept his poise
To the top branches, climbing carefully
With the same pains you use to fill a cup
Up to the brim, and even above the brim.
Then he flung outward, feet first, with a swish,
Kicking his way down through the air to the ground.
So was I once myself a swinger of birches.
And so I dream of going back to be.
It's when I'm weary of considerations,
And life is too much like a pathless wood
Where your face burns and tickles with the cobwebs
Broken across it, and one eye is weeping
From a twig's having lashed across it open.
I'd like to get away from earth awhile
And then come back to it and begin over.
May no fate willfully misunderstand me
And half grant what I wish and snatch me away
Not to return. Earth's the right place for love:
I don't know where it's likely to go better.
I'd like to go by climbing a birch tree,
And climb black branches up a snow-white trunk
Toward heaven, till the tree could bear no more,
But dipped its top and set me down again.
That would be good both going and coming back.
One could do worse than be a swinger of birches.

Frost agreed with his readership in ranking "Birches" among his strongest poems. Selecting it as his contribution to an anthology in 1933, he justified his choice by making reference to the poem's "vocality and its ulteriority" (*CPP&P*, 731). From a poet who routinely celebrated vocality and ulteriority above almost everything else, the description is not especially helpful, but its pointer toward ulterior interpretations does offer encouragement to those many commentators who seek to locate and explain the poem's parabolic meaning: perhaps "Birches" is about a loss of faith, perhaps the poem exemplifies the power of the redemptive imagination, and so on. As Judith Oster argues, there is no shortage of metaphor, "even metaphor within metaphor and metaphoric playing *in* the poem," but Frost also requires that we consider "the whole poem as metaphor, or, in another word, the story-as-metaphor we term 'parable'" (Oster, 161). The danger, as so often in interpreting Frost's poems, comes from ignoring the literal in favor of the figurative; or, just as damagingly, stressing one figurative reading at the expense of others.

"Birches" tries its best to blur all such distinctions. Richard Poirier pushes a crucial point just slightly too far when he states that Frost's "driftings from one kind of experience to another" make it possible to forget that the birches "are bent because of ice storms and not because boys have been swinging in them" (Poirier, 275). Early on, Frost's speaker admits that he "like[s] to think some boy's been swinging them," but that actually the birches are permanently bent only by ice storms. Later, having given himself license to be "poetical," Frost imagines a boy "subdu[ing] his father's trees / By riding them down over and over again," and finally recognizes himself in that boy: "So was I once myself a swinger of birches." Imagination creates a reality capable of replacing (not merely forgetting) that oppressively capitalized "Truth," and leaves the reader unsure about whether or not the boy did bend the birches out of shape. The "matter-of-fact" which burdens adulthood can be evaded by means of poetry: the return to childhood also marks a return to a more intimately experienced fantasy-reality.

But even the dichotomy between the matter-of-fact and the poetical is negated by the poem's own practice, because the matter-of-fact turns out to be, after all, profoundly metaphorical and allusive. Ice crystals onomatopoeically "click upon themselves" and "turn many-colored / As the stir cracks and crazes their enamel"; their fall comes with another rush of sound effects as the sun makes them "shed crystal shells / Shattering and avalanching." Metaphor adds layer to metaphor when they fall as "broken glass" and it seems that "the inner dome of heaven had fallen." The allusion spotted by several critics is to "Adonais," Shelley's great elegy for Keats, in which "Life, like a dome of many-colour'd glass, / Stains the white radiance of Eternity, / Until Death tramples it to fragments." (The grand diction of Shelley's poem is comically undercut in Frost's by the need to tidy up the mess afterward: "Such heaps of broken glass to sweep away.") The birches themselves are no less metaphorically rich and allusive. In a lovely sensuous image, they are "Like girls on hands and knees that throw their hair / Before them over their heads to dry in the sun." Here, Helen Bacon has detected an allusion to *The Bacchae* by Euripides, in which can be found "the motif of the tree bent down to earth and in some sense functioning as an intermediary between earth and heaven" (Bacon, 84). Through metaphor and allusion, almost everything in the poem *is,* or *is like,* another thing, with the consequence that Truth must obey the shape-changing logic of the poetic imagination.

Randall Jarrell offers a lone voice of dissent when he complains about "the taste of 'Birches' in our mouth—a taste a little brassy, a little sugary" (Jarrell 1952, 538). The sugariness to which he objects must come from—if indeed it comes from the poem and not the poem's reception—a certain kind of sentimentality in "Birches," a nostalgia for childhood. That Romantic connection between the poet's vision and the child's, or at least between the child and the poet who wants to return to childhood, provides most of the poem's structuring *topoi.* Yet it is never so simple as to deserve dismissal as "sugary." Frost's fully realized account of the boy's swinging is produced "With the same pains you use to fill a cup / Up to the brim, and even above the brim." That moment of fine excess describes the boy's careful climbing, but it also serves as

Frost's own modus operandi in a poem which celebrates a sense of liberation via poise and endeavor. "It was almost sacrilegious," Frost told one audience, "climbing a birch tree till it bent, till it gave and swooped to the ground. But that's what boys did in those days" (Parini, 22). The anecdote might effectively stand for the skill of a poem like "Birches," as the careful pains of Frost's iambic pentameter allow a sudden release which is (paradoxically) dependent on its continuing rootedness. Like so many of Frost's poems, "Birches" encodes its own aesthetics.

The poem's attraction to transcendence never once forgets that need to remain rooted. (The previous poem in *Mountain Interval* is titled "Bond and Free.") Shelley's "Adonais" ends with the mournful poet ready to shed the "last clouds of cold mortality" and join "The soul of Adonais" which "Beacons from the abode where the Eternal are." Frost, in "Birches" as many times elsewhere, alludes to a Romantic precursor only to reject the earlier vision, this time by risking one of his plainest theological observations: "Earth's the right place for love: / I don't know where it's likely to go better." The man who fantasizes about climbing a tree "*Toward* heaven" (in an echo of "After Apple-Picking" with its ladder "sticking through a tree / Toward heaven still") has no desire to arrive at that particular destination, as his italics are designed to emphasize. This is, after all, a subject about which misunderstanding would prove fatal. Frost's song of the earth seeks only a temporary (and, even then, still connected) respite from the soil, a guarantee that by "going" he will soon be "coming back." "One could do worse than be a swinger of birches," transcendent yet rooted, bond and free, like a poet.

Putting in the Seed

You come to fetch me from my work to-night
When supper's on the table, and we'll see
If I can leave off burying the white
Soft petals fallen from the apple tree.

(Soft petals, yes, but not so barren quite,
Mingled with these, smooth bean and wrinkled pea;)
And go along with you ere you lose sight
Of what you came for and become like me,

Slave to a springtime passion for the earth.
How Love burns through the Putting in the Seed
On through the watching for that early birth
When, just as the soil tarnishes with weed,

The sturdy seedling with arched body comes
Shouldering its way and shedding the earth crumbs.

"The sonnet is the strictest form I have behaved in," Frost told Louis Untermeyer late in life, "and only then by pretending it wasn't a sonnet" (*LU*, 381). The third of four sonnets in *Mountain Interval*, "Putting in the Seed" epitomizes his tendency to mix traditional rhyme schemes, as if to assert free agency against the external impositions of form. This time the closest model is the Shakespearean sonnet. Frost's significant adjustment is to link his first and second quatrains through rhyme (*abab abab*), thereby ensuring that the new rhymes of the third quatrain mark a turn which is reinforced by a noticeable shift to higher diction. A poem which begins with an informal tone akin to "The Pasture" sounds very different when Frost switches his attention, after a winding sentence, to "How Love burns through the Putting in the Seed." The little domestic drama promised by the opening lines has become, quite unexpectedly, a paean to the wonders of natural reproduction (from sowing or conception, through gestation, to a birth which rhymes gloriously with "earth"). Richard Poirier has called this shift "rather abrupt," and concludes that the poem "is not wholly at ease with its own ambitions" (Poirier, 219), but that may be to underestimate Frost's mischievousness. "Putting in the Seed" exemplifies his desire to "trip the reader head foremost into the boundless" (*SL*, 344). We begin by wondering whether or not the poem's persona will let his dinner go cold, and end up with considerably more than we had bargained for: a Song of the Earth.

"Putting in the Seed" invites an apparently simple question: what exactly has been born here? Never satisfied with saying one thing when he could be saying two or more, Frost encourages multiple answers without giving precedence to any of them. Poetry, after all, "provides the one permissible way of saying one thing and meaning another" (*CPr*, 104). "Putting in the Seed" has cause to be interested in the "permissible," because its ulteriority permits the poem to broach a topic which would otherwise be *impermissible:* human sexuality. Frost's lifelong opposition to explicitly sexualized subject matter is well attested: for example, he fell out irremediably with Edward Thomas's widow over her frank memoirs describing the couple's courtship and marriage. Yet the ulterior permits the treatment of sexuality in a number of Frost's poems ("Mowing," "The Subverted Flower," and so on); and "Putting in the Seed" barely holds at bay that figurative reading as the "arched body comes / Shouldering its way" into a poem supposedly focused on vegetative generation.

All the same, to find "Putting in the Seed" chosen by Robert Pinsky for an anthology titled *Great Poems About Sex* is to see a boundary wrongly exceeded. What is successful in Frost's poem is precisely the subtlety, the uncertainty and the understatement which such an anthology must, by the promise of its title, opt to ignore. "Putting in the Seed" is not so much *about* sex as craftily aware of it, and to praise it on more explicit terms is to miss its strengths, just as to censor it would be to risk being condemned as dirty-minded. Frost's act of saying without saying begins with the suggestive title, and leads the attentive reader even to wonder about the "smooth bean and wrinkled pea." Later in the poem, references to birth and the physicality of the body can be excused as metaphor, but by now it is no longer clear which is the literal and which the figurative interpretation.

The relationships between farmer as planter, husband as lover, and poet as maker interfuse without ever quite becoming synonymous, and are held in teasing tension as "Putting in the Seed" moves between metaphors and registers. Frost famously wrote that a poem's "figure is the same as for love." But by "love"—if a conversation recalled by Lawrance Thompson is to be trusted—Frost seems to have specifically meant the physical act of love: "[Frost] said he remembered saying to F. S. Flint in England, long ago, that there was something wrong with a writer who couldn't get into his subject and screw it to a climax: if you were going to find metaphors for the artistic process in the functions of the body, that was the way you ought to do it" (*CPr*, 296). The harvest which results (whether it be plant, child, or poem) seems in this poem like the product of exclusively male activity. As Mark Richardson has noted, "Putting in the Seed" is "a poem about 'husbandry' in every sense of the word: man is to woman as farmer is to field" (Richardson 1997, 46). While the addressee concentrates on the traditionally feminine domestic chores like preparing supper, the man sows and makes and impregnates, driven by his "springtime passion." And so the cycle begins again, as the "white / Soft petals" from the tree help to generate that startlingly corporeal seedling which shakes off the earth in the process of being born from it.

The Cow in Apple Time

Something inspires the only cow of late
To make no more of a wall than an open gate,
And think no more of wall-builders than fools.
Her face is flecked with pomace and she drools
A cider syrup. Having tasted fruit,
She scorns a pasture withering to the root.
She runs from tree to tree where lie and sweeten
The windfalls spiked with stubble and worm-eaten.
She leaves them bitten when she has to fly.
She bellows on a knoll against the sky.
Her udder shrivels and the milk goes dry.

Frost wrote and published "The Cow in Apple Time" in England in late 1914. Although he claimed that the poem had been inspired by a runaway cow on his farm in Derry, he also acknowledged a debt to the "heroic cow" portrayed in the group of animals at the base of the Albert Memorial in London (Thompson 1966, 605). What he neglected to mention was that the "cow" in question is being ridden by Europa—it is a bull.

The appropriate form for this heroic cow is the heroic couplet, although Frost's variations on it are more likely to suggest mock heroism. The feminine rhyme "sweeten"/"worm-eaten" works to underline the cow's foolishness, and the anapestic feet in the poem's second line— "of a wáll than an ópen gáte"—comically transgress the iambic meter as they enact the cow's own comic transgression of the proper boundaries. "Mending Wall" had begun with an aphorism: "Something there is that doesn't love a wall." One such thing is a cow, although the "Something" which "inspires" *her* is never identified. The speaker of "Mending Wall" had gone on to wonder why good fences make good neighbors: "Isn't it / Where there are cows? But here there are no cows." Where there are no cows, there is no need for good fences. As "The Cow in

Apple Time" demonstrates, where there are cows even walls fail to keep them out.

In a notebook entry, Frost describes two kinds of poem: "A poem containing metaphors or a poem that is a metaphor. The latter may be spread thin so that the canvas almost shows through" (*N*, 173). Although "The Cow in Apple Time" belongs to that second category, as metaphor stretches into conceit or even allegory, Frost's readers have failed to agree on any ulterior interpretation. Thompson considers this "characteristically puritanical farm fable" to be "a figurative portrait of a young married woman who runs away from home and suffers the consequences of a sinfully rebellious life" (Thompson 1966, 605). John R. Woznicki sums up the arguments of other commentators who "have noted the Edenic motif of this poem, one complete with the eating of forbidden fruit, the 'windfalls' of modernity that ironically are rotten, growing not in a lush garden but in a wasteland, 'a pasture withering to the root'" (Woznicki, 67). The arguments share an emphasis on sin: the cow, whomever or whatever she may represent, tastes forbidden fruit, even if (in fact) that fruit grows in a "withering" pasture which sounds anything but Edenic. One of Frost's later poems, worrying about the damage done to a peach tree planted too far north, belatedly acknowledges that "There are roughly zones whose laws must be obeyed" (*CPP&P*, 278). His anarchic cow refuses to recognize any such laws, and as a consequence she crosses into a zone ill-suited to sustain her.

Frost thought about walls at the cellular and at the bodily level: "All life is cellular. No living particle of matter however small has yet been found without a skin—without a wall" (*N*, 638). That microscopic level of organization informed and justified his defense of nationalism:

> Look! First I want to be a person. And I want you to be a person, and then we can be as interpersonal as you please. We can pull each other's noses—do all sorts of things. But, first of all, you have got to have the personality. First of all, you have got to have the nations and then they can be as international as they please with each other. (*CPr*, 110)

The wall gives form and identity; paradoxically, it is the prerequisite which makes love and friendship between individuals and nations possible, because without differentiation there can be no collaboration. "A Time to Talk," the poem which precedes "The Cow in Apple Time" in *Mountain Interval,* describes a break from work to speak to a passing friend: "I go up to the stone wall / For a friendly visit." This is a visit all the more "friendly" for staying within its own demarcated territory.

Frost's cow is anything but friendly: she thinks of wall builders as "fools." But she is the foolish one, invading terrain which isn't hers and doesn't suit her, being driven out ("she has to fly"), and suffering the intimate consequences of her greed: she cannot provide nourishment. Writing the poem just weeks after the outbreak of the First World War, Frost provides a devastating warning about the dangers of breaching a neighbor's territorial integrity. His omission of Europa from that reference to the Albert Memorial is the most revealing of disguises, for what is the poem about if not the onset of hostilities on the continent to which Europa gives her name?

To which Frost might reply, as he was wont to reply in similarly literal terms whenever an ulterior meaning was proposed for one of his poems, that it is about a cow which runs amok in an orchard.

An Encounter

Once on the kind of day called "weather breeder,"
When the heat slowly hazes and the sun
By its own power seems to be undone,
I was half boring through, half climbing through
A swamp of cedar. Choked with oil of cedar
And scurf of plants, and weary and over-heated,
And sorry I ever left the road I knew,
I paused and rested on a sort of hook
That had me by the coat as good as seated,
And since there was no other way to look,
Looked up toward heaven, and there against the blue,
Stood over me a resurrected tree,
A tree that had been down and raised again—
A barkless spectre. He had halted too,
As if for fear of treading upon me.
I saw the strange position of his hands—
Up at his shoulders, dragging yellow strands
Of wire with something in it from men to men.
"You here?" I said. "Where aren't you nowadays
And what's the news you carry—if you know?
And tell me where you're off for—Montreal?
Me? I'm not off for anywhere at all.
Sometimes I wander out of beaten ways
Half looking for the orchid Calypso."

"An Encounter" has endured a thoroughgoing neglect: most critical studies of Frost fail to mention it even in passing. That seems a shame, because the poem is the strongest of three in *Mountain Interval* which chart the march of technology across the natural world. (The others are "The Telephone" and "The Line-Gang.") Not only that, it performs the great drama of romantic pastoral as found several times in Frost's work—the individual's journey into wilderness. Its botanical quest brings to mind those other orchis hunts in Frost's work; and the comically futile attempt at conversation points up the challenge to a poetry which thrives on human speech delivered face to face. How, "An Encounter" asks, does a body of poetry such as Frost's, inspired by the wellsprings of human speech and the natural landscape, come to terms with the threat posed to each by the telephone?

"The Telephone" and "The Line-Gang" answer that question straightforwardly: the first dispenses with the need for a telephone altogether as long-distance communication takes place via flowers (" 'leaning with my head against a flower / I heard you talk' "); and the second records the destruction wreaked by line gangs as they "plant dead trees for living" and "set the wild at naught" to "bring the telephone and telegraph." "An Encounter" is more richly enigmatic—a cursory reading of the poem might fail to solve the mystery of the "resurrected tree" with its "yellow strands / Of wire." And that word "resurrected," coupled with the appearance of the telegraph pole against the blue "heaven," gives it at least the impression of sanctity. True, it is subsequently described as a "barkless spectre," and it hooks the unfortunate botanist by the coat, but these negative connotations are counterbalanced by its being seen to have thoughtfully "halted . . . As if for fear of treading upon me." It certainly seems kinder than the swamp which (rather like the "pathless wood" in "Birches") chokes and wearies and overheats. The resurrected tree's mockery of the natural processes of death and decay, in such circumstances, is a victory against a malignant enemy.

The hostility of the natural world creates kinship between those otherwise antagonistic alien invaders, the human and the technological. The botanist regrets having "left the road [he] knew" (the road *more* traveled by), and his encounter with the telegraph pole provides some welcome respite from his ordeal. That resurrected tree has no such concerns, having become all-pervasive: " 'Where aren't you nowadays,' " the botanist wonders, after initial surprise. Even the weather marks the transition to a new and omnipresent deity: a "weather breeder" is a day of calm which foreshadows storms. At the same time as the telegraph pole attracts religious connotations, reliance on the sun is shown to be misplaced. Technology is a "strange" god, miraculous in its ability to carry news and yet itself utterly uncommunicative. It is always "off for" somewhere, nonchalantly breaching national boundaries (in this case, it reaches Montreal) as it strides across even the most inhospitable of terrains. The swamp may seem more immediately threatening, but it is an honest enemy, with nothing of that strange and sinister unwillingness to engage.

Nature, in any case, has good reason to feel defensive. The botanist tells of his purpose in the concluding lines:

> ["]Sometimes I wander out of beaten ways
> Half looking for the orchid Calypso."

Calypso comes from the Greek, meaning "I will conceal." Given the efforts taken by the botanist as he goes "half boring through, half climbing through / A swamp of cedar," his claim to be only "Half looking" sounds disingenuous at best. He searches for the very thing which nature determines to conceal, and the rhyme of Calypso with "know" confirms his desire for that forbidden knowledge. (The verb "wander," with its echo of the end of *Paradise Lost*, further implies the sinfulness of the quest.) Carrying news, the telegraph pole opens communication between people and nations; the botanist, by contrast, is more interested in the secretive and the private. In exploring the difficult interactions between the human, the technological, and the natural world, "An Encounter" raises the possibility that the most iniquitous and damaging of all is the human.

The Bonfire

"Oh, let's go up the hill and scare ourselves,
As reckless as the best of them to-night,
By setting fire to all the brush we piled
With pitchy hands to wait for rain or snow.
Oh, let's not wait for rain to make it safe.
The pile is ours: we dragged it bough on bough
Down dark converging paths between the pines.
Let's not care what we do with it to-night.
Divide it? No! But burn it as one pile
The way we piled it. And let's be the talk
Of people brought to windows by a light
Thrown from somewhere against their wallpaper.
Rouse them all, both the free and not so free
With saying what they'd like to do to us
For what they'd better wait till we have done.
Let's all but bring to life this old volcano,
If that is what the mountain ever was—
And scare ourselves. Let wild fire loose we will . . ."
"And scare you too?" the children said together.

"Why wouldn't it scare me to have a fire
Begin in smudge with ropy smoke and know
That still, if I repent, I may recall it,
But in a moment not: a little spurt
Of burning fatness, and then nothing but
The fire itself can put it out, and that
By burning out, and before it burns out
It will have roared first and mixed sparks with stars,
And sweeping round it with a flaming sword,
Made the dim trees stand back in wider circle—
Done so much and I know not how much more
I mean it shall not do if I can bind it.

Well if it doesn't with its draft bring on
A wind to blow in earnest from some quarter,
As once it did with me upon an April.
The breezes were so spent with winter blowing
They seemed to fail the bluebirds under them
Short of the perch their languid flight was toward;
And my flame made a pinnacle to heaven
As I walked once round it in possession.
But the wind out of doors—you know the saying.
There came a gust. You used to think the trees
Made wind by fanning since you never knew
It blow but that you saw the trees in motion.
Something or someone watching made that gust.
It put that flame tip-down and dabbed the grass
Of over-winter with the least tip-touch
Your tongue gives salt or sugar in your hand.
The place it reached to blackened instantly.
The black was all there was by day-light,
That and the merest curl of cigarette smoke—
And a flame slender as the hepaticas,
Blood-root, and violets so soon to be now.
But the black spread like black death on the ground,
And I think the sky darkened with a cloud
Like winter and evening coming on together.
There were enough things to be thought of then.
Where the field stretches toward the north
And setting sun to Hyla brook, I gave it
To flames without twice thinking, where it verges
Upon the road, to flames too, though in fear
They might find fuel there, in withered brake,
Grass its full length, old silver golden-rod,
And alder and grape vine entanglement,
To leap the dusty deadline. For my own
I took what front there was beside. I knelt

And thrust hands in and held my face away.
Fight such a fire by rubbing not by beating.
A board is the best weapon if you have it.
I had my coat. And oh, I knew, I knew,
And said out loud, I couldn't bide the smother
And heat so close in; but the thought of all
The woods and town on fire by me, and all
The town turned out to fight for me—that held me.
I trusted the brook barrier, but feared
The road would fail; and on that side the fire
Died not without a noise of crackling wood—
Of something more than tinder-grass and weed—
That brought me to my feet to hold it back
By leaning back myself, as if the reins
Were round my neck and I was at the plow.
I won! But I'm sure no one ever spread
Another color over a tenth the space
That I spread coal-black over in the time
It took me. Neighbors coming home from town
Couldn't believe that so much black had come there
While they had backs turned, that it hadn't been there
When they had passed an hour or so before
Going the other way and they not seen it.
They looked about for someone to have done it.
But there was no one. I was somewhere wondering
Where all my weariness had gone and why
I walked so light on air in heavy shoes
In spite of a scorched Fourth-of-July feeling.
Why wouldn't I be scared remembering that?"

"If it scares you, what will it do to us?"

"Scare you. But if you shrink from being scared,
What would you say to war if it should come?

That's what for reasons I should like to know—
If you can comfort me by any answer."

"Oh, but war's not for children—it's for men."

"Now we are digging almost down to China.
My dears, my dears, you thought that—we all thought it.
So your mistake was ours. Haven't you heard, though,
About the ships where war has found them out
At sea, about the towns where war has come
Through opening clouds at night with droning speed
Further o'erhead than all but stars and angels,—
And children in the ships and in the towns?
Haven't you heard what we have lived to learn?
Nothing so new—something we had forgotten:
War is for everyone, for children too.
I wasn't going to tell you and I mustn't.
The best way is to come up hill with me
And have our fire and laugh and be afraid."

"What disheartened me about this Bonfire," Frost wrote in 1916 to Louis
Untermeyer, "was that it made everyone think or so many think that it
was saying something on one side or the other of a 'question of the day.'
Dammit" (*LU,* 36). The following year, Frost described "The Bonfire"
to Amy Lowell as his only poem about the First World War, although
"more of New England than of what is going on over yonder" (*SL,* 220).
That point is borne out by the poem's autobiographical source. Accord-
ing to Lawrance Thompson, it remembers a lucky escape in 1906, when
Frost made a bonfire out of leaves and branches he had gathered with
his children. The fire almost ran out of control, and the children "could
scarcely believe that so much of their pasture had been burned black in
so short a time" (Thompson 1966, 301).

In some respects, "The Bonfire" seems to be another throwback to *North of Boston*. The poem is a dialogue so one-sided that it comes close to monologue, so rare are the children's interjections. Yet there are subtle differences, too. Frost's persona in *North of Boston* was typically the quester and the interrogator, learning from the more native wisdom of the locals he encountered. In "The Bonfire," readers are obliged to join the ranks of the children taught by someone considerably older, someone who goes unnamed but whose relationship to the children mirrors the poet's relationship to his readers: reference to Hyla brook deliberately raises the possibility that Frost is encouraging identification between speaker and poet. Whereas in *North of Boston,* the poetic voice sought knowledge, "The Bonfire" hands it down. Thompson misses the point when he recounts that Frost chose "his war poem entitled 'The Bonfire' [and] his education poem, 'The Axe-Helve'" (Thompson 1970, 81) to read at the Phi Beta Kappa Society at Harvard in 1916. (The Phi Beta Kappa poem traditionally takes as its subject the life of learning.) Describing and constituting an educational process, "The Bonfire" raises questions about education and ethics. To what extent ought children to be exposed to risk? What role should art play in education? How best to prepare children for a world of grown-up violence? Too various and exhilarating a drama to be *reduced* to those debates, "The Bonfire" nevertheless requires that they be addressed.

The presence of war in "The Bonfire" has troubled several commentators, most notably George Monteiro: "One can say with sureness that [Frost], almost shamefully, tries to 'fetch' war into [the poem]." For Monteiro, Frost "does little apart from linking fire and war," that link being "too easy" (Monteiro, 70–71). But this criticism, articulated with no matter how much "sureness," is founded on a false premise: that references to the war have been inappropriately superimposed on what would otherwise have been a perfectly viable poem about bonfires. Rather, the fact of war—especially when technology has enabled it to invade the homes of children—necessitates an education which experiences, manages, and survives risk. What is most terrifying about the Zeppelin raids is that the enemy comes "Through opening clouds at night with droning speed," to attack indiscriminately and without warning. The lighting and putting out of bonfires is a way of coping psychically with danger and regaining control. Prepare children for risk, the speaker argues, by exposing them to it: " 'if you shrink from being scared, / What would you say to war if it should come?' "

Frost makes no attempt to purify this educational instinct. Its motives coexist with a destructive impulse manifested as pyromania, and the laughter of the poem's final line is of satanic transgression and empowerment as well as fear and nervousness. "The Bonfire" saves its most lovingly exultant lines for the fire itself, which can mix " 'sparks with stars,' " its " 'flaming sword' " making a " 'pinnacle to heaven' " and inspiring an eschatological awe: " 'the sky darkened with a cloud / Like winter and evening coming on together.' " David Bromwich finds in the enticing brilliance of the conflagration a fable about the ability of art to "bring its audience close to a scene of risk" (Bromwich 2001, 234–235); the bonfire is both fire and poem. Frost may offer (in Bromwich's words) "all the proper machinery of disapproval"—the relentless speaker, the vulnerable children, the angry and frightened townspeople, the inestimable damage if the fire gets away. But like the children, the reader is seduced from the dully responsible by the reckless, so entrancing is the poem's account of fire. And in this respect, though not in the simplistic way condemned by Monteiro, the fire becomes like war. " 'I walked once round it in possession,' " the speaker remembers of a previous bonfire, the word "possession" bringing together ownership with something like its opposite: the sense of having been taken over by a greater force. That double meaning is the logical conclusion of the fire's capacity to attract oxymoron: it is terrible and beautiful, pleasurable and scary, fascinating and appalling, its flames heavenly yet demonic. Who, the poem wants to ask, would not choose to release such a force whatever the risk? To start a fire and then conquer it is to have the experience of " 'walk[ing] so light on air in heavy shoes / In spite of a scorched Fourth-of-July feeling.' "

Remembering the bonfire which almost ran out of control, Frost's speaker describes how an unusual gust suddenly came on the stillest of days: "'Something or someone watching made that gust.'" The spreading blackness smoldered with

> "the merest curl of cigarette smoke—
> And a flame slender as the hepaticas,
> Blood-root, and violets so soon to be now."

Frost's otherwise puzzling metaphor ("hepaticas" are flowers) closely parallels a famous passage from Shelley's *Defence of Poetry:* "The mind in creation is a fading coal which some invisible influence, like an inconstant wind, awakens to transitory brightness; this power arises from within like the colour of a flower which fades and changes as it is developed." By shadowing Shelley's theory of inspiration, the poem reveals its ulteriority: Frost represents his speaker as a kind of poet, playing a dangerous game which is seen to be leading the young astray, and appearing to be creative and destructive simultaneously. The wind causing the conflagration of his art remains mysterious in origin even to him. Only the scorched aftermath testifies to the intensity of its burning, but it serves as powerful evidence (to those bravely fearful enough to pay heed) of art's ability to warn, prepare, and educate in time of war.

"Out, Out—"

The buzz-saw snarled and rattled in the yard
And made dust and dropped stove-length sticks of wood,
Sweet-scented stuff when the breeze drew across it.
And from there those that lifted eyes could count
Five mountain ranges one behind the other
Under the sunset far into Vermont.
And the saw snarled and rattled, snarled and rattled,
As it ran light, or had to bear a load.
And nothing happened: day was all but done.
Call it a day, I wish they might have said
To please the boy by giving him the half hour
That a boy counts so much when saved from work.
His sister stood beside them in her apron
To tell them "Supper." At that word, the saw,
As if to prove saws knew what supper meant,
Leaped out at the boy's hand, or seemed to leap—
He must have given the hand. However it was,
Neither refused the meeting. But the hand!
The boy's first outcry was a rueful laugh,
As he swung toward them holding up the hand
Half in appeal, but half as if to keep
The life from spilling. Then the boy saw all—
Since he was old enough to know, big boy
Doing a man's work, though a child at heart—
He saw all spoiled. "Don't let him cut my hand off—
The doctor, when he comes. Don't let him, sister!"
So. But the hand was gone already.
The doctor put him in the dark of ether.
He lay and puffed his lips out with his breath.
And then—the watcher at his pulse took fright.
No one believed. They listened at his heart.
Little—less—nothing!—and that ended it.

No more to build on there. And they, since they
Were not the one dead, turned to their affairs.

Allusive titles in Frost's work are few and far between, but the quotation marks around "'Out, Out—'" immediately alert the reader to the existence of a source. Frost refers to Macbeth's speech after he has been told the news of his wife's death:

> Tomorrow, and tomorrow, and tomorrow
> Creeps in this petty pace from day to day
> To the last syllable of recorded time;
> And all our yesterdays have lighted fools
> The way to dusty death. Out, out, brief candle,
> Life's but a walking shadow . . .

Frost's title, then, draws attention to the transience of life, and the ease with which it can be snuffed out. But such a familiar argument hardly requires the authority of a Shakespearean allusion to sustain it. In fact, the reference delivers surprisingly more than it may appear to promise, complicating the poem's attitude to the boy's untimely death. What Frost wrote of metaphor applies equally, and for the same reasons, to allusion: "All metaphor breaks down somewhere. That is the beauty of it. It is touch and go with the metaphor, and until you have lived with it long enough you don't know when it is going. You don't know how much you can get out of it and when it will cease to yield" (*CPr*, 107). Comparisons between "'Out, Out—'" and *Macbeth* seem to break down almost straightaway, because they are obliged to yoke the innocent boy's fate to the death of a great and vicious regicide. Yet Frost makes those comparisons continue to yield, because his poem's recurrent mention of the word "hand"—six times in twelve lines—brings inevitably to mind Lady Macbeth's compulsive washing of her guilty hands. In her hallucinations she sees spots of blood—"Out, damned spot! Out, I say"—

thereby foreshadowing her husband's reaction to her death ("Out, out, brief candle"). Frost's title may allude to Macbeth's speech, but it betrays in its shared motifs a remembrance of Lady Macbeth's self-inflicted demise. To draw that parallel is to raise the issue of culpability, as Lady Macbeth's desperate desire for restoration of a pristine innocence speaks fittingly to the boy's catastrophe.

Double-tongued as it is, the allusion to Shakespeare provides an appropriate title for a poem which—if the polarized reactions to its final lines are to be judged—must negotiate between pity and cruelty. Seamus Heaney is representative in seeking to disengage Frost from the poem's apparent attitudes, insisting that no one should "mistake the wintry report of what happened at the end for the poet's own callousness" (Heaney, 86). Jay Parini goes farther, by suggesting that the dead boy's fellow workers, despite appearances to the contrary, are compassionate: "However heartless these lines have sounded to some ears, Frost is making a point about a way of dealing with grief" (Parini, 70). But where in the text can such sympathies be found? And on the basis of what supporting evidence might poet or poem be absolved from a Neronic pleasure in the suffering of others, or at least from indifference to it? Frost said that " 'Out, Out—' " was "a poem [he] never read in public—too cruel" (Sergeant, 82); that nice hesitation did not extend to writing or publishing the poem, which by this measure must become acts of cruelty. Parini finds similarities between " 'Out, Out—' " and the grieving father of "Home Burial," who takes comfort from manual labor, but that is to overlook crucial linguistic and tonal differences. Through its allusion, its double meanings, and its dark renovation of cliché, " 'Out, Out—' " pushes away the sympathy which readers, disconcerted to find absent from the poem, are keen to compensate it for lacking.

The poetic voice explicitly intervenes only once in the unfolding of events: "Call it a day, I wish they might have said." That is the strongest expression of regret in what is otherwise an extraordinarily detached account. Until that point, the poem had switched cinematically between the majestic long shot of the mountain ranges "Under the sunset far into Vermont" and the dangerous proximity of the snarling rattling buzz saw.

But as soon as the threat implicit in the saw's persistence is realized, and the boy receives his fatal injury, the poem's linguistic choices ensure that pathos is held at bay. First, there is the saw biting into human flesh, "As if to prove saws knew what supper meant" (the saw is obviously hungry); the boy "must have given the hand," with Frost barely skirting round cliché in order to pursue the possibility that the boy willingly contributed to his death; and finally, there is the ghastly repeated pun—"Then the boy *saw* all," "He *saw* all spoiled" (my italics)—which seems in such bad taste that it can barely be recognized as present. Yet the poem is an exercise in (or at least, an exploration of) bad taste: it exposes the ways in which the best intentions of language and art, faced with such appalling circumstances, betray themselves with a horrible comedy.

As Frost makes his language trip itself up, the poem becomes increasingly incapable of describing the accident. It is never made clear, for example, whether the boy's hand has been mangled or completely severed. He "swung toward them holding up the hand"—a line rich in ambiguity, as is the matter-of-fact vagueness of "the hand was gone already." Elsewhere, as even the un-Shakespearean dash in the title suggests, the poem leaves hints and gaps and obliges the reader to complete them. Reuben Brower points out, "At many points in the narrative we have this sensation of being pulled up in sound by contrast with the spreading flow of feeling" (Brower, 170)—although that "spreading flow" might equally well be the blood which the poem replaces with a squeamish euphemism: "to keep / The life from spilling." ("Spilling" and "spoiled" sit together with an awful awkwardness.) Certainly, there is more evidence of withdrawal and retraction, as epitomized in the diminuendo of "Little—less—nothing!—and that ended it." The greater the desire to "fill in" the poem's gaps and reluctances with "feeling" (as Brower puts it), the more the poem's determined resistance to feeling must be admitted.

" 'Out, Out—' " seems remarkably vague, too, about the poem's various protagonists. Only the boy is described at all, and then in the most generic of ways: "Since he was old enough to know, big boy / Doing a man's work, though a child at heart." (This brings to mind the cliché "young at heart," and foreshadows a literal concern for the boy's heart seven lines later.) Sister and doctor are nondescript, as are the faceless "they" who "turned to their affairs." The last word is also the poem's last twist of the knife. Think how differently their actions might be construed had they turned to their labors, their tasks, or even their homes. But "affairs"—standing out as the only polysyllable in the final two lines— sounds more vague and more frivolous, and not merely because of the word's association with affairs of the heart. The dying are often said to want to put their affairs in order; in an astonishing redirection of that desire, the boy's sudden death prompts them to turn to their *own* affairs. Turn, not turn back or return; they have new preoccupations. " 'Out, Out—' " is a brutal poem because it scorns the ameliorative effects of art and human sympathy. To impose compassion on it, as so many readers have done, is to defuse the very danger which gives the poem its terrible power.

The Gum-Gatherer

There overtook me and drew me in
To his down-hill, early-morning stride,
And set me five miles on my road
Better than if he had had me ride,
A man with a swinging bag for load
And half the bag wound round his hand.
We talked like barking above the din
Of water we walked along beside.
And for my telling him where I'd been
And where I lived in mountain land
To be coming home the way I was,
He told me a little about himself.
He came from higher up in the pass
Where the grist of the new-beginning brooks
Is blocks split off the mountain mass—
And hopeless grist enough it looks
Ever to grind to soil for grass.
(The way it is will do for moss.)
There he had built his stolen shack.
It had to be a stolen shack
Because of the fears of fire and loss
That trouble the sleep of lumber folk:
Visions of half the world burned black
And the sun shrunken yellow in smoke.
We know who when they come to town
Bring berries under the wagon seat,
Or a basket of eggs between their feet;
What this man brought in a cotton sack
Was gum, the gum of the mountain spruce.
He showed me lumps of the scented stuff
Like uncut jewels, dull and rough.

It comes to market golden brown;
But turns to pink between the teeth.

I told him this is a pleasant life
To set your breast to the bark of trees
That all your days are dim beneath,
And reaching up with a little knife,
To loose the resin and take it down
And bring it to market when you please.

"The Gum-Gatherer" is modeled on Wordsworth's poems of encounter, whereby the poetic persona interrogates solitary figures met amid natural surroundings, and gains insights into their lives and his own. Frost especially has in mind Wordsworth's "Resolution and Independence," titled "The Leech-Gatherer" in its earliest version. Besides the similarities between gum gatherer and leech gatherer—and their poetically unprepossessing occupations—several of Frost's lines echo Wordsworth's. "Resolution and Independence" mentions in its first six stanzas a "pleasant noise of waters," "the pleasant season" and "pleasant thought, / As if life's business were a summer mood." That last example prompts Frost's "I told him this is a pleasant life"; and the "pleasant noise of waters," elsewhere described in Wordsworth's poem as "distant waters" which "roar," can be heard in Frost's "din / Of water."

Frost is never content to accept his Romantic inheritance uncritically. The greater his indebtedness, the more he determines to expose the frailties of his source. Whereas "An Old Man's Winter Night" had reprised Coleridge's "Frost at Midnight" only to reject that poem's optimism, "The Gum-Gatherer" lays bare the bleak anxieties and agonies of "Resolution and Independence" by celebrating an untroubled way of life. For all his initial cheeriness, the persona of Wordsworth's poem struggles with "dejection," "fears," "Dim sadness," and "blind thoughts," while his leech gatherer faces "hardships" in his "Employment hazardous and wearisome." Frost's gum gatherer has a "down-hill, early-morning stride"; Wordsworth's "decrepit" leech gatherer is "motionless," "bent double," "not all alive nor dead." The breezy pace of Frost's four-beat lines serves as a riposte to the "solemn order" of Wordsworth's rhythms.

Yet whether "The Gum-Gatherer" sustains the positive and rather presumptuous verdict voiced in its final lines is doubtful. The visual separation of the conclusion into its own strophe encourages questions about its appropriateness: does it follow logically from what the gum gatherer has divulged, or is it an unwarranted addition which ignores the evidence? Frost's persona may announce, apparently without disagreement, that the gum gatherer's way of life is "pleasant," but his subject's own report seems more ambivalent. Talk of his "stolen shack," and reference to the nervousness of "lumber folk" at the prospect of apocalyptic fires ("Visions of half the world burned black"—as if remembering "The Bonfire" several poems previous), make his vocation sound precarious and unwelcome among the landowners whose trees provide his living. It is never clear how lucrative that living may be. There is something of the outlaw about the gum gatherer—stolen shacks and uncut jewels. Although the "blocks split off the mountain mass" may be "hopeless" for grinding to "soil for grass," the gum gatherer is involved in a more successful conversion—the conversion into money of "the gum of the mountain spruce." Despite the gum gatherer's clues, the poem's last line indicates that the economic impulse of his work has altogether escaped his interlocutor's dreamy fantasies.

These hints that Frost's persona is guilty of misjudgment throw into relief his relationship with the rural community. In *North of Boston*, Frost's speakers had typically found that relationship to be distant. As Lawrence Buell puts it, "the persona [of *North of Boston*] pictures himself as less embedded in its premises than its local characters are," whereas the attitudes adopted in *Mountain Interval* are more often those of a "naturalized villager" (Buell, 108). "The Gum-Gatherer" presents an exchange between equals: the persona "lives[s] in mountain land," and in return for explaining his circumstances, the gum gatherer replies with "a little about himself." The consequence is a newfound authority which has recourse to the first-person plural to emphasize local knowledge: "*We* know who when they come to town / Bring berries under the wagon seat" (my italics). This persona knows the ways of the marketplace, and he knows the people who sell their produce there (although, strangely, he does not recognize the gum gatherer). And he knows that gum "comes to market golden brown; / But turns to pink between the teeth." Frost described "The Gum-Gatherer" as a favorite of his, "if for no other reason than because it is the only poem I know of that has found a way to speak poetically of chewing gum" (*SL, 233*).

Not for the first time, there is a distant echo of Wordsworth's infamously bathetic lines describing a "little muddy pond" in "The Thorn": "I've measured it from side to side: / 'Tis three feet long, and two feet wide." In Frost, as in Wordsworth, the description reinforces the authority of the persona, who has gone to the effort of finding out for himself and speaking from experience. But Frost's poem creates a drama out of that claim to authority. "The Gum-Gatherer" obliges readers to decide for themselves whether it has been sufficiently earned, or whether the poem's conclusion comes rather too tritely, exposing an unreliable narrator whose self-assurance is profoundly misplaced.

The Vanishing Red

He is said to have been the last Red Man
In Acton. And the Miller is said to have laughed—
If you like to call such a sound a laugh.
But he gave no one else a laugher's license.
For he turned suddenly grave as if to say,
"Whose business,—if I take it on myself,
Whose business—but why talk round the barn?—
When it's just that I hold with getting a thing done with."

You can't get back and see it as he saw it.
It's too long a story to go into now.
You'd have to have been there and lived it.
Then you wouldn't have looked on it as just a matter
Of who began it between the two races.

Some guttural exclamation of surprise
The Red Man gave in poking about the mill
Over the great big thumping shuffling mill-stone
Disgusted the Miller physically as coming
From one who had no right to be heard from.

"Come, John," he said, "you want to see the wheel pit?"

He took him down below a cramping rafter,
And showed him, through a manhole in the floor,
The water in desperate straits like frantic fish,
Salmon and sturgeon, lashing with their tails.
Then he shut down the trap door with a ring in it
That jangled even above the general noise,
And came up stairs alone—and gave that laugh,
And said something to a man with a meal-sack

That the man with the meal-sack didn't catch—then.
Oh, yes, he showed John the wheel pit all right.

A long entry in one of Frost's notebooks, written around 1950, begins with a question: "What is your attitude toward our having robbed the Indians of the American Continent?" (*N*, 564). In reply, Frost praises what little has been absorbed of their bloodline and culture, and celebrates their bravery, but adds, "Our rivalry with the Indians race with race is over however and not worth our lingering regret." If that sounds reserved or even brusque, at least it matches a credo followed by Frost in his personal life. As he had told Edward Thomas thirty-five years earlier, "I dont [*sic*] suppose I was ever sorry for anything I ever did except by assumption to see how it would feel" (Spencer, 70). Regret, in Frost's view, is a self-indulgent emotion which does nothing to assist those who have been wronged.

In his notebook entry, Frost explains the "rivalry" between races in terms of Darwinian natural selection. He also wonders why he should be obliged to respond to the question at all, given that his poetry has already provided the answer: "The first poem I ever wrote, La Noche Triste still extant would show where my sympathies lie and so also would several later" [*sic*] (*N*, 564). Among those "several" must be "The Vanishing Red," the most easily available of Frost's poems on the subject. ("La Noche Triste," Frost's first published poem, was not collected in his lifetime; nor was "Genealogical," a poem about Frost's Indian-killing ancestor.) But whether "The Vanishing Red" shows "where [Frost's] sympathies lie"—at least in quite the way which he implies—remains moot. Discussion of "The Vanishing Red" has paralleled that of " 'Out, Out—.' " In each case, concerns have been commonly expressed that the poet, describing a brutal event, fails to intervene with a sufficiently emotional reaction. Richard Wakefield summarizes and supports received opinion of "The Vanishing Red": "Not only is there no sign of hesitation or remorse on the murderer's part, but there is no indication of moral repugnance on the poet's part, either" (Wakefield, 394).

The title is already unsettling in its doubleness. That "vanishing red" could be an entire race, but is just as likely to refer to the individual who vanishes as if magically, there being no witness to his fate except his murderer. The poem suggests first a national disappearance ("the last Red Man") and, with the aid of a surprising enjambment, a merely local disappearance ("the last Red Man / In Acton"). The fate of the individual becomes a synecdoche for that of his race: murder is genocide writ small, or to express it the other way, genocide is the accumulation of the hundreds and thousands of murders like this one in Acton. "The Vanishing Red" conveys just how temptingly straightforward those murders are—a sudden push through a trapdoor, with the perpetrator confident in the knowledge that he will never be held accountable. The Miller is prepared to make joking remarks about his crime, although he sees it as a strictly private matter ("'Whose business,—if I take it on myself, / Whose business—'"). To accept even the approval of others would be to allow himself to be judged.

The Miller's hesitations and lacunae point to his failure to find a form of words capable of exonerating his deeds. They precede a long rush of monosyllables—"'When it's just that I hold with getting a thing done with'"—in a line which captures as well as anything in Frost's work his belief that "the sentence sound often says more than the words. It may even as in irony convey a meaning opposite to the words" (*SL*, 113). The special pleading, the attempt to close down a topic accidentally opened, the resorting to cliché, the clumsy repetition, the flat rhythm—all point to a deep anxiety barely hidden behind arrogance and aggression. (Lurking in the shadows of the Miller's euphemism about "'getting a thing done with'" is another poem of murder, Robert Browning's "Porphyria's Lover": "I found / A thing to do," the speaker says, the "thing" being to strangle his lover with her own hair.) Yet the Miller never speaks the words attributed to him: "He turned suddenly grave *as if* to say" (my italics). Frost damns the Miller by translating nothing more sinister than a "grave" look into three lines of verbal self-incrimination.

The passage which follows, amounting to a much more explicit intervention by the poet, has often been quoted against Frost as proof of his failure to display the required moral repugnance:

> You can't get back and see it as he saw it.
> It's too long a story to go into now.
> You'd have to have been there and lived it.
> Then you wouldn't have looked on it as just a matter
> Of who began it between the two races.

These lines tempt the reader with a Faustian pact which has not always been declined: "What the poem catches," Reuben Brower states, "is . . . the belief, not entirely unfounded, that Indians were not civilized" (Brower, 121). Frost's passage does not mean quite what Brower and others have assumed: far from encouraging readers not to judge, it criticizes us for a failure to engage. Had we "been there and lived it," then we "wouldn't have looked on it as just a matter / Of who began it between the two races." In other words, we are *more* likely, with the distant perspective of hindsight, to miss the significance of the Red Man's death ("just a matter / Of"), and to exonerate the individual by displacing responsibility onto the undiscoverable origins of the conflict ("who began it between the two races"). Human agency gives way to historical necessity. The verb tense—"Then you wouldn't have looked on it"—informs us that, by understanding events in that way, we are guilty of a serious error which the poet is now obliged to correct.

Having explained that "You can't get back and see it as [the Miller] saw it," the poem grants the reader exactly that privilege, by becoming sole witness to what transpired between murderer and victim. But seeing it as the Miller saw it accentuates the picture of motiveless malignity. He offers a reason for his actions which is condemned by a network of incriminating sounds: the repeated grunting *uh* in "Some guttural exclamation," which so appalls the Miller, is picked up by the noise of the "thumping shuffling" millstone and by the Miller's own "Disgusted" reaction. He and his mill are associated with the same guttural sounds as the Red Man supposedly emits. The awkward articulation—"coming / From one who had no right to be heard from"—satirically reproduces the Miller's earlier problem with prepositions: " 'When it's just that I hold with getting a thing done with.' " This is not so much the language of the unschooled (which Frost often strained to capture in his Wordsworthian belief that it came closer to the language of poetry) as the language of the thuggishly self-righteous. And after fatally tricking the Red Man with a façade of hospitality (" 'Come, John,' he said, 'you want to see the wheel pit?' "), the Miller is given further opportunity to damn himself with his own smug reaction:

> [he] gave that laugh,
> And said something to a man with a meal-sack
> That the man with the meal-sack didn't catch—then.
> Oh, yes, he showed John the wheel pit all right.

Bullying, opinionated, pompous—the Miller is Frost's devastating portrait of the banality of evil. That Frost chose to leave that portrait "where people would be pretty sure to fall forward over [it] in the dark" (*SL*, 344) makes it incumbent on his audience to be alert to its nuances, lest we should imagine ourselves to have found justification for murder and racial hatred in its lines.

The Sound of the Trees

I wonder about the trees.
Why do we wish to bear
Forever the noise of these
More than another noise
So close to our dwelling place?
We suffer them by the day
Till we lose all measure of pace,
And fixity in our joys,
And acquire a listening air.
They are that that talks of going
But never gets away;
And that talks no less for knowing,
As it grows wiser and older,
That now it means to stay.
My feet tug at the floor
And my head sways to my shoulder
Sometimes when I watch trees sway,
From the window or the door.
I shall set forth for somewhere,
I shall make the reckless choice
Some day when they are in voice
And tossing so as to scare
The white clouds over them on.
I shall have less to say,
But I shall be gone.

This final poem of *Mountain Interval* was written in 1914 for his friend, the poet Lascelles Abercrombie. Frost claimed that the poem was the "only one [he] wrote in England that had an English *subject*" (Sergeant, 146)—the subject being a group of elms near Abercrombie's cottage. It was first published as "The Sound of Trees" in December 1914. Frost's two minds about the poem's title suggest an indecision in choosing between specificity ("The Sound of the Trees") and universality ("The Sound of Trees").

Each of Frost's first three volumes charts a journey of departure and return through its judicious choice of opening and closing poems. *A Boy's Will* begins by fantasizing about escape ("Into My Own"), and the adventure is eventually undertaken, only for "Reluctance" to bring Frost's persona regretfully "by the highway home." *North of Boston* invites the reader to accompany the poet-farmer outside ("The Pasture"), and ends in "Good Hours" with a solitary journey back. The positioning of "The Road Not Taken" at the start of *Mountain Interval* looks to augur a break from the pattern: "I doubted if I should ever come back." But "The Sound of the Trees" finds the poet as rooted as ever in his "dwelling place," seeming to describe his own situation as he describes the trees: "They are that that talks of going / But never gets away."

Trees feature prominently in Frost's work. They can be swung on ("Birches"); bartered over ("Christmas Trees"); cut down and resurrected as telegraph poles ("An Encounter"); used for firewood ("The Axe-Helve"), or gum ("The Gum-Gatherer"), or even new human life ("Paul's Wife"); they can provide mysterious inspiration for children's names ("Maple"); and, in "Tree at My Window," they can offer companionship and a sense of shared purpose ("Your head so much concerned with outer, / Mine with inner, weather"). That last example comes closest to "The Sound of the Trees" in its identification of a special relationship. No animal or flower in Frost's work approaches the same intimacy with humans. Trees are secret-sharers which require us to develop "a listening air," the implication being that as they grow "older and wiser," we can learn from their talk and their example.

The identification with trees is so extensive that it becomes unconscious and physical. When he watches trees sway, Frost's persona admits, his feet "tug at the floor" as if rooted there, and his "head sways to [his] shoulder." He is enthralled to the point of hypnotic trance. However, such slavish imitation is preceded and followed by signs of resistance. "Why do we wish to bear / Forever the noise of these," the poem puzzles, with "bear" and "noise" each carrying negative associations. "We suffer them by the day"—"suffer," especially after "bear," meaning *endure* more than it means *allow*. There is even an implication that trees pose a particular threat to poetic composition because they cause us to "lose all measure of pace," with "measure" relating etymologically to meter and "pace" to poetic feet. Even as the poet mimics and identifies with the trees, he appreciates the necessity of escaping from their "noise."

The poem ends with a resolution, albeit one couched in the vaguest of terms:

> I shall set forth for somewhere,
> I shall make the reckless choice
> Some day when they are in voice
> And tossing so as to scare
> The white clouds over them on.
> I shall have less to say,
> But I shall be gone.

"I shall be gone" may be a fitting way to end a volume of poetry, but words like "somewhere" and "Some day" cast doubt on whether the ambition will be fulfilled. As Richard Poirier states, "the reader is deceived into visions by Frost and by his own pretense, as he lets the sentences move casually past the subordinated, dependent, muted reservations that are being made" (Poirier, 82). Even so, fear of the trees, and the desire to avoid them, are unmistakably present in that transference of terror onto the clouds. (Given that the movement of clouds and trees has the same cause, the poet's imputation seems all the more revealing of his own anxieties.) Because they are scary, the trees provoke the clouds to move on. If only he can escape his rootedness, they might provoke Frost's persona to do the same; he might yet make "the reckless choice," like the speaker of "The Bonfire," who urges the children to be " 'As reckless as the best of them to-night.' " Enacting that eventuality of disappearance, the poem dwindles toward its vanishing point, its short lines of trimeter contracting first into dimeter ("I shall have less to say" is mimetic of its own prediction) and finally challenging the reader to find even two stresses in "But I shall be gone." And so the trees are vanquished. They may have plenty to say, but they can never leave. Having stated his ambition to go, the poet has nothing more to add, and ends as if liberated at last.

NEW HAMPSHIRE

PUBLISHED IN 1923, *New Hampshire* was and would remain Frost's largest single volume of poetry. Its subtitle, "A Poem with Notes and Grace Notes," hinted at the volume's tripartite structure: the first section comprised the title poem; there followed a thirteen-poem section titled "Notes," then the "Grace Notes," which added a further thirty poems. The book was widely praised, and won Frost the first of his four Pulitzer Prizes.

Although he would later list "The Grindstone," "Paul's Wife," "The Witch of Coös," and "Two Look at Two" as poems to be included in an expanded *North of Boston (CPr, 344)*, Frost does not seem to have felt any dissatisfaction with *New Hampshire* as a coherent volume. Authorial design is more prominent here than in *Mountain Interval*. A number of footnotes in the title poem direct the reader to poems in the "Notes" section, so that the effect is of a shared inspiration, the poems commentating on each other in ways which are mutually illuminating. Admittedly, "New Hampshire" exhibits worrying early signs of what Randall Jarrell would call the "Yankee Editorialist side of Frost" (Jarrell 1952, 538), with the natural consequence that the "Notes" are a greater achievement than the long poem which they are hypothetically noting. Among them can be found such masterpieces as "Maple," "Paul's Wife," and "The Witch of Coös"—the last of which providing the best evidence for Frost's belief that some of his poems were "a little nearer one act plays than eclogues" (*CPr,* 196).

A "grace note" is a musical ornament which embellishes a harmony or melody without being essential to it. Frost reserves this final section of *New Hampshire* for short lyrics, including what have since become staple anthology poems like "Fire and Ice" (the first of the "grace notes" in the selection given here) and "Stopping by Woods on a Snowy Evening," as well as "To E. T.," Frost's only overt elegy for an individual, his friend Edward Thomas, who had been killed at Arras in 1917.

A Star in a Stone-boat

(*for Lincoln MacVeagh*)

Never tell me that not one star of all
That slip from heaven at night and softly fall
Has been picked up with stones to build a wall.

Some laborer found one faded and stone cold,
And saving that its weight suggested gold,
And tugged it from his first too certain hold,

He noticed nothing in it to remark.
He was not used to handling stars thrown dark
And lifeless from an interrupted arc.

He did not recognize in that smooth coal
The one thing palpable besides the soul
To penetrate the air in which we roll.

He did not see how like a flying thing
It brooded ant-eggs, and had one large wing,
One not so large for flying in a ring,

And a long Bird of Paradise's tail,
(Though these when not in use to fly and trail
It drew back in its body like a snail);

Nor know that he might move it from the spot
The harm was done: from having been star-shot
The very nature of the soil was hot

And burning to yield flowers instead of grain,
Flowers fanned and not put out by all the rain
Poured on them by his prayers prayed in vain.

He moved it roughly with an iron bar,
He loaded an old stone-boat with the star
And not, as you might think, a flying car,

Such as even poets would admit perforce
More practical than Pegasus the horse
If it could put a star back in its course.

He dragged it through the plowed ground at a pace
But faintly reminiscent of the race
Of jostling rock in interstellar space.

It went for building stone, and I, as though
Commanded in a dream, forever go
To right the wrong that this should have been so.

Yet ask where else it could have gone as well,
I do not know—I cannot stop to tell:
He might have left it lying where it fell.

From following walls I never lift my eye
Except at night to places in the sky
Where showers of charted meteors let fly.

Some may know what they seek in school and church,
And why they seek it there; for what I search
I must go measuring stone walls, perch on perch;

Sure that though not a star of death and birth,
So not to be compared, perhaps, in worth
To such resorts of life as Mars and Earth,

Though not, I say, a star of death and sin,
It yet has poles, and only needs a spin
To show its worldly nature and begin

To chafe and shuffle in my calloused palm
And run off in strange tangents with my arm
As fish do with the line in first alarm.

Such as it is, it promises the prize
Of the one world complete in any size
That I am like to compass, fool or wise.

Frost valued "A Star in a Stone-boat" highly enough to consider making it the title poem of a volume of lyrics (Thompson 1970, 239). However, despite sharing motifs soothingly familiar to Frost's readers (walls and wall building, the laborer, the stars), this poem in rhyming triplets is so intensely metaphorical that it has proved recalcitrant to any but the most determined analysis. No longer is there an emphasis on the rhythms of speech. The poem can seem concise to the point of brusqueness, even bookishness: "The one thing palpable besides the soul"; "Such as even poets would admit perforce"; "But faintly reminiscent of the race"; "Yet ask where else it could have gone as well." "A Star in a Stone-boat" is deliberately written in this high-flown register, as if wanting to place itself in the orbiting "arc" from which the star has been "interrupted." The poet-persona's detachment from everyday concerns—and certainly from the concerns of the laborer who acts as counterpart—is given expression in his linguistic choices.

   The poem begins unpropitiously with the complication of a double negative, as the oddity of maintaining that no "star" has ever been used to build a wall is trumped by the still greater oddity that the poet should feel the preemptive need to prohibit such a claim. The mazy logic of the poem's opening allows Frost to assert as fact, under cover of his negatives, the assumption that stars must indeed have been "picked up . . . to build a wall." Having settled the issue before an audience assumed to be skeptical, in the second stanza Frost is free to adopt a tone of reportage and to detail one such instance of star finding. But the phrase "Some laborer" remains sufficiently offhand and imprecise (as well as being rather dismissive) to remind us that the account is, after all, purely an act of imagination.

The title had pointed up the poem's negotiations between the heavenly and the earthly—between a "star" which is also variously a meteorite and a comet, and a "stone-boat" made (usually) of wood and shaped like a low sled for shifting large rocks from fields. There is one further clue to the ulterior meaning of that star. It is described as "faded and stone cold," and several lines later as a "smooth coal." Once again, Frost has in mind Shelley's account of inspiration: "The mind in creation is as a fading coal." Frost's coal has now lost all its warmth, and yet it endures as a remnant and reminder of that creativity. The power lingers only in its having turned the soil "hot // And burning to yield flowers instead of grain"—those flowers, as so often in Frost's work, might be emblems for poetry itself. So a question posed by "A Star in a Stone-boat," albeit in a typically parabolic way, is: to what uses ought art to be put? The laborer seems philistine in his unappreciative hunt for raw materials, as he is reminiscent of the "old-stone savage armed" in "Mending Wall." But he does use the "star" to construct something larger. The poet is more akin to the laborer than he admits, because he constructs a poem (the poem we are reading) out of his quest to "right the wrong," and that righting / writing gives the stone-boat a billing alongside the star.

If anything, the poet seems rather too starstruck. The special pleading at the start of the poem encourages suspicion of his flights of fancy, and suspicion becomes justified when the stone is described as "brood[ing] ant-eggs," having "one large wing, / One not so large," and retracting its "Bird of Paradise's tail" back into its body. Frost's ulteriority will never accept that a stone is a stone is a stone: he mockingly toys with Gertrude Stein's "A rose is a rose is a rose" in a later poem, "The Rose Family." Yet the issue of the stone's identity is reminiscent of Frost's 1919 "Remarks on Form in Poetry":

> A man who makes really good literature is like a fellow who goes into the fields to pull carrots. He keeps on pulling them patiently enough until he finds a carrot that suggests something else to him. It is not shaped like other carrots. He takes out his knife and notches it here and there, until the two pronged roots become legs and the carrot takes on something of the semblance of a man. The real genius takes hold of that bit of life which is suggestive to him and gives it form. But the man who is merely a realist, and not a genius, will leave the carrot just as he finds it. The man who is merely an idealist and not a genius, will try to carve a donkey where no donkey is suggested by the carrot he pulls. (*CPr*, 79)

Evidently, the laborer fails that first test: despite the gold weight of the stone, he cannot recognize its extraterrestrial origins because he does not allow it to suggest "something else to him." But the poet risks failure as well. In trying to turn a stone into a star, or into a comet complete with wings and retractable tail, he seems more like Frost's "idealist" than his "genius."

His idealism comes across as self-indulgence. The poetic persona's supposed concession to pragmatism—that a "flying car" would be "More practical than Pegasus the horse"—is merely an argument between two learned poeticisms. (The phrase "even poets would admit" implies that they are the most impractical of creatures.) The poet cuts a comic figure throughout, compulsively going "as though / Commanded in a dream" on a quest to scour walls for misappropriated stars. That search for the extraordinary within the ordinary—a Frostian search for inspiration among mundane surroundings—is his substitute for "school and church," making clear that the poet's vocation is allied to, but set apart from, each. There is a sense of superiority in the comparison: the poet is to the educator or the preacher as the "race / Of jostling rock in interstellar space" is to the star's slow drag "through the plowed ground" on a stone-boat. All the same, it is hard to take very seriously anyone who alludes to "such resorts of life as Mars and Earth." Richard Poirier points out that "A Star in a Stone-boat" comes "close at times to self-ridicule" (Poirier, 312); on more than one occasion the poem walks straight into it.

Poirier finds that the poem "de-accelerates" in its final stanza. He is undoubtedly right to draw attention to the many kinds of motion described; but the final stanzas seek to reenergize and to move from stasis toward a new inspiring momentum:

> Though not, I say, a star of death and sin,
> It yet has poles, and only needs a spin
> To show its worldly nature and begin
>
> To chafe and shuffle in my calloused palm
> And run off in strange tangents with my arm
> As fish do with the line in first alarm.
>
> Such as it is, it promises the prize
> Of the one world complete in any size
> That I am like to compass, fool or wise.

The enjambment across a stanza break ("begin // To chafe"), and the sudden unpunctuated reliance on conjunction ("and only needs," "and begin," "and shuffle," "And run off") point to a quickening of pace, as the poet fantasizes about reinvigorating the becalmed star. That word "worldly" reconciles the heavens (the star is its own world) and the Earth (the star is part of, or similar to, this world), just as the poem's title now looks like an act of reconciliation rather than juxtaposition: the star in the stone-boat represents a literal but also a truly *poetic* transport, not least because "stone-boat" is alive with its own nautical metaphoricity. Frost's angling simile confirms that watery undercurrent, and the arm which is taken in "strange tangents" is also the arm of a writer whose inspiration quickens into unexpected territories. The faded coal may not be able to resume its extraterrestrial journey, but in the poet's hands it can at least be made to remember something of its former glory. Enjoying the kinetic force of inspiration, Frost "compass[es]" the poem which he himself has created, leaving the final verdict on his achievement to others: "fool or wise."

Maple

Her teacher's certainty it must be Mabel
Made Maple first take notice of her name.
She asked her father and he told her "Maple—
Maple is right."

        "But teacher told the school
There's no such name."

          "Teachers don't know as much
As fathers about children, you tell teacher.
You tell her that it's M-A-P-L-E.
You ask her if she knows a maple tree.
Well, you were named after a maple tree.
Your mother named you. You and she just saw
Each other in passing in the room upstairs,
One coming this way into life, and one
Going the other out of life—you know?
So you can't have much recollection of her.
She had been having a long look at you.
She put her finger in your cheek so hard
It must have made your dimple there, and said,
'Maple.' I said it too: 'Yes, for her name.'
She nodded. So we're sure there's no mistake.
I don't know what she wanted it to mean,
But it seems like some word she left to bid you
Be a good girl—be like a maple tree.
How like a maple tree's for us to guess.
Or for a little girl to guess sometime.
Not now—at least I shouldn't try too hard now.
By and by I will tell you all I know
About the different trees, and something, too,
About your mother that perhaps may help."

Dangerous self-arousing words to sow.
Luckily all she wanted of her name then
Was to rebuke her teacher with it next day,
And give the teacher a scare as from her father.
Anything further had been wasted on her,
Or so he tried to think to avoid blame.
She would forget it. She all but forgot it.
What he sowed with her slept so long a sleep,
And came so near death in the dark of years,
That when it woke and came to life again
The flower was different from the parent seed.
It came back vaguely at the glass one day,
As she stood saying her name over aloud,
Striking it gently across her lowered eyes
To make it go well with the way she looked.
What was it about her name? Its strangeness lay
In having too much meaning. Other names,
As Lesley, Carol, Irma, Marjorie,
Signified nothing. Rose could have a meaning,
But hadn't as it went. (She knew a Rose.)
This difference from other names it was
Made people notice it—and notice her.
(They either noticed it, or got it wrong.)
Her problem was to find out what it asked
In dress or manner of the girl who bore it.
If she could form some notion of her mother—
What she had thought was lovely, and what good.
This was her mother's childhood home;
The house one story high in front, three stories
On the end it presented to the road.
(The arrangement made a pleasant sunny cellar.)
Her mother's bedroom was her father's still,
Where she could watch her mother's picture fading.
Once she found for a bookmark in the Bible

A maple leaf she thought must have been laid
In wait for her there. She read every word
Of the two pages it was pressed between
As if it was her mother speaking to her.
But forgot to put the leaf back in closing
And lost the place never to read again.
She was sure, though, there had been nothing in it.

So she looked for herself, as everyone
Looks for himself, more or less outwardly.
And her self-seeking, fitful though it was,
May still have been what led her on to read,
And think a little, and get some city schooling.
She learned shorthand, whatever shorthand may
Have had to do with it—she sometimes wondered.
So, till she found herself in a strange place
For the name Maple to have brought her to,
Taking dictation on a paper pad,
And in the pauses when she raised her eyes
Watching out of a nineteenth story window
An airship laboring with unship-like motion
And a vague all-disturbing roar above the river
Beyond the highest city built with hands.
Someone was saying in such natural tones
She almost wrote the words down on her knee,
"Do you know you remind me of a tree—
A maple tree?"

        "Because my name is Maple?"

"Isn't it Mabel? I thought it was Mabel."

"No doubt you've heard the office call me Mabel.
I have to let them call me what they like."

They were both stirred that he should have divined
Without the name her personal mystery.
It made it seem as if there must be something
She must have missed herself. So they were married,
And took the fancy home with them to live by.

They went on pilgrimage once to her father's
(The house one story high in front, three stories
On the side it presented to the road)
To see if there was not some special tree
She might have overlooked. They could find none,
Not so much as a single tree for shade,
Let alone grove of trees for sugar orchard.
She told him of the bookmark maple leaf
In the big Bible, and all she remembered
Of the place marked with it—"Wave offering,
Something about wave offering, it said."

"You've never asked your father outright, have you?"

"I have, and been put off sometime, I think."
(This was her faded memory of the way
Once long ago her father had put himself off.)

"Because no telling but it may have been
Something between your father and your mother
Not meant for us at all."

                    "Not meant for me?
Where would the fairness be in giving me
A name to carry for life, and never know
The secret of?"

"And then it may have been
Something a father couldn't tell a daughter
As well as could a mother. And again
It may have been their one lapse into fancy
'Twould be too bad to make him sorry for
By bringing it up to him when he was too old.
Your father feels us round him with his questing,
And holds us off unnecessarily,
As if he didn't know what little thing
Might lead us on to a discovery.
It was as personal as he could be
About the way he saw it was with you
To say your mother, had she lived, would be
As far again as from being born to bearing."

"Just one look more with what you say in mind,
And I give up"; which last look came to nothing.
But, though they now gave up the search forever,
They clung to what one had seen in the other
By inspiration. It proved there was something.
They kept their thoughts away from when the maples
Stood uniform in buckets, and the steam
Of sap and snow rolled off the sugar house.
When they made her related to the maples,
It was the tree the autumn fire ran through
And swept of leathern leaves, but left the bark
Unscorched, unblackened, even, by any smoke.
They always took their holidays in autumn.
Once they came on a maple in a glade,
Standing alone with smooth arms lifted up,
And every leaf of foliage she'd worn
Laid scarlet and pale pink about her feet.
But its age kept them from considering this one.
Twenty-five years ago at Maple's naming

It hardly could have been a two-leaved seedling
The next cow might have licked up out at pasture.
Could it have been another maple like it?
They hovered for a moment near discovery,
Figurative enough to see the symbol,
But lacking faith in anything to mean
The same at different times to different people.
Perhaps a filial diffidence partly kept them
From thinking it could be a thing so bridal.
And anyway it came too late for Maple.
She used her hands to cover up her eyes.
"We would not see the secret if we could now:
We are not looking for it any more."

Thus had a name with meaning, given in death,
Made a girl's marriage, and ruled in her life.
No matter that the meaning was not clear.
A name with meaning could bring up a child,
Taking the child out of the parents' hands.
Better a meaningless name, I should say,
As leaving more to nature and happy chance.
Name children some names and see what you do.

"All metaphor breaks down somewhere," wrote Robert Frost. "You don't
know how much you can get out of it and when it will cease to yield. It is
a very living thing. It is as life itself" (*CPr*, 107). His remarks underscore
the central interpretive challenge of his poetry—to insist on the pres-
ence of ulterior meaning without overinsisting, to balance detection with
restraint. "Maple" examines how metaphor can govern a life, and how
the woman whose fate is to bear and become that metaphor—*nomen est
omen*—must continually puzzle over what can be got out of it and how
far it ought to be taken. It can, after all, be taken too far, because every

metaphor "breaks down somewhere." A woman is not literally a tree, although three poems later in *New Hampshire,* "Paul's Wife" playfully resists that statement of the obvious by making a woman out of a tree. In a figurative sense, Maple is also made from a tree, but how and why and to what extent that insight should be pursued are matters left "for us to guess" along with Maple and her husband.

"Maple" comes filled with clues about stories hidden beneath stories. Not for nothing does Frost describe the family home as "one story high in front, three stories / On the end it presented to the road"; and to make sure that the pun is not missed, he repeats the description almost verbatim forty lines later. So ostentatious as to be funny, that emphasis draws attention to other hints throughout the poem: the father's unfulfilled promise to tell something about the mother " 'that perhaps may help,' " which the poem's narrator describes as "Dangerous . . . words"; the father's subsequent guilt at having not told Maple "Anything further"; the maple bookmark in the Bible and the reference to a "wave offering"; the possibilities mooted by her husband that the secret had to do with " 'Something between your father and your mother,' " or " 'Something a father couldn't tell a daughter / As well as could a mother.' " Maple is herself ambivalent about her quest for meaning. Having found the maple bookmark, she seems too keen to dismiss its significance: "She was sure, though, there had been nothing in it." And having stumbled on that most sensually "bridal" of maples—"every leaf of foliage she'd worn / Laid scarlet and pale pink about her feet"—Maple covers her eyes and calls off the search. When she tells her husband, " 'We are not looking for [the secret] any more,' " it sounds less like a statement of fact than a hidden imperative. Maple has come to fear what she may find.

The temptation for the reader is to identify the secret. Katherine Kearns has argued that the clues point to "the passionate extramarital circumstances of [Maple's] birth," and more plainly, to the mother's "marital infidelity" (Kearns, 100). She acknowledges that there are at least nine mentions of "wave offerings" in the Bible, but believes that the maple leaf had marked one particular offering, in Numbers 5:12–31, "made when a woman was thought to have been unfaithful to her husband" (Kearns, 20). Those "scarlet" leaves also evoke erotic and illicit passion, and they bring to mind Hawthorne's novel in which the product of an adulterous union is given another name with "too much meaning": Pearl. But enticing though it may seem, Kearns's case is as unprovable as it is irrefutable. The poem tantalizes with the possibility of a truth which can be glimpsed only out of the corner of the eye. Is Maple's mother a faithful wife taken tragically young in the aftermath of childbirth, or a scarlet woman destroyed with biblical wrath for her infidelity? To solve that mystery would be to distort it. As Frost said in an interview late in life, "Families break up when people take hints you don't intend and miss hints you do intend" (CPP&P, 888). "Maple" requires the reader to take the hint but take it no farther.

Metaphor can serve as a form of shorthand. Maple, the poem tells us, "learned shorthand, whatever shorthand may / Have had to do with it." Shorthand has everything to do with it. It makes multiple and concentrated connections which lend themselves to being teased out by tactful judgment rather than scientific measurement. After all, the image of the "airship laboring with unship-like motion" is Frost's reminder of metaphor's limitations and (on occasion) inadequacies in negotiating between likeness and unlikeness. An airship is and is not a ship. The *extent* to which Maple resembles a maple tree is not so urgently addressed as the *ways* in which she is like the tree, but the airship's conspicuous difference (akin to the stone-boat's, earlier in *New Hampshire*) provides both a warning and an opportunity: Maple need not allow her identity to be subsumed into her name. She can, if she chooses, be like a maple tree as an airship is like a ship; she invests her name with a significance which it need not possess. Who is to say that the father has not invented the story about the mother's act of naming; or has not misheard her in her final illness (a neat irony given the number of people in the poem who reportedly hear Maple as Mabel); or, for that matter, that the mother was not thinking more about maple syrup—the baby looking so sweet—than about the tree itself? And so on, *ad absurdam*. Like Kearns choosing one wave offering to the exclusion of eight others, Maple dismisses any connection to maples when they "Stood uniform in buckets, and the steam / Of sap and snow rolled off the sugar house." She and her husband "made her related to the maples"—implying that the evidence is being forced—and then not to any maple but only "the tree [of] autumn fire." Maple pursues a myth of origins which allows her to select her own meanings, until those decisions lead her to a shockingly erotic image from which she must retreat. The poem certainly suggests that Maple is "near discovery," and that the "bridal" image carries an important truth about the ability for things to mean "The same at different times to different people." Nevertheless, the question of whether she has taken the metaphor too far, or not far enough, goes unanswered.

The narrative voice which oversees Maple's journey from birth to married womanhood identifies itself as authorial. "Maple" is written in Frost's trademark blank verse, even down to the characteristic tendency to allow one extra unstressed syllable at the end of lines (for example, the opening line: "Her teacher's certainty it must be Mabel"). More overtly, the observation that "Other names, / As Lesley, Carol, Irma, Marjorie, / Signified nothing" lists the forenames of Frost's surviving children. Macbeth may be making a point about the meaningless of existence when he states that life is "a tale / Told by an idiot, full of sound and fury, / Signifying nothing," but Frost's allusion carries across none of that despair. Names *should* signify nothing, or so at least the author wants to be seen to conclude:

> Thus had a name with meaning, given in death,
> Made a girl's marriage, and ruled in her life.
> No matter that the meaning was not clear.
> A name with meaning could bring up a child,
> Taking the child out of the parents' hands.
> Better a meaningless name, I should say,
> As leaving more to nature and happy chance.
> Name children some names and see what you do.

The commentary brings a bathetic end to such an intriguing quest. A name which helps to raise a girl whose mother had died in childbirth, and which makes for her what is seemingly a happy marriage, has done less harm than good. However, the authorial voice remains firm: "Better a meaningless name." And the poem's final line—its last word on the matter—pronounces a piece of homely (not to say homiletic) wisdom which makes its pitch to future books of quotations. Even so, "Maple" does not belong among those of Frost's poems in which the author "comes out and tells you the point after it's been made—and comes out and tells you in such trudging doctrinaire lines" (Jarrell 1952, 538). The wrench between Maple's quest and the author's words of counsel becomes part of the poem's unsettling drama. The authorial persona, like Maple, finds or creates meanings for himself, and in doing so, excludes any possibility which does not serve his agenda. The passage is another of Frost's traps. His "innate mischievousness," as he himself described it, ensures that in "Maple" the reader can trust neither the tale nor the teller.

The Axe-Helve

I've known ere now an interfering branch
Of alder catch my lifted axe behind me.
But that was in the woods, to hold my hand
From striking at another alder's roots,
And that was, as I say, an alder branch.
This was a man, Baptiste, who stole one day
Behind me on the snow in my own yard
Where I was working at the chopping-block,
And cutting nothing not cut down already.
He caught my axe expertly on the rise,
When all my strength put forth was in his favor,
Held it a moment where it was, to calm me,
Then took it from me—and I let him take it.
I didn't know him well enough to know
What it was all about. There might be something
He had in mind to say to a bad neighbor
He might prefer to say to him disarmed.
But all he had to tell me in French-English
Was what he thought of—not me, but my axe;
Me only as I took my axe to heart.
It was the bad axe-helve someone had sold me—
"Made on machine," he said, plowing the grain
With a thick thumbnail to show how it ran
Across the handle's long drawn serpentine,
Like the two strokes across a dollar sign.
"You give her one good crack, she's snap raght off.
Den where's your hax-ead flying t'rough de hair?"
Admitted; and yet, what was that to him?

"Come on my house and I put you one in
What's las' awhile—good hick'ry what's grow crooked,
De second growt' I cut myself—tough, tough!"

Something to sell? That wasn't how it sounded.

"Den when you say you come? It's cost you nothing.
To-naght?"

As well to-night as any night.

Beyond an over-warmth of kitchen stove
My welcome differed from no other welcome.
Baptiste knew best why I was where I was.
So long as he would leave enough unsaid,
I shouldn't mind his being overjoyed
(If overjoyed he was) at having got me
Where I must judge if what he knew about an axe
That not everybody else knew was to count
For nothing in the measure of a neighbor.
Hard if, though cast away for life with Yankees,
A Frenchman couldn't get his human rating!

Mrs. Baptiste came in and rocked a chair
That had as many motions as the world:
One back and forward, in and out of shadow,
That got her nowhere; one more gradual,
Sideways, that would have run her on the stove
In time, had she not realized her danger
And caught herself up bodily, chair and all,
And set herself back where she started from.
"She ain't spick too much Henglish—dat's too bad."
I was afraid, in brightening first on me,
Then on Baptiste, as if she understood
What passed between us, she was only feigning.
Baptiste was anxious for her; but no more
Than for himself, so placed he couldn't hope

To keep his bargain of the morning with me
In time to keep me from suspecting him
Of really never having meant to keep it.

Needlessly soon he had his axe-helves out,
A quiverful to choose from, since he wished me
To have the best he had, or had to spare—
Not for me to ask which, when what he took
Had beauties he had to point me out at length
To insure their not being wasted on me.
He liked to have it slender as a whipstock,
Free from the least knot, equal to the strain
Of bending like a sword across the knee.
He showed me that the lines of a good helve
Were native to the grain before the knife
Expressed them, and its curves were no false curves
Put on it from without. And there its strength lay
For the hard work. He chafed its long white body
From end to end with his rough hand shut round it.
He tried it at the eye-hole in the axe-head.
"Hahn, hahn," he mused, "don't need much taking down."
Baptiste knew how to make a short job long
For love of it, and yet not waste time either.

Do you know, what we talked about was knowledge?
Baptiste on his defence about the children
He kept from school, or did his best to keep—
Whatever school and children and our doubts
Of laid-on education had to do
With the curves of his axe-helves and his having
Used these unscrupulously to bring me
To see for once the inside of his house.
Was I desired in friendship, partly as some one
To leave it to, whether the right to hold

Such doubts of education should depend
Upon the education of those who held them?

But now he brushed the shavings from his knee
And stood the axe there on its horse's hoof,
Erect, but not without its waves, as when
The snake stood up for evil in the Garden,—
Top-heavy with a heaviness his short,
Thick hand made light of, steel-blue chin drawn down
And in a little—a French touch in that.
Baptiste drew back and squinted at it, pleased;
"See how she's cock her head!"

Frost must have had "The Axe-Helve" in mind during an interview given in April 1916: "[Poetry is] in the axe-handle of a French Canadian woodchopper. . . . You know the Canadian woodchoppers [make their own] axe-handles, following the curve of the grain, and they're strong and beautiful. Art should follow lines in nature, like the grain of an axe-handle. False art puts curves on things that haven't any curves" (Thompson 1970, 77). Frost spelled out the allegory again when he annotated a friend's copy of the poem: "This is as near as I like to come to talking about art, in a work of art" (Parini, 188). Undoubtedly, "The Axe-Helve" belongs among that sizable number of Frost's poems which discuss their own aesthetic practices—poems which, as Frost put it elsewhere, have "a lot of literary criticism in them—*in them*" (Poirier, 313). Yet his insistence ought not to overshadow the poem's explicit interest in education (which is itself bound up with artistic questions), nor its comedy of manners as neighbors struggle to be neighborly.

Generosity drives the plot: Baptiste invites his neighbor round for a new axe helve which he has made by hand, the ones " 'Made on machine' " being of poor quality. That act of kindness must overcome considerable mistrust, and its beneficiary never stops worrying that a quid pro quo will be required. Initially but indirectly, Baptiste is portrayed as "interfering," like the alder branch which can "catch" a "lifted axe"; and he steals up on Frost's speaker in the manner of a thief or an assailant. Instinctively antagonistic, such vocabulary may explain why Baptiste takes hold of the axe "to calm" him, and why the speaker continues to see the axe's potential as a weapon: "There might be something / He had in mind to say to a bad neighbor / He might prefer to say to him disarmed." Violence and confrontation are the assumed motives, based on no evidence other than Baptiste's unheralded arrival. (Ironically, Baptiste's stated intention is to *prevent* wounding, as he fears that a broken axe helve will cause the axe head to fly—with a scalping pun—"'t'rough de hair.'") And even when such anxieties can be allayed, they are replaced first by a fear of Baptiste's as-yet-unexplained interest in the axe ("what was that to him?"), and then by the suspicion that Baptiste may have "Something to sell." More friendly and more emotionally intuitive than his neighbor, Baptiste immediately senses how best to reassure: "'It's cost you nothing.'"

Baptiste's accent, conveyed phonetically to emphasize its otherness, marks him out as the interloper "cast away for life with Yankees." However, his language corresponds to his woodcraft, following the grain and "slender as a whipstock," its curves "no false curves." The few lines attributed to him have an eloquence lacking in the stuffy verbosity of Frost's speaker, whose syntax can sound absurdly labyrinthine:

> So long as he would leave enough unsaid,
> I shouldn't mind his being overjoyed
> (If overjoyed he was) at having got me
> Where I must judge if what he knew about an axe
> That not everybody else knew was to count
> For nothing in the measure of a neighbor.

The penultimate line of that passage exemplifies *in extremis* Frost's comment that "the possibilities for tune from the dramatic tones of meaning struck across the rigidity of a limited meter are endless" (*CPr,* 131).

The "limited meter" of "The Axe-Helve" (as of every poem preceding it in *New Hampshire*) is iambic pentameter, but the caesura which the meaning requires after "knew" makes the line unrhythmical and nigh-on impenetrable. The horrible clunking phrase "measure of a neighbor" in the following line betrays a machine-made language which, like the speaker's axe, is not strong enough to labor with.

The speaker persists in his opinion that he is the generous one bestowing the favor of his presence on Baptiste, who is allowed to feel "overjoyed" at the honor. But suspicions remain: perhaps Baptiste's wife understands more than she pretends; and perhaps Baptiste has behaved "unscrupulously" in using his axe helves to tempt the speaker into his house. Even the display of consummate craftsmanship—his poetic expressing of lines "native to the grain"—does not forestall that particular allegation. Under such circumstances, Baptiste cannot be blamed for having fetched out the axe helves "Needlessly soon" to dispel any fear that he would fail to "keep his bargain."

The poem's analogy between artisan and artist is clearly signaled: Baptiste's practices and principles would hold true for any artist in any medium. But Frost complicates that narrative by introducing for comparison a third subject: education. Frost's speaker cannot articulate the relationship, wondering what it might be that "school and children and our doubts / Of laid-on education had to do / With the curves of his axe-helves." (Frost delivered "The Axe-Helve" as the Phi Beta Kappa poem at Harvard in June 1916 to an audience which may have been wondering something similar.) In attributing to Baptiste so many base motives, he misses the fact that Baptiste is a teacher as well as a craftsman; instead of simply donating an axe helve to his neighbor, he wants to show him how it is made. School-educated children, we are encouraged to recognize, are like attenuated and machine-made tools; the "false curves / Put on [axe helves] from without" are akin to "laid-on education." Home education allows the expression of innate characteristics which develop strength "For the hard work." No wonder Frost should have confided to Louis Untermeyer that "except by a stretch of the words" (*LU*, 37), "The Axe-Helve" could not be described as an "appropriate" choice for the

Phi Beta Kappa poem at that pinnacle of the education establishment, Harvard. "That much," he mischievously added, "may be said in [its] favor."

The final stanza returns to the physical object in its finished glory, although the speaker's description of an axe with a horse's hoof and waves like a snake's does not greatly assist the process of visualization. His reference to the Garden of Eden seems tainted by the thought that all labor is the product of the Fall, and that art must therefore embody original sin. Such a characteristically suspicious response stands at odds with Baptiste's concise pride, as winding syntax gives way to the poem's only foreshortened line: " 'See how she's cock her head!' " Quite what creature Baptiste has in mind never becomes clear, but by animating his axe as female (*hache,* in French, is a feminine noun), he conveys a sensuous delight far different from the undispelled wariness of his guest. Challenged at every point in his acts of generosity and creativity, he is allowed a simple and final expression of pleasure.

The Grindstone

Having a wheel and four legs of its own
Has never availed the cumbersome grindstone
To get it anywhere that I can see.
These hands have helped it go, and even race;
Not all the motion, though, they ever lent,
Not all the miles it may have thought it went,
Have got it one step from the starting place.
It stands beside the same old apple tree.
The shadow of the apple tree is thin
Upon it now, its feet are fast in snow.
All other farm machinery's gone in,
And some of it on no more legs and wheel
Than the grindstone can boast to stand or go.
(I'm thinking chiefly of the wheelbarrow.)
For months it hasn't known the taste of steel,
Washed down with rusty water in a tin.
But standing outdoors hungry, in the cold,
Except in towns at night, is not a sin.
And, anyway, its standing in the yard
Under a ruinous live apple tree
Has nothing any more to do with me,
Except that I remember how of old
One summer day, all day I drove it hard,
And someone mounted on it rode it hard,
And he and I between us ground a blade.

I gave it the preliminary spin,
And poured on water (tears it might have been);
And when it almost gayly jumped and flowed,
A Father-Time-like man got on and rode,
Armed with a scythe and spectacles that glowed.
He turned on will-power to increase the load

And slow me down—and I abruptly slowed,
Like coming to a sudden railroad station.
I changed from hand to hand in desperation.
I wondered what machine of ages gone
This represented an improvement on.
For all I knew it may have sharpened spears
And arrowheads itself. Much use for years
Had gradually worn it an oblate
Spheroid that kicked and struggled in its gait,
Appearing to return me hate for hate;
(But I forgive it now as easily
As any other boyhood enemy
Whose pride had failed to get him anywhere).
I wondered who it was the man thought ground—
The one who held the wheel back or the one
Who gave his life to keep it going round?
I wondered if he really thought it fair
For him to have the say when we were done.
Such were the bitter thoughts to which I turned.

Not for myself was I so much concerned.
Oh no!—although, of course, I could have found
A better way to pass the afternoon
Than grinding discord out of a grindstone,
And beating insects at their gritty tune.
Nor was I for the man so much concerned.
Once when the grindstone almost jumped its bearing
It looked as if he might be badly thrown
And wounded on his blade. So far from caring,
I laughed inside, and only cranked the faster,
(It ran as if it wasn't greased but glued);
I'd welcome any moderate disaster
That might be calculated to postpone
What evidently nothing could conclude.

The thing that made me more and more afraid
Was that we'd ground it sharp and hadn't known,
And now were only wasting precious blade.
And when he raised it dripping once and tried
The creepy edge of it with wary touch,
And viewed it over his glasses funny-eyed,
Only disinterestedly to decide
It needed a turn more, I could have cried
Wasn't there danger of a turn too much?
Mightn't we make it worse instead of better?
I was for leaving something to the whetter.
What if it wasn't all it should be? I'd
Be satisfied if he'd be satisfied.

~ ⚡ ~

"The Grindstone" is reminiscent of earlier poems by Frost in which the working environment becomes a site of deliberate or accidental violence. "The Code," "The Self-Seeker," "The Vanishing Red," and "'Out, Out—'" belong to that group, and even "Mending Wall" and "The Axe-Helve" carry the unrealized threat of bloodshed. Put men together as laborers, Frost's work suggests, and you encourage competition and confrontation; put them next to machines and, sooner or later, flesh will be mutilated. The animosity in "The Grindstone" between human and human, and between human and a machine which returns "hate for hate," finally does no physical damage. However, one worker "[gives] his life"—figuratively this time—to keep the wheel "going round," and encourages the grindstone to come off its bearing so as to injure his coworker.

Frost is never sentimental enough to ignore the casual indifference, and sometimes cruelty, with which people treat each other's sufferings. In an interview he situates that hostility at the heart of his creativity: "When they want to know about inspiration, I tell them it's mostly animus" (*CPP&P*, 893). Frost talks on occasion about "animus" as "the spirit that breaks the form" (*CPr*, 305), but the context of the interview makes plain that he also has *animosity* in mind. "The Grindstone" displays plenty of animus in both senses, fittingly for a poem named after a machine used to sharpen a blade. Yet Frost's "mostly" expresses a crucial reservation about the complex relationship between conflict and creation. Untempered animus is destructive: lacking the ability to shape that impulse into form, the workers jeopardize their product, "wasting precious blade."

A drama of "motion," embodied in the poem's rhythms and rhymes, is overtly established from the start: the grindstone races but is "cumbersome," and the many "miles it may have thought it went" have never yet budged it from its "starting place." That starting place under an apple tree carries the slightest suggestion of the Fall. Like "The Axe-Helve" before it, but less conspicuously, "The Grindstone" reminds us that labor is a consequence of man's first disobedience. As if on cue, "sin" appears soon enough in the poem, if only to be dismissed in a wry aside about social injustice: "But standing outdoors hungry, in the cold, / Except in towns at night, is not a sin." That is as close as the poem comes to questions of social or religious justice, because almost immediately, the mature poet's memories of youth bring the grindstone to life:

> I remember how of old
> One summer day, all day I drove it hard,
> And someone mounted on it rode it hard,
> And he and I between us ground a blade.

The repetitions in rhythm and rhyme convey a grim relentlessness which is hammered home by heavy alliterations: day, day, drove, hard, and, rode, hard, and, ground, blade. This is "hard" and never-ending work, and the growing sense of discord is confirmed by the poet's failure to find a rhyme for "blade"—the only unrhymed line in the poem. Appropriately, when "blade" is used again much later as an end-word, it is made to rhyme with "afraid." All that risk and all that endeavor go toward the making of something fearfully disharmonious.

Frost is reported by Elizabeth Sergeant to have referred to the grindstone as a "symbol of the great round earth" (Sergeant, 265). An "oblate / Spheroid" given a "preliminary spin," it seems to be kin to the fallen meteorite of "A Star in a Stone-boat," which "only needs a spin / To show its worldly nature." Just as the spinning meteorite would have "run off in strange tangents with my arm," so the grindstone's spinning causes it to jump and flow and shock the human body with a sudden momentum; and to add to the mock allegory, this particular world is presided over by a "Father-Time-like man" who has the power to slow it when he chooses. It is a comically grim vision, in which the music of the spheres is replaced by a "gritty tune," and the workers grind "discord"—almost anagrammatically—out of the "grindstone." The point could not be more clearly spelled out: labor causes conflict. The poem's final lines may masquerade as a desire to please, but they disguise frustration and aggression:

> I was for leaving something to the whetter.
> What if it wasn't all it should be? I'd
> Be satisfied if he'd be satisfied.

For all the verbal parallels, there is no sincere wish to mirror the feelings of the coworker. The word "satisfied" carries different nuances of meaning: the wry understatement of its first use contrasts with the bland contentment evoked in the second usage. Each man, at the poem's end, is less than "satisfied"—one with the quality of the job, and the other with his colleague's pernickety judgments. And so the poem ends where the labor cannot. Frost is on record as having said that "literature is a kind of forgiveness. Something happens to you and it hurts too much at first to do anything about it, but after a while you write a poem about it—when there is only just enough sting left to make you eloquent, and then you find it doesn't bother you any more" (*CPr*, 265). "The Grindstone" does not seem to deliver that kind of release. The mature poet's distant memory of the grindstone leaves him trapped in an earthly hell of discord and discontent "which evidently nothing could conclude."

Paul's Wife

To drive Paul out of any lumber camp
All that was needed was to say to him,
"How is the wife, Paul?"—and he'd disappear.
Some said it was because he had no wife,
And hated to be twitted on the subject.
Others because he'd come within a day
Or so of having one, and then been jilted.
Others because he'd had one once, a good one,
Who'd run away with some one else and left him.
And others still because he had one now
He only had to be reminded of,—
He was all duty to her in a minute:
He had to run right off to look her up,
As if to say, "That's so, how is my wife?
I hope she isn't getting into mischief."
No one was anxious to get rid of Paul.
He'd been the hero of the mountain camps
Ever since, just to show them, he had slipped
The bark of a whole tamarack off whole,
As clean as boys do off a willow twig
To make a willow whistle on a Sunday
In April by subsiding meadow brooks.
They seemed to ask him just to see him go,
"How is the wife, Paul?" and he always went.
He never stopped to murder anyone
Who asked the question. He just disappeared—
Nobody knew in what direction,
Although it wasn't usually long
Before they heard of him in some new camp,
The same Paul at the same old feats of logging.
The question everywhere was why should Paul
Object to being asked a civil question—

A man you could say almost anything to
Short of a fighting word. You have the answers.
And there was one more not so fair to Paul:
That Paul had married a wife not his equal.
Paul was ashamed of her. To match a hero,
She would have had to be a heroine;
Instead of which she was some half-breed squaw.
But if the story Murphy told was true,
She wasn't anything to be ashamed of.

You know Paul could do wonders. Everyone's
Heard how he thrashed the horses on a load
That wouldn't budge until they simply stretched
Their rawhide harness from the load to camp.
Paul told the boss the load would be all right,
"The sun will bring your load in"—and it did—
By shrinking the rawhide to natural length.
That's what is called a stretcher. But I guess
The one about his jumping so's to land
With both his feet at once against the ceiling,
And then land safely right side up again,
Back on the floor, is fact or pretty near fact.
Well this is such a yarn. Paul sawed his wife
Out of a white-pine log. Murphy was there,
And, as you might say, saw the lady born.
Paul worked at anything in lumbering.
He'd been hard at it taking boards away
For—I forget—the last ambitious sawyer
To want to find out if he couldn't pile
The lumber on Paul till Paul begged for mercy.
They'd sliced the first slab off a big butt log,
And the sawyer had slammed the carriage back
To slam end on again against the saw teeth.
To judge them by the way they caught themselves

When they saw what had happened to the log,
They must have had a guilty expectation
Something was going to go with their slambanging.
Something had left a broad black streak of grease
On the new wood the whole length of the log
Except, perhaps, a foot at either end.
But when Paul put his finger in the grease,
It wasn't grease at all, but a long slot.
The log was hollow. They were sawing pine.
"First time I ever saw a hollow pine.
That comes of having Paul around the place.
Take it to hell for me," the sawyer said.
Everyone had to have a look at it,
And tell Paul what he ought to do about it.
(They treated it as his.) "You take a jack-knife,
And spread the opening, and you've got a dug-out
All dug to go a-fishing in." To Paul
The hollow looked too sound and clean and empty
Ever to have housed birds or beasts or bees.
There was no entrance for them to get in by.
It looked to him like some new kind of hollow
He thought he'd *better* take his jack-knife to.
So after work that evening he came back
And let enough light into it by cutting
To see if it was empty. He made out in there
A slender length of pith, or was it pith?
It might have been the skin a snake had cast
And left stood up on end inside the tree
The hundred years the tree must have been growing.
More cutting and he had this in both hands,
And, looking from it to the pond near by,
Paul wondered how it would respond to water.
Not a breeze stirred, but just the breath of air
He made in walking slowly to the beach

Blew it once off his hands and almost broke it.
He laid it at the edge where it could drink.
At the first drink it rustled and grew limp.
At the next drink it grew invisible.
Paul dragged the shallows for it with his fingers,
And thought it must have melted. It was gone.
And then beyond the open water, dim with midges,
Where the log drive lay pressed against the boom,
It slowly rose a person, rose a girl,
Her wet hair heavy on her like a helmet,
Who, leaning on a log looked back at Paul.
And that made Paul in turn look back
To see if it was anyone behind him
That she was looking at instead of him.
Murphy had been there watching all the time,
But from a shed where neither of them could see him.
There was a moment of suspense in birth
When the girl seemed too water-logged to live,
Before she caught her first breath with a gasp
And laughed. Then she climbed slowly to her feet,
And walked off talking to herself or Paul
Across the logs like backs of alligators,
Paul taking after her around the pond.

Next evening Murphy and some other fellows
Got drunk, and tracked the pair up Catamount,
From the bare top of which there is a view
To other hills across a kettle valley.
And there, well after dark, let Murphy tell it,
They saw Paul and his creature keeping house.
It was the only glimpse that anyone
Has had of Paul and her since Murphy saw them
Falling in love across the twilight mill-pond.
More than a mile across the wilderness

285   *Paul's Wife*

They sat together half-way up a cliff
In a small niche let into it, the girl
Brightly, as if a star played on the place,
Paul darkly, like her shadow. All the light
Was from the girl herself, though, not from a star,
As was apparent from what happened next.
All those great ruffians put their throats together,
And let out a loud yell, and threw a bottle,
As a brute tribute of respect to beauty.
Of course the bottle fell short by a mile,
But the shout reached the girl and put her light out.
She went out like a firefly, and that was all.

So there were witnesses that Paul was married,
And not to anyone to be ashamed of.
Everyone had been wrong in judging Paul.
Murphy told me Paul put on all those airs
About his wife to keep her to himself.
Paul was what's called a terrible possessor.
Owning a wife with him meant owning her.
She wasn't anybody else's business,
Either to praise her, or so much as name her,
And he'd thank people not to think of her.
Murphy's idea was that a man like Paul
Wouldn't be spoken to about a wife
In any way the world knew how to speak.

Like many of Frost's poems, "Paul's Wife" brings classical traditions to
bear on American subjects. The myth of the heroic lumberjack Paul Bun-
yan was new, current, and extremely popular in the early decades of the
twentieth century. Paul's feats of slipping "The bark of a whole tamarack
off whole," and of forcing horses to pull a load by letting the sun shrink

their "rawhide harness," are recounted by the poem as familiar lore ("Everyone's / Heard"). But to these old "yarn[s]," Frost adds and adapts the story of Pygmalion—the sculptor who fell in love with his statue of a female form, and whose prayers were answered when Venus took pity and brought it to life. Frost dispenses with any divine intervention but keeps the sensual metamorphosis, as Paul becomes an artist who must (literally) live with the consequences of his act of creation.

The circumstances of this birth are confided to the poem's narrator by their sole witness: Paul's sometime colleague, Murphy. That such a "stretcher" of a story should come secondhand is entirely appropriate, and Murphy's reliability is further called into question by the account of subsequent events: "Next evening Murphy and some other fellows / Got drunk." The drunkards become "witnesses that Paul was married," although the strange events that they report do not support either that contention or the moralizing judgments about Paul's character which lead from it. Murphy is reported as implying that "Everyone had been wrong in judging Paul," but his own judgments about Paul seem wayward to the point of eccentricity. A man with such a "wife" can hardly be called "a terrible possessor" given her supernatural origins and her unfortunate encounter with the "great ruffians." Frost himself claimed that the poem was "merely about the kind of person who refuses to share socially in his spiritual possessions" (Cramer, 69), the emphasis falling on "spiritual." This is no ordinary wife, and society is not fit for her, least of all the raucous society of the lumber camp.

The language of "Paul's Wife," whether the narrator's own or the narrator reporting Murphy ("let Murphy tell it"), is plain even by Frost's standards. The line about slipping "The bark of a whole tamarack off whole," with its repetition of "of . . . off" and "whole," sounds like a deliberate violation of good writing. Other lines level the iambic beat of the blank verse: "All that was needed was to say to him"; "As was apparent from what happened next"; "She wasn't anything to be ashamed of" (a line repeated almost verbatim later); "She wasn't anybody else's business." From a poet who contended that the second line of Shakespeare's Sonnet 18, "Thou art more lovely and more temperate," carried only two "rhythmical accents" (lóvely, témperate) (*CPr*, 295), these seem like attempts to write lines devoid of any stress whatsoever. Frost's matter-of-fact descriptions of "wonders," in a diction simpler than Wordsworth's and a rhythm which courts bathos, make the impossible seem credible: this tall tale does not strain for effect, and situates its magic in an easily recognizable world of gossip and drunkenness and backbiting. The transformation of "pith" into woman is achieved via something as simple as a repetition of pronouns:

> Not a breeze stirred, but just the breath of air
> He made in walking slowly to the beach
> Blew it once off his hands and almost broke it.
> He laid it at the edge where it could drink.
> At the first drink it rustled and grew limp.
> At the next drink it grew invisible.
> Paul dragged the shallows for it with his fingers,
> And thought it must have melted. It was gone.

The word "it" appears nine times, drawing emphatic attention to the inanimate pith and particularly to its *status* as inanimate. "It" starts as the object of the sentences—carried, almost broken, laid at the edge of the water. Gradually, almost imperceptibly, "it" acquires agency, until "It slowly rose a person"—still gender neutral—but then, magnificently, "rose a girl." Frost's genius is to understate at the moment of revelation. The transformation into a living being plays out as a drama of pronouns, through which "it" metamorphoses into "she" and "her."

Pronouns seem as close as language is capable of getting to the identity of Paul's "wife." The poem's title borrows Murphy's normalizing assumptions about her relationship with Paul, and she is never identified more precisely than that. Her origins obscure ("pith, or was it pith?"), she is that vaguest and all-encompassing of terms—a "creature"—and certainly nothing so definitive as a dryad or wood nymph. Paul does nothing to dispel the mystery, refusing to let others "praise her, or so much as name her." Whereas Maple was named after a tree, and lived with the burden of that name, Paul's wife is born out of a tree—the vaginal "hollow" or "opening" in the pine through which the pith is first glimpsed—but manages to avoid any name which would fix her identity. She would be as vulnerable to fallen language as to fallen society, and Paul's belief (attributed to him by Murphy) that she cannot be spoken about "In any way the world knew how to speak" gives protection to her primal innocence. Paul seems like the perfect match, because despite being surrounded by garrulous rumors and drunken "shout[s]" and "yell[s]," he is never heard to speak. All the motives ascribed to him come unsupported by evidence. While the newborn woman walks away from the water "talking to herself or Paul," Paul is seen "taking after her around the pond." Taking is so easily mistaken for talking that the significance of Paul's silence can be missed. He refuses to stand by while others contaminate the identity of his "wife" with language—a response interpreted by Murphy as "put[ting] on all those airs." Far from "Owning a wife," he ensures her freedom by keeping her apart from a society and a language that would name and claim her.

Place for a Third

Nothing to say to all those marriages!
She had made three herself to three of his.
The score was even for them, three to three.
But come to die she found she cared so much:
She thought of children in a burial row;
Three children in a burial row were sad.
One man's three women in a burial row
Somehow made her impatient with the man.
And so she said to Laban, "You have done
A good deal right; don't do the last thing wrong.
Don't make me lie with those two other women."

Laban said, No, he would not make her lie
With anyone but that she had a mind to,
If that was how she felt, of course, he said.
She went her way. But Laban having caught
This glimpse of lingering person in Eliza,
And anxious to make all he could of it
With something he remembered in himself,
Tried to think how he could exceed his promise,
And give good measure to the dead, though thankless.
If that was how she felt, he kept repeating.
His first thought under pressure was a grave
In a new boughten grave plot by herself,
Under he didn't care how great a stone:
He'd sell a yoke of steers to pay for it.
And weren't there special cemetery flowers,
That, once grief sets to growing, grief may rest:
The flowers will go on with grief awhile,
And no one seem neglecting or neglected?
A prudent grief will not despise such aids.
He thought of evergreen and everlasting.

And then he had a thought worth many of these.
Somewhere must be the grave of the young boy
Who married her for playmate more than helpmate,
And sometimes laughed at what it was between them.
How would she like to sleep her last with him?
Where was his grave? Did Laban know his name?

He found the grave a town or two away,
The headstone cut with *John, Beloved Husband,*
Beside it room reserved, the say a sister's,
A never-married sister's of that husband,
Whether Eliza would be welcome there.
The dead was bound to silence: ask the sister.
So Laban saw the sister, and, saying nothing
Of where Eliza wanted *not* to lie,
And who had thought to lay her with her first love,
Begged simply for the grave. The sister's face
Fell all in wrinkles of responsibility.
She wanted to do right. She'd have to think.
Laban was old and poor, yet seemed to care;
And she was old and poor—but she cared, too.
They sat. She cast one dull, old look at him,
Then turned him out to go on other errands
She said he might attend to in the village,
While she made up her mind how much she cared—
And how much Laban cared—and why he cared,
(She made shrewd eyes to see where he came in.)
She'd looked Eliza up her second time,
A widow at her second husband's grave,
And offered her a home to rest awhile
Before she went the poor man's widow's way,
Housekeeping for the next man out of wedlock.
She and Eliza had been friends through all.
Who was she to judge marriage in a world

Whose Bible's so confused in marriage counsel?
The sister had not come across this Laban;
A decent product of life's ironing-out;
She must not keep him waiting. Time would press
Between the death day and the funeral day.
So when she saw him coming in the street
She hurried her decision to be ready
To meet him with his answer at the door.
Laban had known about what it would be
From the way she had set her poor old mouth,
To do, as she had put it, what was right.

She gave it through the screen door closed between them:
"No, not with John. There wouldn't be no sense.
Eliza's had too many other men."

Laban was forced to fall back on his plan
To buy Eliza a plot to lie alone in:
Which gives him for himself a choice of lots
When his time comes to die and settle down.

Frost is not quite a frequenter of graveyards, but they do make regular
appearances in his imaginative hinterland. From "Ghost House" with
its "stones out under the low-limbed tree," and "The graves of men on
an opposing hill" in "The Vantage Point," to the family plot of "Home
Burial," to *New Hampshire*'s "In a Disused Graveyard," the graveyard
serves (predictably enough) as a memento mori for the living. At a dis-
tance, there seems very little to choose between "the homes of men"
and "The graves of men" ("The Vantage Point"); and even close up,
as in *North of Boston*, Frost records the death-in-life existences of the
entrapped, the bereaved, and the guilt-ridden. Death can invade the
domestic sphere: a graveyard in "Home Burial" seems "not much larger

than a bedroom," and as if reciprocally, the marriage bed has become a grave.

"Place for a Third," described by Frost as one of his "less amiable poems" (*SL,* 243), is *more* amiable than its author suggests, because it risks a comic attitude to serious questions about the responsibilities of the living to the dead. The most fearful thing about death is the etiquette of burial: where, and with whom? How will the arrangements be judged by others, and by the dead themselves? Judgments of various kinds make the poem's drama: Eliza's judgment about the impropriety of a widower lining up his dead wives in a "burial row" (and her "impatien[ce]," as though the decent thing would have been for him to have died by now); her judgment that Laban, having done " 'A good deal right,' " would now be doing something "wrong" if he ignored her wishes: the sister-in-law's judgment of Laban's motives and her final decision that he could not have the plot. The poem opens with husband and wife unable to judge each other because each has had three marriages: "The score was even for them," Frost explains, turning it into a sporting contest. (Christ's comment to the Samaritan woman at Sichar bears on the poem: "For thou hast had five husbands, and he whom thou now hast, is not thy husband" [John 4:17].) "Place for a Third" ends by looking ahead to another judgment, as Laban must decide which wife he would like to be buried next to.

" 'Don't make me lie with those two other women,' " Eliza pleads when she is dying. Lying with someone is a biblical euphemism for sex; it occurs seven times in Genesis, and at least another twenty times through the Old Testament. (To ensure that the point cannot be missed, Frost gives Laban a good Old Testament name: Laban is Rebekah's brother in Genesis.) The impropriety of lying with other women would have strong sexual connotations, which makes Laban's response all the more urgently reassuring: "No, he would not make her lie / With anyone but that she had a mind to." The connection between the grave and the bed—a traditional metaphor but here pursued to the point of sexual disgust—leads Laban's thoughts to turn naturally to Eliza's first husband, "Who married her for playmate more than helpmate." That description reveals just as much about the relationship between Laban and Eliza—practical, affectionate, but not passionately physical. In the phrase "prudent grief" Frost finds the perfect oxymoron for Laban's mourning: willing to go to great pains and great expense in order to "give good measure to the dead," he remains enough of a pragmatist also to consider the need for "special cemetery flowers" which will not need regular tending.

Frost is most likely thinking of the sister-in-law's refusal to allow Eliza to be buried beside her first husband when he calls the poem "one of [his] less amiable." Certainly, the poem sets up the expectation that her answer will be yes. She judges Laban kindly, and through simple mirroring of language the poem presents them as kindred spirits: "Laban was old and poor, yet seemed to care;/And she was old and poor—but she cared, too." She remembers Eliza as a friend. And she acknowledges her own lack of authority: "Who was she to judge?" Yet she must judge, and she passes judgment against the plaintiff, speaking through a "screen" of respectability: " 'Eliza's had too many other men.' " To the reader it may seem a cruel and sudden verdict, but Laban had known what to expect from "the way she had set her poor old mouth,/To do, as she had put it, what was right." That phrase seems to echo Eliza's dying words about Laban having done " 'A good deal right; [so] don't do the last thing wrong.' " Eliza and the old spinster take equally firm positions on what is "right," leaving Laban to follow hints and guesses while muddling his way to an acceptable solution. There is another respect, as well, in which the two women resemble each other. Eliza's horror at the thought of " 'l[ying] with those two other women' " and the spinster's comment that " 'Eliza's had too many other men' " make a further verbal parallel: each woman takes the grave/bed metaphor the same distance, immediately thinking of the sexual implications. Notwithstanding the fact that the poem seems to set them in opposition, with one thwarting what Laban takes to be the other's desire, the women are like-minded and act according to identical motives.

The poem's final lines jokily reinforce the sexual commitments made by the dead. Laban will have "a choice of lots/When his time comes to die and settle down." Death, not marriage, constitutes "set-tl[ing] down." Marriages come and go and they seem like a kind of pro-miscuity, a sowing of wild oats before the final commitment which lasts forever and forsakes all others.

Two Witches

I. The Witch of Coös

Circa 1922

I staid the night for shelter at a farm
Behind the mountain, with a mother and son,
Two old-believers. They did all the talking.

Mother. Folks think a witch who has familiar spirits
She could call up to pass a winter evening,
But won't, should be burned at the stake or something.
Summoning spirits isn't "Button, button,
Who's got the button," I would have them know.

Son. Mother can make a common table rear
And kick with two legs like an army mule.

Mother. And when I've done it, what good have I done?
Rather than tip a table for you, let me
Tell you what Ralle the Sioux Control once told me.
He said the dead had souls, but when I asked him
How could that be—I thought the dead were souls,
He broke my trance. Don't that make you suspicious
That there's something the dead are keeping back?
Yes, there's something the dead are keeping back.

Son. You wouldn't want to tell him what we have
Up attic, mother?

Mother.   Bones—a skeleton.

Son. But the headboard of mother's bed is pushed
Against the attic door: the door is nailed.

It's harmless. Mother hears it in the night
Halting perplexed behind the barrier
Of door and headboard. Where it wants to get
Is back into the cellar where it came from.

Mother. We'll never let them, will we, son? We'll never!

Son. It left the cellar forty years ago
And carried itself like a pile of dishes
Up one flight from the cellar to the kitchen,
Another from the kitchen to the bedroom,
Another from the bedroom to the attic,
Right past both father and mother, and neither stopped it.
Father had gone upstairs; mother was downstairs.
I was a baby: I don't know where I was.

Mother. The only fault my husband found with me—
I went to sleep before I went to bed,
Especially in winter when the bed
Might just as well be ice and the clothes snow.
The night the bones came up the cellar-stairs
Toffile had gone to bed alone and left me,
But left an open door to cool the room off
So as to sort of turn me out of it.
I was just coming to myself enough
To wonder where the cold was coming from,
When I heard Toffile upstairs in the bedroom
And thought I heard him downstairs in the cellar.
The board we had laid down to walk dry-shod on
When there was water in the cellar in spring
Struck the hard cellar bottom. And then someone
Began the stairs, two footsteps for each step,
The way a man with one leg and a crutch,
Or little child, comes up. It wasn't Toffile:

It wasn't anyone who could be there.
The bulkhead double-doors were double-locked
And swollen tight and buried under snow.
The cellar windows were banked up with sawdust
And swollen tight and buried under snow.
It was the bones. I knew them—and good reason.
My first impulse was to get to the knob
And hold the door. But the bones didn't try
The door; they halted helpless on the landing,
Waiting for things to happen in their favor.
The faintest restless rustling ran all through them.
I never could have done the thing I did
If the wish hadn't been too strong in me
To see how they were mounted for this walk.
I had a vision of them put together
Not like a man, but like a chandelier.
So suddenly I flung the door wide on him.
A moment he stood balancing with emotion,
And all but lost himself. (A tongue of fire
Flashed out and licked along his upper teeth.
Smoke rolled inside the sockets of his eyes.)
Then he came at me with one hand outstretched,
The way he did in life once; but this time
I struck the hand off brittle on the floor,
And fell back from him on the floor myself.
The finger-pieces slid in all directions.
(Where did I see one of those pieces lately?
Hand me my button-box—it must be there.)

I sat up on the floor and shouted, "Toffile,
It's coming up to you." It had its choice
Of the door to the cellar or the hall.
It took the hall door for the novelty,
And set off briskly for so slow a thing,

Still going every which way in the joints, though,
So that it looked like lightning or a scribble,
From the slap I had just now given its hand.
I listened till it almost climbed the stairs
From the hall to the only finished bedroom,
Before I got up to do anything;
Then ran and shouted, "Shut the bedroom door,
Toffile, for my sake!" "Company," he said,
"Don't make me get up; I'm too warm in bed."
So lying forward weakly on the handrail
I pushed myself upstairs, and in the light
(The kitchen had been dark) I had to own
I could see nothing. "Toffile, I don't see it.
It's with us in the room though. It's the bones."
"What bones?" "The cellar bones—out of the grave."
That made him throw his bare legs out of bed
And sit up by me and take hold of me.
I wanted to put out the light and see
If I could see it, or else mow the room,
With our arms at the level of our knees,
And bring the chalk-pile down. "I'll tell you what—
It's looking for another door to try.
The uncommonly deep snow has made him think
Of his old song, *The Wild Colonial Boy,*
He always used to sing along the tote-road.
He's after an open door to get out-doors.
Let's trap him with an open door up attic."
Toffile agreed to that, and sure enough,
Almost the moment he was given an opening,
The steps began to climb the attic stairs.
I heard them. Toffile didn't seem to hear them.
"Quick!" I slammed to the door and held the knob.
"Toffile, get nails." I made him nail the door shut,
And push the headboard of the bed against it.

Then we asked was there anything
Up attic that we'd ever want again.
The attic was less to us than the cellar.
If the bones liked the attic, let them like it,
Let them stay in the attic. When they sometimes
Come down the stairs at night and stand perplexed
Behind the door and headboard of the bed,
Brushing their chalky skull with chalky fingers,
With sounds like the dry rattling of a shutter,
That's what I sit up in the dark to say—
To no one any more since Toffile died.
Let them stay in the attic since they went there.
I promised Toffile to be cruel to them
For helping them be cruel once to him.

Son. We think they had a grave down in the cellar.

Mother. We know they had a grave down in the cellar.

Son. We never could find out whose bones they were.

Mother. Yes, we could too, son. Tell the truth for once.
They were a man's his father killed for me.
I mean a man he killed instead of me.
The least I could do was to help dig their grave.
We were about it one night in the cellar.
Son knows the story: but 'twas not for him
To tell the truth, suppose the time had come.
Son looks surprised to see me end a lie
We'd kept all these years between ourselves
So as to have it ready for outsiders.
But tonight I don't care enough to lie—
I don't remember why I ever cared.

Toffile, if he were here, I don't believe
Could tell you why he ever cared himself . . .

She hadn't found the finger-bone she wanted
Among the buttons poured out in her lap.
I verified the name next morning: Toffile.
The rural letter-box said Toffile Lajway.

One of Frost's greatest poems, "The Witch of Coös" is also among his funniest. The point is worth stressing, not least because of Frost's own impatience with criticism which missed the humor of his work. Frost enjoyed goading those whom he called "the humorless in poetry's train (for there are a few such)" (*CPr*, 120). Too often, commentaries on "The Witch of Coös" bear out his case. The poem has been variously described as a study of isolation, mental disturbance, guilt, dementia, madness, hysteria, Oedipal drama, and general horror. Humor and psychological depth need not be mutually exclusive, of course; Frost once observed that "outer seriousness" of style must be accompanied by "inner humor," and "outer humor" by "inner seriousness" (*CPr*, 120). And he knew very well the use of humor as an avoidance strategy: "Humor is the most engaging cowardice" (Barry, 78). Yet this approach would do an injustice to the sophistication of "The Witch of Coös," which broaches its subject by means of humor. The poem's achievement resides in its refusal to take seriousness seriously: the poker-faced readings which it seems to encourage—more or less psychoanalytical readings—become part of the joke.

Frost encodes his own mischievous intentions at the end of the poem, when the speaker reports that he "verified the name" of the dead husband "next morning": "The rural letter-box said Toffile Lajway." Like the friendly neighbor in "The Axe-Helve," Toffile seems to have French origins. His name is an anglicization of "Théophile Lajoie," which manages with wonderful irony to bring together God, love, and joy. Here is a man never fortunate enough for his name to have become his destiny. Frost plays Joycean games (in 1922, this year of *Ulysses*) with the corrupt version, "Toffile Lajway," which, as Mordecai Marcus notes, puns on "To file away" (Marcus, 69–78)—fittingly for a poem in which the theme of repression runs pseudo-seriously throughout. Naming the story's absent protagonist, Frost lets it break into outright comedy: the poem invites psychoanalytical interpretations in order to laugh at them.

There had been no shortage of clues even before Frost's speaker checked the letter box. The only other name in the poem is that of "Ralle the Sioux Control." His identity has caused much puzzlement among scholars, some of whom miss the fact that he is a spirit. A "control" communicates with the medium while she is in her trance, and (as the term would imply) controls her trance state. This Sioux spirit perplexes the witch with his reports of the afterlife:

> He said the dead had souls, but when I asked him
> How could that be—I thought the dead were souls,
> He broke my trance. Don't that make you suspicious
> That there's something the dead are keeping back?
> Yes, there's something the dead are keeping back.

This makes a joke of repression and accidental revelation, as the spirit's response to letting slip a secret is immediately to shut down communication. Claiming to have glimpsed some unexpected truth, the witch conveys her judgment with ponderous repetitions which manage to catch not just her voice and character but the poem's own humor-through-repression: its deadpan expression of farce.

Reporting this exchange with Ralle, at the same time the witch seems unconcerned or unaware that her story about the skeleton flatly contradicts the assumption that the dead are disembodied souls. Commentators who believe that this is a poem of great horror have not paid attention to Frost's delighted metaphors: the bones are variously "like a chandelier," "like lightning or a scribble," a "chalk-pile," and best of all, "like a pile of dishes." They make a noise like "the dry rattling of a shutter." Attempts at horror are halfhearted special effects relegated to parentheses: "(A tongue of fire / Flashed out and licked along his upper teeth. / Smoke rolled inside the sockets of his eyes.)." They inspire such little terror that the witch has the idea to "mow the room" in the dark, arms at knee-level, to bring the skeleton down.

The poem's story of infidelity and murderous retribution raises questions about the paternity of the son who was "a baby" when the skeleton first made its attempted escape. As in "Maple," these must go unanswered (and, except in the reader's mind, unasked), and there is no evidence that the son has even considered the possibility. To pursue the matter too far would be to sound like the absurdly dry detective voice of the narrator, whose response to the story's uproarious entertainment is to "verif[y] the name" on the letter box. The clues to the witch's past sex life and current mental state are so comically conspicuous that they become part of the joke, as does the emphasis on enclosure and entrapment: the attic door "nailed" and bolstered by the "headboard of mother's bed"; the bulkhead double-doors "double-locked / And swollen tight and buried under snow"; the cellar windows—with repetitive emphasis as the witch refuses to rush her telling of the tale—also "swollen tight and buried under snow"; a door downstairs held shut and then flung open; an upstairs door shut to hold the skeleton; an "open door up attic" used—paradoxically—to "trap him." The bones' frantic desire to escape ("He's after an open door to get out-doors"), and the frantic desire of the witch to shut them in, create Frost's poetic equivalent of a French bedroom farce (in which husband and lover never quite meet), as may well be acknowledged in the nod to Toffile's national origins.

Marking the dramatic parts of mother and son as if for theater, "The Witch of Coös" is the consummation of an almost exclusive privileging of the spoken voice first heard in *North of Boston*. Frost's "old-believers" live "Behind the mountain": that geographically unhelpful description brings to mind "The Mountain" itself, with its narrator who (as in "The Witch of Coös") becomes the recorder of an idiomatic oral history. It may seem like an unnecessary provocation to acclaim Frost—poet first and only partially successful playwright—as the most important American dramatist of his century; but "The Witch of Coös" breaks generic distinctions because the beguiling accuracy of its "imagining ear" (*CPP&P,* 687) guarantees Frost's poetry a dialogic drama which few playwrights can match. "The Witch of Coös" needs no acting. Frost writes so that, as he told John T. Bartlett in 1913, "the reader must be at no loss to give his voice the posture proper to the sentence" (*SL,* 80). That proper posture is revealed by the interworkings of an impoverished lexis (as in that great Frostian line, "So as to sort of turn me out of it"), repetition, and the most nuanced modulations of rhythm and meter:

> *Son.* We think they had a grave down in the cellar.
>
> *Mother.* We know they had a grave down in the cellar.
>
> *Son.* We never could find out whose bones they were.
>
> *Mother.* Yes, we could too, son. Tell the truth for once.
> They were a man's his father killed for me.
> I mean a man he killed instead of me.

The mother's trumping of the son's deceits and equivocations is achieved by imposing emphasis on the tonally flat: "We think they had," which is rhythmically if not metrically unstressed, becomes "We knów they had"; "We never could," again unstressed, is transformed into the heavy beat of "Yés, we coúld tóo." Having returned her son's language to him with newly meaningful emphases, the mother does the same to her own, as the adverb "instead" is made to bear a long backstory of betrayal, intimidation, and violent death. The biggest drama turns out to be not the killing itself, nor the identity of the man killed, but that the man was killed *instead* of (that is, in place of) his lover. He becomes the scapegoat, brushing chalky skull with chalky fingers as the woman on the other side of the door, whose life he inadvertently saved in losing his own, repeats her mantra every night: "Let them stay in the attic since they went there."

II. The Pauper Witch of Grafton

Now that they've got it settled whose I be,
I'm going to tell them something they won't like:
They've got it settled wrong, and I can prove it.
Flattered I must be to have two towns fighting
To make a present of me to each other.
They don't dispose me, either one of them,
To spare them any trouble. Double trouble's
Always the witch's motto anyway.
I'll double theirs for both of them—you watch me.
They'll find they've got the whole thing to do over,
That is, if facts is what they want to go by.
They set a lot (now don't they?) by a record
Of Arthur Amy's having once been up
For Hog Reeve in March Meeting here in Warren.
I could have told them any time this twelvemonth
The Arthur Amy I was married to
Couldn't have been the one they say was up
In Warren at March Meeting for the reason
He wa'n't but fifteen at the time they say.
The Arthur Amy I was married to
Voted the only times he ever voted,
Which wasn't many, in the town of Wentworth.
One of the times was when 'twas in the warrant
To see if the town wanted to take over
The tote road to our clearing where we lived.
I'll tell you who'd remember—Heman Lapish.
Their Arthur Amy was the father of mine.
So now they've dragged it through the law courts once
I guess they'd better drag it through again.
Wentworth and Warren's both good towns to live in,
Only I happen to prefer to live
In Wentworth from now on; and when all's said,

Right's right, and the temptation to do right
When I can hurt someone by doing it
Has always been too much for me, it has.
I know of some folks that'd be set up
At having in their town a noted witch:
But most would have to think of the expense
That even I would be. They ought to know
That as a witch I'd often milk a bat
And that'd be enough to last for days.
It'd make my position stronger, think,
If I was to consent to give some sign
To make it surer that I was a witch?
It wa'n't no sign, I s'pose, when Mallice Huse
Said that I took him out in his old age
And rode all over everything on him
Until I'd had him worn to skin and bones,
And if I'd left him hitched unblanketed
In front of one Town Hall, I'd left him hitched
In front of every one in Grafton County.
Some cried shame on me not to blanket him,
The poor old man. It would have been all right
If some one hadn't said to gnaw the posts
He stood beside and leave his trade mark on them,
So they could recognize them. Not a post
That they could hear tell of was scarified.
They made him keep on gnawing till he whined.
Then the same smarty someone said to look—
He'd bet Huse was a cribber and had gnawed
The crib he slept in—and as sure's you're born
They found he'd gnawed the four posts of his bed,
All four of them to splinters. What did that prove?
Not that he hadn't gnawed the hitching posts
He said he had besides. Because a horse
Gnaws in the stable ain't no proof to me

He don't gnaw trees and posts and fences too.
But everybody took it for a proof.
I was a strapping girl of twenty then.
The smarty someone who spoiled everything
Was Arthur Amy. You know who he was.
That was the way he started courting me.
He never said much after we were married,
But I mistrusted he was none too proud
Of having interfered in the Huse business.
I guess he found he got more out of me
By having me a witch. Or something happened
To turn him round. He got to saying things
To undo what he'd done and make it right,
Like, "No, she ain't come back from kiting yet.
Last night was one of her nights out. She's kiting.
She thinks when the wind makes a night of it
She might as well herself." But he liked best
To let on he was plagued to death with me:
If anyone had seen me coming home
Over the ridgepole, 'stride of a broomstick,
As often as he had in the tail of the night,
He guessed they'd know what he had to put up with.
Well, I showed Arthur Amy signs enough
Off from the house as far as we could keep
And from barn smells you can't wash out of plowed ground
With all the rain and snow of seven years;
And I don't mean just skulls of Rogers' Rangers
On Moosilauke, but woman signs to man,
Only bewitched so I would last him longer.
Up where the trees grow short, the mosses tall,
I made him gather me wet snow berries
On slippery rocks beside a waterfall.
I made him do it for me in the dark.
And he liked everything I made him do.

I hope if he is where he sees me now
He's so far off he can't see what I've come to.
You *can* come down from everything to nothing.
All is, if I'd a-known when I was young
And full of it, that this would be the end,
It doesn't seem as if I'd had the courage
To make so free and kick up in folks' faces.
I might have, but it doesn't seem as if.

New Hampshire and subsequent editions group "The Pauper Witch of Grafton" with "The Witch of Coös" under the title "Two Witches." "The Pauper Witch" has suffered from being paired with one of Frost's strongest poems, but it deserves attention as a pure dramatic monologue, and it belongs with a group of poems ("The Hill Wife," "A Servant to Servants," "The Fear") exploring the mental consequences of a woman's isolation. Several critics characterize the pauper witch as "mad," but that hardly seems the adequate word; she is old, and lonely, and unwanted— circumstances which together provoke a bitterness bordering on regret. The Witch of Coös had her son and a passing traveler for company (not to mention the "bones"); by contrast, the pauper witch may make verbal gestures to an audience ("you watch me," "I'll tell you who'd remember," "You know who he was"), but she seems to be speaking into the ether. Dramatic monologue is the appropriate form for someone so bereft of human society. The woman who exercised such bewitching power over men when younger has been abandoned in her dotage.

The pauper witch reminisces fondly of that power, as Frost exposes the self-protective denials of male sexual fantasy: if a woman bewitches a man, it follows that she must be a witch. A similarly perverse logic drives the fantasies of Mallice Huse, an old man with a name punningly raising the question of whose malice is at work: that of the spirited young woman branded a witch, or of the patriarchal society which must guiltily repress and transfer its own desires? Mallice's account that the woman "rode" him all over Grafton County suggests that, unable to acknowledge his urge to be ridden like a horse in the sexual sense, he disguises the figurative in the literal and is ridden *as* a horse, hitched and left to gnaw the posts outside Grafton's various town halls. Similarly, the gnawing of those posts (or rather, of his bedposts which he is later found to have "scarified") is the external manifestation of his own lust gnawing at him. His desire to be naked with her is itself shamefully laid bare. He complains at having been hitched "unblanketed," and the community transfers his shame on to her: "Some cried shame on me not to blanket him." The woman becomes the scapegoat for the town's dark urges. Only one man—a "smarty someone" named Arthur Amy—is rational enough to resist the general denunciation and to locate the source of the outrage in Mallice's own fevered imaginings. His intervention serves as the briefest respite. Having courted and married this "strapping girl of twenty," he connives with her to reestablish her reputation for witchcraft: he "got to saying things / To undo what he'd done and make it right." Making it right means informing the townsfolk that his wife has regularly been "kiting . . . 'stride of a broomstick."

The psychology of the community, potentially sinister but here portrayed comically by Frost, is easier to understand than the married couple's. Why should the woman and her husband actively encourage her branding as a witch? At least her attitude is straightforwardly consistent: she has "the courage / To make so free and kick up in folks' faces," and that rebelliousness is gratified by the label which it attracts. Having demonstrated his ability to regulate her power, Arthur Amy claims her for his own: "That was the way he started courting me," the witch recalls. Only after marriage does he discover the benefits of "having [her] a witch." There are hints that he, too, is keen to resist the community's influence, not only in his lone-voiced interruption of "the Huse business" but also in the paucity of his voting record: "one of the only times" that he voted "was when 'twas in the warrant / To see if the town wanted to take over / The tote road to our clearing where we lived." Beginning with the settling of a dispute about ownership of the pauper witch, the poem emphasizes these conflicts between the individual and the community.

We are not told which way Arthur Amy was inclined to vote, but the fact of his having taken his wife from the disapproving community to a home in a "clearing" linked only by a "tote road" implies the desire to live beyond the town's reach. This liminal status will provoke the legal case between Wentworth and Warren in later years.

The pauper witch offers a glimpse of the married life she and her husband enjoyed outside the community. Arthur Amy "never said much," and the little which he *is* reported as saying, he says to the locals and not to her. Theirs is a nonverbal relationship but an intensely erotic one, and the passage describing their amorous explorations is as sexually charged as anything Frost ever published. The witch remembers that she "showed" her husband

> woman signs to man,
> Only bewitched so I would last him longer.
> Up where the trees grow short, the mosses tall,
> I made him gather me wet snow berries,
> On slippery rocks beside a waterfall.
> I made him do it for me in the dark.
> And he liked everything I made him do.

Randall Jarrell puts it perfectly: "There is more sexuality there than in several hothouses full of Dylan Thomas" (Jarrell 1952, 555). The landscape becomes a bodyscape, and vice versa, and the playing out of the couple's fantasy brings with it exciting dangers as the husband risks "slippery rocks beside a waterfall" in the dark. Even their house in the clearing is not sufficiently remote: they have escaped "Off from the house as far as [they] could keep" and away from "barn smells" which would evoke enclosure and the domestication of nature and reproduction. It is yet another manifestation of a journey into the wilderness in Frost's work which is dreamed of ("Into My Own," "The Sound of the Trees"), and occasionally acted on ("The Wood-Pile," "An Encounter"). The couple live their fantasies outside the conventions which, as the local community shows only too well, would repress and distort natural desires.

The passage is a paean to female sexuality. The woman's bewitching nature is not because of her hackneyed claims about milking bats, or even for her ability to find "skulls of Rogers' Rangers / On Moosilauke." (Rogers' Rangers were a British militia renowned during the French and Indian War for their ability to operate in inhospitable conditions.) She makes her husband do what she chooses; for their mutual pleasure and benefit, she is in control. Dangerous though he may find it, Arthur Amy willingly pays the price of subservience, being the only one who understands the nature of her power. He had demonstrated his authority when intervening in the Mallice Huse affair, and having loosened her hold on the community he had courted and married her; but subsequently he is eager to succumb. No wonder that, reminiscing so fondly, the pauper witch should rue her old age: she has "come down from everything to nothing," her influence having resided in her sexuality rather than any supposed supernatural power. For the towns of Warren and Wentworth, she has become merely an expense to be avoided. Once, Wentworth's claim to their tote road had exercised the husband and wife; now it seeks only to distance itself from the widow. "No memory of having starred / Atones for later disregard," as Frost puts it in a later poem, "Provide, Provide." Proud to the end, the best that the pauper witch can do is cause as much difficulty as possible:

> Right's right, and the temptation to do right
> When I can hurt someone by doing it
> Has always been too much for me, it has.

The final irony for this lifelong enemy of conventions is that her only weapons are the law and a sense that "Right's right."

Fire and Ice

Some say the world will end in fire,
Some say in ice.
From what I've tasted of desire
I hold with those who favor fire.
But if it had to perish twice,
I think I know enough of hate
To know that for destruction ice
Is also great
And would suffice.

Little in Frost's earlier work prepares for "Fire and Ice," perhaps the most epigrammatically memorable of his poems. Here are no New Hampshire landscapes, no minutely observed natural images or carefully recorded tones of speech. The poem stands as an abstract musing on apocalypse, so unconcerned at that prospect that it makes room for a double perishing. Rather than worrying about possibilities of survival, the emphasis is on making sure that these "great" elemental forces of fire and ice are sufficient for the job at hand. That the "destruction" will occur one way or the other is never doubted.

   The poem alludes to contrasting scientific theories about the end of the world: its incineration by an expanding sun; or a new ice age rendering the planet uninhabitable. The astronomer Harlow Shapley remembered that he had explained these possibilities to Frost a year or two before the poem first appeared. Yet science is only the goad for a poem which soon transforms the literal into the figurative. Appropriately given its rhyme, "fire" is associated with "desire," and "ice" with "hate," almost to the point of their becoming synonymous. The poet takes sides in this dispute on the basis of nothing more than personal preference, thereby presenting scientific debate as subjectively partisan: some *favor* fire. Frost adopts his position simply by translating science into metaphor: who would not choose desire rather than hate? That translation, or rather the viewing of science *as* metaphor, is a common theme of Frost's later prose. The best scientific theories, he argues, are conveyed by a "very brilliant metaphor" (*CPr*, 105), and as the metaphor of passionate conflagration is more appealing than that of a paralyzing hatred, his decision is inevitable. It is through metaphor that science is understood, just as Frost chooses in "Fire and Ice" to imagine the unimaginable via personally felt emotions.

Jeffrey Meyers has claimed that "Fire and Ice" has its literary origins in Canto XXXII of Dante's *Inferno,* where sinners in the fires of hell are condemned to be "preserved in ice" (Meyers, 178). Despite Meyers's ingenious reference to the nine circles of Dante's hell and the poem's nine lines, his case is not especially compelling, because the juxtaposition of fire and ice is commonplace in the Petrarchan tradition as well: "I burn, and freeze like ice," Thomas Wyatt writes in "I Find No Peace," describing the oxymoronic effects of love. Frost's persona shows himself to be equally capable of burning and freezing—that is, of desire and of hatred—and if a particular source needs to be found, it is more likely Catullus, one of Frost's favorite classical poets: his Carmen LXXXV begins, famously, "Odi et amo" ("I hate and I love"). "Fire and Ice" creates echoes which incriminate the poem's fourfold "I" in both "fire" and "ice": Frost's first-person voice, the assonance confirms, has tasted desire and hatred. (See, for comparison, "Beyond Words": "That row of icicles along the gutter / Feels like my armory of hate" (*CPP&P*, 356).) He prefers desire, but in no way rejects hatred, and conveys a sense of satisfaction that they bring about the same sufficient result.

The poem switches from tetrameter to dimeter in lines 2, 8, and 9, each foreshortened line describing the work of "ice." Thanks not least to the irresistible logic of rhyme, "ice" will always "suffice," and as such, little more needs to be said. The expansive fires of passion give way to a paralyzed and frozen waste. As if capturing the destruction visually, Frost claimed in public readings that this variation in line lengths had the effect of creating a "jagged lightning" down the poem's right-hand edge. And he compared his poem with Eliot's *The Hollow Men:*

313   *Fire and Ice*

This is the way the world ends
This is the way the world ends
This is the way the world ends
Not with a bang but a whimper.

"Fire and Ice" was "serious," Frost would declare seriocomically, but "not quite as serious" as that.

To E. T.

I slumbered with your poems on my breast
Spread open as I dropped them half-read through
Like dove wings on a figure on a tomb
To see, if in a dream they brought of you,

I might not have the chance I missed in life
Through some delay, and call you to your face
First soldier, and then poet, and then both,
Who died a soldier-poet of your race.

I meant, you meant, that nothing should remain
Unsaid between us, brother, and this remained—
And one thing more that was not then to say:
The Victory for what it lost and gained.

You went to meet the shell's embrace of fire
On Vimy Ridge; and when you fell that day
The war seemed over more for you than me,
But now for me than you—the other way.

How over, though, for even me who knew
The foe thrust back unsafe beyond the Rhine,
If I was not to speak of it to you
And see you pleased once more with words of mine?

"To E. T." stands apart as Frost's only overt elegy for an individual—in
this case, the English poet Edward Thomas, who had been killed at the
Battle of Arras in April 1917. Frost and Thomas had met in London dur-
ing October 1913, and quickly developed what Frost's granddaughter,
Lesley Lee Francis, has described as "one of the great literary friendships

of British and American letters" (Francis, 81.) Thomas's death prompted Frost to mourn "the only brother [he] ever had" (*SL*, 217), and he addresses Thomas directly as "brother" in the poem.

After Frost's return to the States in early 1915, Thomas wrote "A Dream," a sonnet in which the two friends walk together through "known fields." Dream potentially has the power to reunite those who are separated by distance or by death. Such is the hope expressed in "To E. T."—that a dream prompted by reading his friend's poetry might provide the opportunity to say things to him which were "Unsaid" during his life. Whether communication through dream does successfully take place between living and dead is never spelled out. The desire is reported, the outcome not. Poetry becomes yet another channel for this communication: like a dream, elegy can address the dead directly. Frost's insistent repetitions of "you" (nine times) and "your" (three) read like attempts to conjure the friend into being through force of will; but this dialogue must remain one-sided, the poet's fraternal message possibly undelivered. As Frost writes in 1948 about the gulf between Britain and America, "I wish Edward Thomas (that poet) were here to ponder gulfs in general with me. . . . But now I do not know the number of his mansion to write him so much as a letter of enquiry" (*CPr*, 158). There are some gulfs, it seems, too great to be bridged.

Jay Parini has stated that "Frost was never quite able to express his deepest feelings about Thomas in poetry" (Parini, 181). Certainly, there is a tonal instability in the poem which is rarely encountered elsewhere in Frost's work. "I slumbered with your poems on my breast" is an example of poetry on its best behavior, trying too hard to sound sincere, and straining for effect through that stuffy word "slumbered" and the all-too-poetical "breast." "On my breast" seems more like an image of maternal nurturing (why not chest?), but before that bizarre possibility is allowed to develop, the dropped book is compared to "dove wings on a figure on a tomb." This is the closest Frost's elegy is allowed to come to Christian consolation; it also has the curious effect of making Frost himself the "figure" adorning Thomas's tomb. Briefly, "To E. T." conjures an image of what John Hollander has called "notional ekphrasis"—the verbal description of an imaginary work of art. Running counter to these awkward attempts at the language of mourning is the slightly comical realization that reading his friend's poetry seems to have made Frost nod off.

After Thomas's death, Frost wrote to his widow, "I want to see him to tell him something. I want to tell him, what I think he liked to hear from me, that he was a poet. . . . I had meant to talk endlessly with him still" (*SL,* 216). "To E. T." attempts to fulfill that ambition, albeit by bringing Thomas's status as "poet" together with his soldiering: "First soldier, and then poet, and then both." Frost does not quite say that it is sweet and decorous to die "a soldier-poet of your race," but says that joining of vocations through the hyphen is meant to serve as a glorious epitaph. And although "*your* race" threatens to divide the friends, Frost emphatically reconciles them with the word "brother" two lines later. "I fail to see how we can have been so much to each other, he an Englishman and I an American" (*SL,* 217), Frost wrote in the month of Thomas's death, raising the drawbridge of nationality only to point out how it had been breached in ways that are still mysterious to him.

There is "one thing more" which Frost knows when he writes "To E. T.," and which he hadn't known in April 1917: that Thomas fought and died for a cause which proved to be victorious. This is the news which the poem must pass on. In one sense, the war is over for soldiers who are killed; in another sense, it never ends, because they hear nothing about the subsequent peace. That, at least, seems to be the meaning of Frost's cumbersome fourth quatrain, but he immediately revises his position in the final lines:

> How over, though, for even me who knew
> The foe thrust back unsafe beyond the Rhine,
> If I was not to speak of it to you
> And see you pleased once more with words of mine?

This distinguishes itself with alternating rhymes: previously, the quatrains had rhymed *xaxa*. That extra rhyme is "knew" / "you," its past tense poignantly exposing the poem's hope that Thomas can still be addressed in the present. Throughout, the poem is couched in conditionals and negatives—"if," "not," "nothing," "not," "If," "not,"—as if the impossible might yet be taken by surprise through grammatical sleights of hand. So the last two lines imply the possibility of a satisfactory resolution: *as long as I speak of it to you, I will see you pleased once more with words of mine.* The poet frees himself from the war, and discharges his duty, by writing the poem; even while imagining the cost of a failure to communicate with his dead friend, he tries to persuade himself that he *is* communicating. So the dialogue is established: the poem opens with Frost reading Thomas's words, and it ends by raising the prospect of Thomas being "pleased once more" with Frost's.

Stopping by Woods on a Snowy Evening

Whose woods these are I think I know.
His house is in the village though;
He will not see me stopping here
To watch his woods fill up with snow.

My little horse must think it queer
To stop without a farmhouse near
Between the woods and frozen lake
The darkest evening of the year.

He gives his harness bells a shake
To ask if there is some mistake.
The only other sound's the sweep
Of easy wind and downy flake.

The woods are lovely, dark and deep.
But I have promises to keep,
And miles to go before I sleep,
And miles to go before I sleep.

Frost considered "Stopping by Woods" to be his "best bid for remembrance" (*LU*, 163). At the very least, it takes its place among those dozen or so poems which Frost successfully lodged "where they will be hard to get rid of" (*CPP&P*, 744). The poem is at once disarmingly simple and temptingly ulterior: we are invited to understand that much more is at stake than a snowy nocturnal journey through an attractive landscape, but we may be less certain about how to define or characterize that ulterior meaning, or even on what textual basis we are entitled to try. Properly concerned with negotiating a path between saying too little and insisting too much, literary criticism encounters some of its greatest challenges when it must discuss ulteriority in poems such as this. Frank Lentricchia, one of Frost's subtlest critics, makes a revealing leap of faith: "If with many of Frost's readers we take the woods to represent some sort of death-wish—and I think we have to, Frost's humorous public protestations to the contrary . . ." (Lentricchia, 96). That is, although the poem never mentions death, *we have to* assume that it embodies a death wish within it. On what textual basis we make that assumption, Lentricchia never explains, but he is in good company: Richard Poirier speaks of "some furtive impulse toward extinction" (Poirier, 181); Katherine Kearns finds that Frost's protagonist must "resist that furtive invitation to nothingness" (Kearns, 10); and many others have referred to "Stopping by Woods" as a suicide poem, a poem of self-annihilation or self-eradication. Frost himself is reported to have given a biographical source, describing how he once broke down in tears on the way back from market during a difficult winter. As they passed some woods, his horse slowed and then stopped: "It knew what [Frost] had to do. He had to cry, and he did" (Bleau, 174–177).

Yet there are no tears shed during "Stopping by Woods." The poem may be set in the "darkest evening of the year," but if "darkest" is meant to imply depression and despair—a dark night of the soul—it seems strange that the woods should be described as "lovely, dark and deep." (Here are "those dark trees" of "Into My Own" once again.) The woods cast their shadow of ulteriority, but shadows are intangible: here, as elsewhere in Frost's work, the more that an ulterior meaning is pursued, the more that the poem, not wanting to be betrayed by interpretation, evades the reader's grasp. In the spirit of such paradoxes, Frost himself expressed a faux-naïf concern about people "pressing ['Stopping by Woods'] for more than it should be pressed for. It means enough without its being pressed. . . . I don't say that somebody shouldn't press it, but I don't want to be there" (Cook 1956, 52). Or as he put it in his notebooks, "What can you do with a poem besides read it without offending against refinement of feeling" (*N*, 235).

As all readings are interpretations, offense against "refinement of feeling" may prove unavoidable. But "Stopping by Woods" actively encourages such offense, from the moment when it withholds knowledge about the owner of the woods, to the vague reference to "promises" which must be kept. Frost raises these subjects as provocations, pricking interest with their latent significance. The interactions between horse and human, which constitute a quarter of the poem, comically represent the dangers of elaborating on these clues: apparently on the basis of nothing more than a "shake" of the harness bells, the human thinks that the horse is thinking that it cannot understand the human's thoughts. That clumsy dance of intellects is a warning against presumption, although the glorious mood music of "easy wind and downy flake" immediately intervenes to "sweep" the misunderstandings away.

Straying only infrequently from a four-beat iambic meter, Frost's first three quatrains also establish a regular (if novel) rhyming pattern: lines 1, 2, and 4 of each stanza rhyme, while the third line establishes the rhyme for the succeeding stanza. This presents a problem, because the pattern cannot be sustained in a finite poem: the third line of the final stanza will have no subsequent stanza with which to rhyme. Ironically, a poet who declares himself to have "promises to keep" must therefore break a formal promise in the next line. Frost described his difficulty and attempted solutions at some length:

> A dead [that is, unrhymed] line in the last stanza alone would have been a flaw. I considered for a moment four of a kind in the last stanza but that would have made five including the third in the stanza before it. I considered for a moment winding up with a three line stanza. The repetend was the only logical way to end such a poem. (Thompson 1970, 596)

The drafts reveal that Frost first considered rhyming his final stanza's third line with a rhyme from the previous stanza: "The woods are lovely dark and deep / But I have promises to keep / That bid me give the reins a shake." Dissatisfied with that, he tried a "dead line," replacing those shaken reins with "That bid me on, and there are miles." Finally, the repetend (or refrain) solves the problem: repetition is "the only logical way" to fill the gap in the rhyme scheme.

Frost's account risks making "Stopping by Woods" seem like an arithmetical exercise: it has four beats to the line, four lines to the stanza, four stanzas to the poem, and were it not that the pattern must plunge in medias res, every rhyme would have four distinct rhyme-words. (At a pinch, "miles to go" does fulfill that pattern through an internal rhyme with "know," "though," and "snow.") To consider a pun on the repeated and iambic word "be*fore*" may be to press for more than should be pressed for, but the poem's foursquare regimentation does resist a studied vagueness in the opening and closing lines. Whose woods *are* these? Why does the poet only *think* he knows who owns them? *How many* miles to go?

Elizabeth Sergeant draws a parallel between Frost's final stanza and the opening lines of Keats's sonnet, "Keen, fitful gusts" (Sergeant, 251):

> Keen, fitful gusts are whisp'ring here and there
> Among the bushes half leafless, and dry;
> The stars look very cold about the sky,
> And I have many miles on foot to fare.

Even while acknowledging differences (bushes aren't trees, gusts aren't a "sweep / Of easy wind," "on foot" isn't on horseback), it is possible to appreciate the echo: "And I have many miles on foot to fare" sounds in "And miles to go before I sleep." Keats's protagonist, distant from "home's pleasant lair," is "brimful of the friendliness" that he has found in his books, and as a consequence feels "little of the cool bleak air." Frost's Keatsian cadences lack this purposeful well-being: the woods may be filling with snow, but they are more appealing, and certainly less chilly, than those "promises" which need to be kept. The repetend is a formal dramatization of the poem's conflict between motion and stasis, and (if we should allow the ulterior meaning) between life and death. Is repetition a reiterated determination to move on, or is it a failure to progress as the poem's speaker finds the woods too "lovely" to resist? Ominously, at the moment when the journey must continue, the poem comes to a halt.

For Once, Then, Something

Others taunt me with having knelt at well-curbs
Always wrong to the light, so never seeing
Deeper down in the well than where the water
Gives me back in a shining surface picture
Me myself in the summer heaven godlike
Looking out of a wreath of fern and cloud puffs.
Once, when trying with chin against a well-curb,
I discerned, as I thought, beyond the picture,
Through the picture, a something white, uncertain,
Something more of the depths—and then I lost it.
Water came to rebuke the too clear water.
One drop fell from a fern, and lo, a ripple
Shook whatever it was lay there at bottom,
Blurred it, blotted it out. What was that whiteness?
Truth? A pebble of quartz? For once, then, something.

Initially titled "Well" and then "Wrong to the Light," "For Once, Then, Something" was (Frost confessed) "calculated to tease the metrists" (*SL*, 248). The poem is a virtuoso performance, its Phalaecean hendecasyllabic verse an homage to Catullus, who wrote more than forty surviving poems in that meter. Frost's choice may have been determined by the tradition which associates the meter with poems of rebuttal. Phalaecean hendecasyllabics have not only "tease[d]" but confused many of Frost's commentators, who have variously described the meter as accentual or syllabic. Frost himself joked, in an unpublished lecture from 1947, that he had never received proper credit: "Everybody just thinks it's my kind of blank verse." Hendecasyllabic verse as used here is more accurately described as an example of quantitative meter; although (like much of Frost's work) each line has eleven syllables, in this case the syllables are measured by duration. Insofar as the accentual rhythms of the English language allow, Frost follows Catullus's scheme fairly strictly. So, to take just the first half of the line, he starts with a trochaic foot ("Others," "Always," "Deeper"), and follows with a choriamb (a classical foot of four syllables in the pattern long, short, short, long): "taunt me with hav-"; "wrong to the light"; "down in the well"; "back in a shin-." Frost uses substitutions more freely at the line's end, where the required spondee is present in "wéll-cúrbs" and "cloúd púffs" but is usually replaced by trochee ("seéing," "wáter").

"For Once, Then, Something" has claims to be the most classical of Frost's works. The aphorism attributed to the Greek philosopher Democritus, that truth lies at the bottom of a well, merges with the myth of Narcissus entranced by his own reflection. Seamus Heaney's "Personal Helicon" (an early poem heavily indebted to Frost) makes that myth explicit as he stares down into wells, a "big-eyed Narcissus." Heaney's untypically clumsy poem only emphasizes how lightly "For Once, Then, Something" wears its classical learning. Not one to flaunt what he calls his "loyalty to the untranslated classics" (Brower, 139), Frost writes a poetry which engages with those traditions without abandoning its New Hampshire farm or its commitment to the New Hampshire farmer's vocabulary.

Yet "For Once, Then, Something" does signal its ulteriority in the opening lines. "Others taunt me with having knelt at well-curbs / Always wrong to the light": wrong-angled observations at the edges of wells seem an unlikely, and certainly an insufficient, cause for others to start "taunt[ing]." The literal meaning is flimsy enough for the reader to understand straightaway that more must be at stake. Frost is preoccupied with different kinds of vision—a vision which claims to penetrate through to profound truths, against a vision which is apparently superficial and narcissistic. In an astonishing switch of perspective, the poet who sees only his own image ("Me myself in the summer heaven godlike / Looking out of a wreath of fern and cloud puffs") allows the reader to view him from below. He becomes his own work of art, framed by the circle of the well and foregrounded against "fern and cloud puffs" as if peering down at his audience from a Renaissance fresco. "Picture," thrice used to allow no ambiguity, comes from the Latin *pictura*—that is, painting. Those unidentified "Others," then, criticize a poet who is in their judgment limited to artistic self-projection and unable to see past that self into greater depths. The phrase "Always wrong to the light" implies a theological motive for such criticism. Although Lawrance Thompson contextualizes "For Once, Then, Something" as Frost's playful contribution to an ongoing religious debate with his atheistical wife (Thompson 1970, 561–562), the poem's inability to see what is seen by the "Others" sounds more like a disagreement with believers confident in their faith. (Frost's doubt makes belief and unbelief seem equally false.) The poet who portrays himself as "godlike" has no need for another deity.

Fifteen lines long, unrhymed, and in quantitative meter, the poem has been mistaken for a sonnet by at least one commentator (Buell, 111). It does share with the sonnet a turn, or *volta,* as Frost begins line 7 with an italicized "*Once,*" which moves the poem from the general state of affairs to one particular occasion. What follows is a partial concession to the poet's detractors, but it concedes only so as to damage their arrogance more than his skepticism. At last, positioning himself with chin on well curb, the poet discerns (or rather, *thinks* he discerns, adding another layer of doubt) "a something white, uncertain, / Something more of the depths." This briefest of glimpses into profundity offers little in the way of illumination: "something" (which appears three times, and a fourth time in the poem's title) could be almost anything. As water rebukes water, the physical world rushes to cover up a mystery which should never have been exposed.

When the poet spies that "something white, uncertain," he makes a claim far more radically skeptical than a transferred epithet would grant. The observer may be "uncertain," but the syntax cannot be plainer: the "something" at the bottom of the well—Democritus's irretrievable truth—is itself also "uncertain." Truth is not to do with answers, or revelations, or certainties, but with questions and doubts and uncertainties. As Amelia Klein has argued, "Truth, for Frost, requires the recognition of limitation, of the contingency of knowledge" (Klein, 22). So protean is its nature that its presence can never be confidently asserted: perhaps it is merely "a pebble of quartz." Frost ends the poem tentatively but defiantly. For once, there was something where truth is meant to be. What it was, he cannot say for sure; and because he cannot say for sure, it was truthful.

The Onset

Always the same, when on a fated night
At last the gathered snow lets down as white
As may be in dark woods, and with a song
It shall not make again all winter long
Of hissing on the yet uncovered ground,
I almost stumble looking up and round,
As one who overtaken by the end
Gives up his errand, and lets death descend
Upon him where he is, with nothing done
To evil, no important triumph won,
More than if life had never been begun.

Yet all the precedent is on my side:
I know that winter death has never tried
The earth but it has failed: the snow may heap
In long storms an undrifted four feet deep
As measured against maple, birch and oak,
It cannot check the peeper's silver croak;
And I shall see the snow all go down hill
In water of a slender April rill
That flashes tail through last year's withered brake
And dead weeds, like a disappearing snake.
Nothing will be left white but here a birch,
And there a clump of houses with a church.

***

"The Onset" is chilled by the weather of *New Hampshire:* nineteen of
the volume's poems mention snow. It also seems to hark back to "Stop-
ping by Woods on a Snowy Evening," especially in the opening stanza's
"dark woods" and the speaker's temptation to give up his "errand" (from
the Old English meaning *mission* or *message*) and succumb to "death."

Reuben Brower finds that the natural scene is "definitely unpleasant" (Brower, 97), but that is to miss the considerable temptations on offer. The "hissing" sibilance throughout the poem, finally embodied as a "disappearing snake," joins with the reference to "stumbl[ing]" to evoke the Fall. Were the setting as unpleasant as Brower suggests, there would be no danger; but the allure of the siren "song" makes it nigh-on irresistible. "I almost stumble," Frost states, barely kept on his feet by that precarious "almost": the "important triumph[s]" of life seem distantly abstract compared with the sensuous delights of song and snow.

The poem's hissing sound effects are complemented by serpentine syntax, winding the first stanza into just one sentence. One consequence is to create ambiguity about the song, which initially seems to allude to the noise of snow against "uncovered ground," but which belatedly picks up the subject of its clause in the sixth line: "I." Poet and snow are strangely of one voice in a death song which does not so much terminate life as erase it from the record. Triumph implies struggle; by opting out of that struggle, the "one" who "lets death descend / Upon him where he is," and disappears under the snow, somehow leaves less of a mark than if he had never been born. The poem's only rhyming tercet ("done" / "won" / "begun") allows form to replace logic in hammering home the incontrovertibility of that argument.

Because most readings of "The Onset" concur with Brower's belief that the setting is "unpleasant"—Lentricchia speaks of it being "bathed in fear" (Lentricchia, 94)—they have taken heart from Frost's "Yet" at the start of the second stanza. Here is the turn from fear to hope: far from being the "end," winter must itself give way to spring, and snow to thaw. With poetical legerdemain, the seasons become a metaphor for human life, which is no longer a linear "errand" toward death but a cyclical pattern in which rebirth is always promised. The snake of temptation disappears, and the death wish vanishes with it. However, while seeming to mark the defeat of "winter death," the second stanza is almost entirely given over to memory of its power and to its lingering effects (including the sibilant hiss of the snow's song). "[F]our feet deep" is not quite six feet under, although the echo resonates; the devastated vegetation is described as "withered brake / And dead weeds," with no mention of green shoots; and even the flimsy evidence of "the peeper's silver croak" conveys mortality in its pun on "croak." The meltwater is alive, the natural landscape dead.

Like "To E. T.," "The Onset" proceeds by way of negatives ("not," "uncovered," "nothing," "never," "never," "undrifted," "cannot," "Nothing"), the cumulative weight of which burdens the second stanza's attempt at optimism. Unable to assert the positive, Frost takes whatever cold comfort can be mustered by pointing out what winter cannot do. The poem's final couplet sets out to limit the extent of the snow's lingering springtime presence:

> Nothing will be left white but here a birch,
> And there a clump of houses with a church.

This, of course, alludes to the coloring of a silver birch and to white-washed buildings, but even as it does so, it makes those croaking peepers seem even more doomed: if a silver birch is white, then their "silver croak" is a death rattle contaminated by the snow's fatal whiteness. The snow's springtime retreat also exposes some disturbing affiliations: the birch "here," and the habitations of people and their God "there," display that same whiteness. The snow may have gone, but ominously, its haunting pallor has been "left" on the natural world, the human and the divine.

A Hillside Thaw

To think to know the country and not know
The hillside on the day the sun lets go
Ten million silver lizards out of snow!
As often as I've seen it done before
I can't pretend to tell the way it's done.
It looks as if some magic of the sun
Lifted the rug that bred them on the floor
And the light breaking on them made them run.
But if I thought to stop the wet stampede,
And caught one silver lizard by the tail,
And put my foot on one without avail,
And threw myself wet-elbowed and wet-kneed
In front of twenty others' wriggling speed,—
In the confusion of them all aglitter,
And birds that joined in the excited fun
By doubling and redoubling song and twitter,
I have no doubt I'd end by holding none.

It takes the moon for this. The sun's a wizard
By all I tell; but so's the moon a witch.
From the high west she makes a gentle cast
And suddenly, without a jerk or twitch,
She has her spell on every single lizard.
I fancied when I looked at six o'clock
The swarm still ran and scuttled just as fast.
The moon was waiting for her chill effect.
I looked at nine: the swarm was turned to rock
In every lifelike posture of the swarm,
Transfixed on mountain slopes almost erect.
Across each other and side by side they lay.
The spell that so could hold them as they were
Was wrought through trees without a breath of storm

To make a leaf, if there had been one, stir.
It was the moon's: she held them until day,
One lizard at the end of every ray.
The thought of my attempting such a stay!

"A Hillside Thaw" is one of Frost's overlooked poems. It treats a moment when seasonal change becomes evident; and as the springtime answer to winter's first snowfall it might serve as a companion piece for "The Onset." That first poem, set on the "fated night" when snow starts to cover the ground, looks ahead to the April thaw when the meltwater runs downhill like "a disappearing snake." Not content with just one snake, "A Hillside Thaw" takes inflationary delight in describing "Ten million silver lizards" suddenly released by "some magic of the sun." Yet their freedom proves temporary: that night the moon casts her spell, and "the swarm [is] turned to rock."

The poem begins and ends with rhyming triplets ("know" / "go" / "snow"; "day" / "ray" / "stay") which frame a more fluid and irregular pattern of rhymes. The temptation is to understand rhyme as the poet's playful means of "holding" and "ma[king] . . . run." Such power can be attained only through poetry: in the first stanza the poet imagines himself trying to "stop the wet stampede," and the "confusion" of the lizards' "wriggling speed" is mimicked in a rhythm which runs relentlessly through its nine-line sentence to the final disappointed bathos of defeat: "I have no doubt I'd end by holding none." The sun, as a "wizard" imposing its "magic" on the natural world, has the same effect on the thawed rhythms of Frost's poetry, making them run.

Nevertheless, the poem admits to other and deeper affinities. Frost's persona wants to resist the sun's magic, although he may appear ridiculous in the attempt. The power which he seeks for himself is the moon's. Her witchcraft is to undo the sun's work, and to hold "Transfixed" what the sun had previously released. Again, the spell affects the poem's rhythms, which are continually checked and halted by syntactical requirements. Tellingly, the first stanza consists of four sentences; the second stanza, ten. The "thought" of stopping the daytime stampede returns at the end of the poem: "The thought of my attempting such a stay!" But the aspirational has joined—if not entirely replaced—the farcical. However absurd the idea of acquiring the moon's power may sound, the poet cannot bring himself to renounce it.

"Like a piece of ice on a hot stove the poem must ride on its own melting" (*CPr*, 133). Frost's famous injunction in "The Figure a Poem Makes" seems to speak to "A Hillside Thaw" in finding poetry at the precarious point where form meets fluidity, where fire meets ice and the sun's magic meets the moon's. Yet a phrase from earlier in the same essay confirms that, in "A Hillside Thaw" at least, Frost is not so evenhanded. When he calls poetry "a momentary stay against confusion" (*CPr*, 132) he describes another dynamic perfection which must be, by its very nature, transitory. This time, however, the "stay" against confusion is the poem's (and poet's) act of resistance against a universal force which can be only momentarily defied. "A Hillside Thaw" moves from the "confusion" of lizards to the moon's admired ability to make them "stay." Although the final victory will always be the sun's, the moon's power of resistance is the power sought by the poet, whose poem performs the very "stay" which the final line wistfully desires.

The Need of Being Versed in Country Things

The house had gone to bring again
To the midnight sky a sunset glow.
Now the chimney was all of the house that stood,
Like a pistil after the petals go.

The barn opposed across the way,
That would have joined the house in flame
Had it been the will of the wind, was left
To bear forsaken the place's name.

No more it opened with all one end
For teams that came by the stony road
To drum on the floor with scurrying hoofs
And brush the mow with the summer load.

The birds that came to it through the air
At broken windows flew out and in,
Their murmur more like the sigh we sigh
From too much dwelling on what has been.

Yet for them the lilac renews its leaf,
And the aged elm, though touched with fire;
And the dry pump flung up an awkward arm;
And the fence post carried a strand of wire.

For them there was really nothing sad.
But though they rejoiced in the nest they kept,
One had to be versed in country things
Not to believe the phoebes wept.

The italicized finale of *New Hampshire,* "The Need of Being Versed in Country Things" is a refusal to mourn which, like many such refusals, acknowledges even in its denial the occurrences which make mourning inevitable. That tension between restraint and release is heard in the rhythms themselves. The poem's tetrameter varies between the heavy stresses of the opening line ("The hoúse had góne to bríng agaín") and the anapests of the third ("Now the chímney was áll of the hoúse that stoód") to establish poles of sonorous regularity and hurried reportage. Whereas the simple rhyming pattern insists on closure with its masculine monosyllables ("glow"/"go," "flame"/"name," and so on), that which is enclosed is never metrically tamed. Nature resists the impositions of the sentimental perspective. The barn seems "forsaken," especially so when memories of its busy history are evoked as contrast; and the birds' murmur sounds like a nostalgic sigh. The reality is very different. "For them there was really nothing sad": the birds' existences defy the human meaning which seeks to colonize them.

Abandoned houses, and other long-forgotten remnants of human habitation, seem to have carried a particular poignancy for Frost, littering his landscapes from an early poem like "Ghost House" to the late master-piece "Directive" ("There is a house that is no more a house / Upon a farm that is no more a farm / And in a town that is no more a town"). One critic has drawn comparison with Emerson's "Hamatreya," in which Death adds men to their own land, "a lump of mould the more" (Smith, 225). Yet Frost does not strain to mock the vanity of human wishes; his target is our habit of understanding (or, rather, *mis*understanding) the natural world as sympathetic to our own desires and defeats. "The Need of Being Versed in Country Things" belongs to that tendency in Frost's work to challenge the Romantic construction of a relationship between humanity and nature. The birds delight in their own habitation, indifferent to the destruction of the human residence.

The poem's voice is caught between a keenness to find signs of sorrow in the natural world and a realization that nature does not share that sorrow. The third stanza cradles its nostalgia, calling to mind the teams of horses bringing in the summer harvest. "No more it opened with all one end," Frost says of the barn, his inversion lending a grammatical antiquity to the scene described. Now, only birds enter the barn, their murmur "more like the sigh we sigh / From too much dwelling on what has been." That "too much" acknowledges an excess of regret: the sighing sounds overly attractive, bringing to mind the more famous "sigh" (or mock sigh, as Frost insisted) in "The Road Not Taken." Frost himself was scathing about the usefulness of regret as a human emotion, but here he tempers his criticism with a full disclosure of its pleasures. Misplaced and inherently futile it may be, and it may encourage us to distort our appreciation of the natural world, but it proves irresistible: when Frost writes of "the sigh *we* sigh" (my italics), he incriminates his own self-indulgence along with that of his species.

Products of human endeavor disintegrate: the barn's broken windows, the "dry pump," and the fence post with just a single "strand of wire" bear witness to the general deterioration. The poem opens by suggesting a consonance between the man-made and the natural world: the burned house's chimney stands "Like a pistil after the petals go." However, whereas human alterations to the landscape fall into irreversible decline, seasonal change in nature ensures that rebirth follows death. The birds are more wisely attuned to natural cycles than we are. In the penultimate stanza, Frost uses anaphora to make the point with devastating irony. His threefold repetition of "And" draws rhetorical equivalence between things which are, truly, opposites. The lilac and the "aged elm" renew themselves "for" the birds, who nest among the ruins; by comparison, the dry pump and fence post are incongruous remnants.

However, the poem never shakes off its instinct for nostalgia, nor its desire that some presence in the natural world should acknowledge and share that human sadness. Having apparently given up on any emotional kinship from the birds, Frost's speaker turns to them again in the final lines: "One had to be versed in country things / Not to believe the phoebes wept." (Phoebes are flycatchers, their name imitative of their call.) The poet who knows better, and who is himself "versed" (with its clear double meaning) in "country things," nevertheless reiterates the possibility of sympathy in nature even if only to deny it. The poem's rhetorical trick, as summed up in the final line, is to keep evoking that which it knows to be untrue. So the poem has it both ways, bringing together the blunt fact that nature is indifferent to our suffering, and the Romantic assumption that it sympathizes.

LATER POEMS

T HE POEMS INCLUDED in this final section have been
selected from four of Frost's later volumes. "Acquainted with
the Night" was published in *West-Running Brook* (1928); "Two
Tramps in Mud Time," "Desert Places," "Neither Out Far Nor
In Deep," and "Design" in *A Further Range* (1936); "The Silken Tent,"
"The Most of It," "The Subverted Flower," and "The Gift Outright" in
A Witness Tree (1942); and "Directive" in *Steeple Bush* (1947). In several
cases, the dates can mislead: "The Subverted Flower" and an early ver-
sion of "Design" were already available to Frost, if he had wanted to use
them, when he was compiling his manuscript of *A Boy's Will*.

Awards and honors were bestowed on Frost during the latter part
of his career. Like *New Hampshire* before them, *A Further Range* and *A
Witness Tree* won the Pulitzer Prize, as did his *Collected Poems* in 1931;
and the culminating honor came in 1961 when Frost recited "The Gift
Outright" at John F. Kennedy's inauguration. Reviews of each volume
were favorable far more often than not; as Jay Parini notes in his account
of *Steeple Bush*'s reception, "Frost had by now built up such a layer
of goodwill among critics that he was generally praised" (Parini, 369).
Hearing of Frost's death in January 1963, John Berryman reacted with a
literary-political question which had not previously needed to be asked:
"It's scary. Who's number one?"

Notwithstanding the scale of public recognition, the consensus
view that Frost's strongest books came early in his career as a published
poet is hard to dispute. Even so, each of his volumes manages to lodge
at least one or two lyrics where they have proven hard to get rid of. The
ten poems chosen here belong among Frost's very best.

Acquainted with the Night

I have been one acquainted with the night.
I have walked out in rain—and back in rain.
I have outwalked the furthest city light.

I have looked down the saddest city lane.
I have passed by the watchman on his beat
And dropped my eyes, unwilling to explain.

I have stood still and stopped the sound of feet
When far away an interrupted cry
Came over houses from another street,

But not to call me back or say good-bye;
And further still at an unearthly height,
One luminary clock against the sky

Proclaimed the time was neither wrong nor right.
I have been one acquainted with the night.

Frost claimed that "Acquainted with the Night" was "written for the tune," and is reported to have identified the tower of the Washtenaw County Courthouse as the location of the "luminary clock" (Parini, 246). Despite the precision of that detail, the poem has in common with other anthology pieces—"The Road Not Taken," "Stopping by Woods on a Snowy Evening"—a lack of specificity which encourages metaphysical speculations. Ulteriority is allowed to run wild, because the poem's various elements (the night, the city lane, the rain, the watchman, the clock, the "interrupted cry") connote far more than they denote. The debate among critics over whether the poem describes "a purely urban wasteland" or a "cosmic, even astrological darkness" (Adams, 2) therefore seems beside the point, because such possibilities are not mutually exclusive.

This fourteen-liner is not a sonnet according to any but the most unhelpfully arithmetical of definitions. Written in Dante's *terza rima* (*aba bcb cdc*), the poem faces the formal challenge of bringing that pattern to an end. Frost solved a similar problem in a similar way when he used repetend in "Stopping by Woods," repeating the line "And miles to go before I sleep." "Acquainted with the Night" concludes by repeating not just the opening *line* but the opening *rhyme:* "height," "right," and "night" echo back to the first rhyme of "night" / "light," as the poem begins and ends nocturnally. Frost marries the potentially endless Dantean structure with the sonnet's economy. But when Randall Jarrell described "Acquainted with the Night" as "a poem in Dante's own form and with some of Dante's own qualities" (Jarrell 1952, 552), he was exaggerating a point: desolate rather than horrifying, brief rather than expansive, it lacks the impetus to do more than gesture toward that epic journey.

The closest precursors are earlier poems by Frost. "Good Hours," as Frank Lentricchia noticed, seems like "a preliminary study" (Lentricchia, 76) for "Acquainted with the Night": the walker of the earlier poem deliberately strays beyond his community on his evening walk "till there were no cottages found"; and, now, Frost's protagonist reports having "outwalked the furthest city light." Whereas the speaker of "Good Hours" "turned and repented," the later poem seems to be suffused with an imprecise shame: "I have passed by the watchman on his beat / And dropped my eyes, unwilling to explain." Shunning the orthodox comforts of home and the community, the nightwalker cannot meet the gaze of those who would question his motives. Frost's watchman seems to be Blake's "Accuser who is The God of This World" writ small; and although the phrase "unwilling to explain" suggests a refusal to elaborate to such a figure, the poem also implies inability. To the question "Why?" readers are given no more answer than the watchman.

That this is a poem of profound melancholia is proven by the rhythmical resignation, and by the transferred epithet in "saddest city lane."

Thompson is probably right to propose that the word "acquainted" should bring to mind the reference in Isaiah 53:3 to "a man of sorrows, and acquainted with grief" (Thompson 1970, 627). The quest has no grail, unless it be the attempt to discover meaning in what otherwise seems like a meaningless universe. The deliberate avoidance of engagement with humans is reciprocated by that "interrupted cry" which invites the possibility of communication only to dash the prospect instantly with an emphatic denial: "not to call me back or say good-bye." It matters to no one whether the protagonist comes back. As Mary Adams argues, words and phrases like "out," "outwalked," "furthest," "passed by," "far away," and "further still" show him "pass[ing] beyond society's meaning-making apparatus without a specific destination" (Adams, 2). He is like the solitary figure in Frost's later poem, "The Most of It," who listens for a "voice in answer" to his own, but who never finds that "counter-love" which he craves.

Meaning is sought, perhaps, in the "luminary clock," the adjective "luminary" suggesting both the clock's inspirational and its light-giving qualities. ("Luminary" is a Frostian mot juste because it gives equal weight to the literal and the figurative.) The clock might be expected to proclaim the time; better still, the *right* time. Yet it stands at an "unearthly height," distant from the affairs of men. Ignoring its basic function, this clock strays into portentousness only to deliver a uselessly equivocal judgment, that the time is "neither wrong nor right." The clock cannot tell the time, and it cannot *right* the time. It may give light, but it is not illuminating, and seems like a poor substitute for sun and moon. And so the poem only describes a circular journey, ending where it began, with no meaning found or wisdom gained. The restrained formal patternings signal the pressure of the protagonist's desperation. His repeated line, "I have been one acquainted with the night," is understated almost to the point of primness: this "acquaint[ance]" amounts to a painful intimacy with the dark night of the soul.

Two Tramps in Mud Time

Out of the mud two strangers came
And caught me splitting wood in the yard.
And one of them put me off my aim
By hailing cheerily "Hit them hard!"
I knew pretty well why he dropped behind
And let the other go on a way.
I knew pretty well what he had in mind:
He wanted to take my job for pay.

Good blocks of beech it was I split,
As large around as the chopping block;
And every piece I squarely hit
Fell splinterless as a cloven rock.
The blows that a life of self-control
Spares to strike for the common good
That day, giving a loose to my soul,
I spent on the unimportant wood.

The sun was warm but the wind was chill.
You know how it is with an April day
When the sun is out and the wind is still,
You're one month on in the middle of May.
But if you so much as dare to speak,
A cloud comes over the sunlit arch,
A wind comes off a frozen peak,
And you're two months back in the middle of March.

A bluebird comes tenderly up to alight
And fronts to the wind to unruffle a plume,
His song so pitched as not to excite
A single flower as yet to bloom.
It is snowing a flake: and he half knew

Winter was only playing possum.
Except in color he isn't blue,
But he wouldn't advise a thing to blossom.

The water for which we may have to look
In summertime with a witching-wand,
In every wheelrut's now a brook,
In every print of a hoof a pond.
Be glad of water, but don't forget
The lurking frost in the earth beneath
That will steal forth after the sun is set
And show on the water its crystal teeth.

The time when most I loved my task
These two must make me love it more
By coming with what they came to ask.
You'd think I never had felt before
The weight of an axe-head poised aloft,
The grip on earth of outspread feet,
The life of muscles rocking soft
And smooth and moist in vernal heat.

Out of the woods two hulking tramps
(From sleeping God knows where last night,
But not long since in the lumber camps).
They thought all chopping was theirs of right.
Men of the woods and lumberjacks,
They judged me by their appropriate tool.
Except as a fellow handled an axe,
They had no way of knowing a fool.

Nothing on either side was said.
They knew they had but to stay their stay
And all their logic would fill my head:

As that I had no right to play
With what was another man's work for gain.
My right might be love but theirs was need.
And where the two exist in twain
Theirs was the better right—agreed.

But yield who will to their separation,
My object in living is to unite
My avocation and my vocation
As my two eyes make one in sight.
Only where love and need are one,
And the work is play for mortal stakes,
Is the deed ever really done
For Heaven and the future's sakes.

Frost first published "Two Tramps in Mud Time" in 1934. The "tempta-
tion of the times," he had noted that same year, was "to write politics"
(*SL*, 403), and the poem has been taken as evidence that Frost did not
always resist. Lawrance Thompson reports that on at least one occasion
Frost read "Two Tramps in Mud Time" publicly to "clinch his argument
concerning how to cope with the social and economic problems of the
worker" (Thompson 1970, 426). Even so, the evidence is contradictory.
At other readings, Frost described the poem as a "philosophical" rather
than a political statement, and argued that it had "nothing to do with
the times" (*CPP&P*, 766–767).

   The tramps of the title are autochthonous: they come "Out of the
mud." That description places them in time as well as space: "Mud time
is going by," Frost told an audience in 1937, because "few back roads
are left now" (*CPP&P*, 766). So if "Two Tramps" comments on the
Great Depression and the New Deal, it does so obliquely as a period
piece which precedes them both. Privately, Frost's views on poverty and
the New Deal were complex: "For Christ's sake forget the poor some of

the time," he writes twice in his notebooks (*N*, 35, 404), and one note-book entry acknowledges that "poetry has a vested interest in seeing the poor kept poor." After all, poetry "depends as much on the sorrows of poverty as on the sorrows of plenty (if that is an evil)" (*N*, 45). "Two Tramps" remarks on the difficulty for the providers more than for the recipients, but it, too, is inspired by "the sorrows of poverty."

The poem allows Frost to be nostalgic for "those good old days" before the New Deal (*CPP&P*, 766), although it is never so sepia-tinged as to attempt to disguise the desperate poverty which the tramps must endure. The poor, Frost knows, are always with us. Even chopping logs outside an isolated home can become ethically fraught. What price self-reliance, if by acting for ourselves we deprive the less fortunate of a livelihood? But how legitimate are the claims which others hold over us? These are the claims of society and the state over the individual, claims which, from certain perspectives and in certain circumstances, can be perceived as infringing on constitutional rights to liberty and the pursuit of happiness. Not for nothing does the word "right" appear four times in the poem; and not for nothing does Frost invoke the view, which in unpublished talks he ascribes to Jefferson, that the state and the individual are antagonists.

The "philosophical" issue with which "Two Tramps" is concerned, then, could hardly be more pertinent, or, for that matter, more political. The poem tests to destruction two conflicting "right[s]," as aphoristically described in the penultimate stanza: "My right might be love but theirs was need." Theirs, the poet acknowledges, trump his: "Theirs was the better right." Yet Frost will not let the matter rest there. He has already prefaced their case with the comment that "a life of self-control" (such as, implicitly, his own) needs to strike these blows "for the common good"; we all have blows to strike, and if we don't strike them on the "unimportant wood," we will strike them more damagingly elsewhere. His final stanza signals a more overt opposition to the tramps, with a powerful counterargument which, if not quite contradicting the previous stanza, nevertheless seeks to recuse itself from the social contract which the agreement entailed.

This may seem like a heavy load to bear for a poem which describes a scene of woodchopping against a vernal backdrop. Yet from the start of his writing career, work has always been central to Frost's philosophy: "Mowing" and "The Tuft of Flowers" are early indicators that his poetry represents work and represents *itself as* work. The duty of work, the personal satisfaction offered by work, the need to work which may include financial need—more than any other poem by Frost, it is "Two Tramps" which stages the collision of competing motives. The strangers, Frost writes, "caught me splitting wood in the yard"; he has been found out, exposed in the act of doing something improper. The enthusiasm with which one of them encourages him—'"Hit them hard!"'—is interpreted as an act of aggression. The tramp plays to his status as spectator so as to redouble the woodcutter's anxiety and guilt. (Later in the poem, Frost acknowledges that these new arrivals "knew that they had but to stay their stay" in order for their logic to fill his head.) There is also an implied criticism—is he not hitting them hard already?—which provokes the poet to defend his expertise: "every piece I squarely hit / Fell splinterless as a cloven rock." His proud allusion to "Rock of Ages" awards the poet a divine power under the gaze of hostile eyes.

The woodcutter is "caught" in the act; the tramp wants to "take [his] job." The verbs suggest impropriety, even criminality. Although the tension may appear to be dispelled by three stanzas which move from the human to the natural world, those descriptions amount only to war by other means. The poet signs his continued presence: "The lurking *frost* in the earth beneath" may catch the unwary with its "crystal teeth." Lurking under his own text—ready to "steal forth" in a poem concerned with ownership, rights, and theft—Frost alerts the reader to continued dangers in this unexpected interlude.

His reason for doing so is best explained by David Bromwich, who has demonstrated the poem's indebtedness to "Resolution and Independence," Frost's Wordsworth poem of choice; or rather, the poem which inspires and bothers Frost so profoundly that he can neither find a resolution nor assert his independence from it. Bromwich summarizes the "Wordsworthian situation" set out in that earlier poem: "In an unpromising landscape, lit by a change of weather from stormy to fair . . . a poet filled with unsettling thoughts about his vocation is suddenly brought face to face with a common laborer, or one who suffers the common fate of men and not the uncommon fate of poets" (Bromwich 1989, 220). Frost's restaging of this Wordsworthian drama repeats a difference between poet and laborer in their relationship to the natural world. As Bromwich explains, "the pleasures of landscape will belong to the poet alone, and be felt at the intervals of his self-questioning; to the figure who confronts the poet, on the other hand, landscape hardly exists." The tramps may be born from landscape, but they remain unconscious of it. By contrast, the poet becomes preternaturally aware of his surroundings at those moments of tense human interaction. He is both poet *and* laborer, holding the greater claim, and more nearly in sympathy with his environment. He is also Antaean, feeling "The grip on earth of outspread feet," but he draws on a spiritual dimension wholly lacking in those lumpen creatures who interrupt his happiness: "Except as a fellow handled an axe, / They had no way of knowing a fool." The poet has more and better ways than theirs to know a fool when he sees one.

Having apparently succumbed to the tramps' unstated arguments ("Theirs was the better right—agreed"), Frost-as-laborer gives his own "side" the last word. The final stanza has been described by Bromwich as "a fine enough sort of eloquence," but "not quite in earnest" (Bromwich 1989, 226). The cause of Bromwich's unease is Frost's unwillingness to confront what Wordsworth had more willingly admitted: the fact of his being a poet. A writer such as Frost who can define poetry as "words that have become deeds" (*LU*, 10) betrays his profound suspicion of a poetry which has no kinetic force in the world. By speaking of poetry in an ulterior fashion, through mowing, orchis hunting, tree selling, or (here) woodcutting, Frost escapes his own distrust of the sedentary trade. Yet that evasion can come at a cost, and in "Two Tramps" the cost is what Bromwich considers to be "a touch of bad faith": the poet is hidden behind the laborer when he needs to be visible. Frost may seek (when it suits) to align poetry and woodcutting, but the tramps are offering only to chop his wood, not write his poems for him.

Bromwich's demurral touches on the issue central to any consideration of Frost's achievement: how can we know when we should read for ulteriority? When is a woodcutter a woodcutter, and when (and to what extent) is he a poet? After all, the unpardonable sin for the reader of poetry, as Frost argues several times, is to take a hint where none is intended; and he has to "leave it to nice people" to spot intended hints (Thompson 1970, 547). When "Two Tramps" states, "My object in living is to unite / My avocation and my vocation," it chooses not to elaborate on which is the diversion and which the calling. Poetry (words becoming deeds) is inextricably tied with woodchopping (deeds here becoming words). One possible reply to Bromwich, then, is to insist that Frost-as-poet *is* represented in "Two Tramps," and that the poem refuses to separate vocation and avocation. Bromwich argues that "we need to see the poet"; but the paradox of ulteriority is that the poet should be visible never and always. It is the perfect poetic strategy for merging "love" and "need" (or "Heaven" and "the future") into one perspective. Frost described the "object of everything," which he sets out in the final stanza, as "saving your soul some way," by "get[ting] your love and your need together" (*CPP&P*, 767). "It's just that we don't quite do it," he confessed.

Desert Places

Snow falling and night falling fast oh fast
In a field I looked into going past,
And the ground almost covered smooth in snow,
But a few weeds and stubble showing last.

The woods around it have it—it is theirs.
All animals are smothered in their lairs.
I am too absent-spirited to count;
The loneliness includes me unawares.

And lonely as it is that loneliness
Will be more lonely ere it will be less—
A blanker whiteness of benighted snow
With no expression, nothing to express.

They cannot scare me with their empty spaces
Between stars—on stars where no human race is.
I have it in me so much nearer home
To scare myself with my own desert places.

This astonishing poem was one of a number which Frost claimed to have written "without fumbling a sentence" (Thompson 1970, 597). "Desert Places" has been the subject of countless scholarly readings, the most influential of which, by Cleanth Brooks and Robert Penn Warren in their coauthored book *Understanding Poetry,* argues that the poem advocates the need for religious faith. As a result, many subsequent interpretations have focused on the poem's perceived theology. Jonathan N. Barron, for example, maintains that "according to Frost, loneliness is the negative emotion we associate not just with the absence of other people but also with the absence of God" (Barron, 73).

The setting of "Desert Places" is familiar to anyone who has read "Stopping by Woods on a Snowy Evening." That poem was torn between obligation ("promises to keep") and a potentially fatal desire for the dark profundity of the woods as they filled with snow. The death wish had been an act of affirmation, and the "lovely, dark and deep" woods spoke to a human need. Seductively, they stirred the protagonist into a response so intense that he could barely resist their siren song. Far from seeming bleak, "Stopping by Woods" amounted to a kind of celebration; it was a love poem. "Desert Places," by contrast, provides no such relief from its unremitting vision. It contains within itself some of the things which are more terrifying than death.

Just as the protagonist of "Stopping by Woods" is caught between stopping and passing, so "Desert Places" indecisively describes "a field I looked into going past." The absence of a comma after "into" creates the ghost of a contrary reading: "I looked into [the possibility of] going past the field." Even the obvious interpretation—"a field which I looked into as I went past"—seems perplexingly double-tongued, for the field's gravity seems to suck everything into it. Snow falls and night falls "*In* a field I looked *into*"—and apparently nowhere else. Even "go*ing* past" picks up the repetition of "In" and "into." Add those instances to the repeated "falling" of the first line, then "in snow," "in their lairs," "in me," "includes," and perhaps (visually at least) "loneliness." The pattern is reinforced by an extraordinary profusion of /n/ phonemes, as epitomized in "A blanker whiteness of benighted snow." The full weight of "Desert Places" is falling "in," being sucked in, not "going past." And what it is being sucked into is "snow," "night," "loneliness," "nothing." The echo chamber entraps and negates.

To claim to hear "Desert Places" as an expression of the need for faith is to impose a sentimental reading unsupported by, and alien if not anathema to, this insidious music. Better to read it as an expression of the impossibility of faith—faith in God and, more desperately, faith in the self. The third line of each stanza remains unrhymed and unaccommodated, a dead line formally signaling a failure to find harmony or consolatory design. And this is also what the fast-falling snow communicates through refusing to communicate: it says and means nothing. The snow includes things only in their suffocating loneliness, and it does so unthinkingly: both it and the protagonist are left "unawares." Emerson could believe that nature "always speaks of Spirit. It suggests the absolute." In this sense, Frost is profoundly hostile to his forebear; the reassurance provided by the "absolute" is nowhere to be found. Nature suggests only the stubborn absence of the absolute. Indeed, when Frost's protagonist describes himself as "absent-spirited" (desolately replacing the more common "absent-minded"), it may be Emerson's emphasis on "spirit" which Frost has in his sights. Frost asks where the spirit has gone, and for that matter, where the Spirit has gone. Spirit is absent, untrackable, so that the protagonist's personal loss is mirrored by a universal loss: the loss of a God who has abandoned his Creation.

Frost's final stanza alludes (as "An Old Man's Winter Night" may have previously alluded) to Blaise Pascal's confession: "Le silence éternel de ces espaces infinis m'effraie"—the eternal silence of these infinite spaces terrifies me. Yet that sense of terror at cosmic blankness is unshared by the protagonist: "They cannot scare me with their empty spaces / Between stars." More terrifying is the strange kind of loneliness felt on that "star" populated by the "human race." Loneliness is not the absence of the human, not even the absence of the divine (although that is a macrocosmic version of the same crisis), but the absence within the human: "I have it in me" is a phrase which promises possession and delivers only emptiness. Nature's desert is a metonym for human absent-spiritedness, and only secondarily for God's.

Interviewed in 1960, Frost proposed that poetry itself was inevitably affirmative: "If [a] poem expresses grief, it also expresses—as an *act,* as a composition, a performance, a 'making,'—the opposite of grief; it shows or expresses 'what a *hell* of a good time I had writing it'" (Richardson 1997, 192). But in "Desert Places," the failure of that consolation is especially pronounced. A making may imply a maker, but the landscape implies no God; and all the poet does by creating "[his] own desert places"—that is, the poem of that name—is "scare [himself]" and his readers. They may reach for religious faith as a way of controlling the poem's terrors, but "Desert Places" implies that those terrors are far too intimate to be reached or assuaged by any God.

Neither Out Far Nor In Deep

The people along the sand
All turn and look one way.
They turn their back on the land.
They look at the sea all day.

As long as it takes to pass
A ship keeps raising its hull;
The wetter ground like glass
Reflects a standing gull.

The land may vary more;
But wherever the truth may be—
The water comes ashore,
And the people look at the sea.

They cannot look out far.
They cannot look in deep.
But when was that ever a bar
To any watch they keep?

"Neither Out Far Nor In Deep," described by Lionel Trilling as "the most perfect poem of our time" (Trilling, 157), *dares* the reader to interpret it—knowing all the while that interpretation must become interpolation. What does the sea represent, and what the land? Where and what is the "truth"? Are the watchers wasting their time or carrying out a necessary task? These questions seem to require a response, but the poem blankly refuses to support any decisive verdict. Interpretation fills gaps which are also traps. For example, Randall Jarrell concludes that the sea stands for "the infinite that floods over us endlessly, the hypnotic monotony of the universe that is incommensurable with us"; and he goes on to argue that "it would be hard to find anything more unpleasant to say about people than that last stanza" (Jarrell 1952, 539). Yet the sea is not infinite but bounded; it varies less than the land but it is not invariable; far from "flood[ing] over us endlessly," the water merely "comes ashore"; and the "people" who keep watch at the end of the poem seem to be neither criticized nor commended. There is no textual reason to assume that the last stanza is at all "unpleasant" in its attitude, or to agree with Trilling that the poem's effects are "terrifying" and that nothing in it provides warmth "except the energy with which emptiness is perceived" (Trilling, 156–157). Withholding the evidence, "Neither Out Far" refuses to sustain the readings and reactions inspired by it.

Among possible sources has been mentioned Matthew Arnold's "Dover Beach," a poem of religious doubt which would prompt an understanding of "Neither Out Far Nor In Deep" as an allegorical study of faith and skepticism: the watchers wait for a truth to emerge from what Arnold called the "Sea of Faith," a domain beyond human ken. A more easily demonstrated source, given the many verbal echoes and parallels, is Emerson's essay "The Method of Nature":

> The universal does not attract us until housed in an individual. Who heeds the waste abyss of possibility? The ocean is everywhere the same, but it has no character until seen with the shore or the ship. Who would value any number of miles of Atlantic brine bounded by lines of latitude and longitude? Confine it by granite rocks, let it wash a shore where wise men dwell, and it is filled with expression; and the point of greatest interest is where the land and water meet.

Frost's poem encompasses the shore and the ship, the land and the water. It also contains the acknowledgment that "The land may vary more," although that is not absolutist in the way of Emerson's statement: "The ocean is everywhere the same." Emerson locates meaning in the "individual," and dismisses the external world without that human perspective as merely a "waste abyss of possibility" "lacking character." According to

Emerson, it is the universe's meeting with the human—the sea's with the land—which gives it significance. Frost's people disagree. They "turn their back on the land" in a clear gesture of rejection.

Reuben Brower, who draws attention to the allusion, states that "Emerson's moral is a more tranquil one than Frost's" (Brower, 150). But "tranquil" is hardly the right word. Where Frost's poem differs, crucially, is in its willingness to countenance (if not exactly support) an antihumanist worldview. The poem does not know where "the truth may be," but the sea is one possibility. We cannot be certain, because we cannot look out far or in deep. Even so, those watchers, who are in turn watched by the poetic persona, may yet prove to be the "wise men." As for Emerson's confident belief that the "point of greatest interest is where the land and water meet," Frost provides the perfect rebuttal with an image so drab as to be desolate: "The wetter ground like glass / Reflects a standing gull." Reflection is just one kind of repetition, taking its place alongside the description of the ship which "keeps raising its hull." Movement is a regular and repeated pattern, like a wave. Even the people lined across the sand "turn" as if synchronously, mirror images of one another, keeping their vigil as a mass (having only one "back") rather than as individuals.

These synchronized movements befit the repetitions of the poetic form: the spartan trimeter, the subject-verb-object structure, the monosyllabic masculine rhymes, the use of anaphora ("They cannot look out far. / They cannot look in deep"). Aside from a fugitive concession to ulteriority in the reference to "the truth," the poem does not wish to elaborate, and what little it expresses is expressed as if factually and objectively. This is what I can see happening, the poet tells his reader. Make of it what you will.

Design

I found a dimpled spider, fat and white,
On a white heal-all, holding up a moth
Like a white piece of rigid satin cloth—
Assorted characters of death and blight
Mixed ready to begin the morning right,
Like the ingredients of a witches' broth—
A snow-drop spider, a flower like froth,
And dead wings carried like a paper kite.

What had that flower to do with being white,
The wayside blue and innocent heal-all?
What brought the kindred spider to that height,
Then steered the white moth thither in the night?
What but design of darkness to appall?—
If design govern in a thing so small.

"Design" began as a sonnet titled "In White" which was ready to send to editors as early as 1912. That version did not appear until 1965, two years after Frost's death. Heavily revised and with its new title, "Design" was first published in 1922 in an anthology of the year's poetry. Frost finally collected the poem in *A Further Range* (1936), attributing the long delay to his own forgetfulness: he had no memory of the poem until "someone turned it up and it began to get said about" (Cook 1974, 126–127), and having been reminded of its existence, he added "Design" to the next convenient volume. Scholars have considered this account to be an unpersuasive piece of mischief. Perhaps, they speculate, Frost had been for a long time shy of the poem's theological implications and the reaction of his readership to such self-exposure. Or perhaps, as Anne Ferry has proposed, Frost wanted to withhold it "until late in his career," when it could be presented "in the context of other poems compatible with it" (Ferry, 314).

Frost is known to have been anxious that no one should be able to track any "upward Darwinian line" in his work (Burnshaw, 168). But "Design" ought not to have made him hesitate on that account. The poem does not overtly engage with Darwinian evolution. It is more concerned with what M. H. Abrams called "the heterocosmic analogue": the parallel between making a poem and making the universe. The poet is to the poem what God is to the world—a designer, a maker. "I am not undesigning," Frost told a correspondent in July 1913 (*SL*, 84). That being so, Frost pursues the logic of arguments from design to challenge God himself. Design implies a designer, and a bad poem implies a bad poet. By the same measure, if design is evil, or accommodates evil or suffering within it, then the character of the designer must be called urgently into question. The designing spider which entraps the moth may only be participating in a universal pattern of predation and pain.

"In White" had ended with the poet raising a question about his own terminology: "Design, Design! Do I use the word aright?" No such doubt exists in the retitled poem's final version, but this prominent anxiety indicates a concern for the word "design" and a knowledge of its currency in contemporary philosophical and theological discourse. Richard Poirier quotes a passage from William James's *Pragmatism*, which Frost would have encountered:

> The designer is no longer the old man-like deity. His designs have grown so vast as to be incomprehensible to us humans. The *what* of them so overwhelms us that to establish the mere *that* of a designer for them becomes of very little consequence in comparison. We can with difficulty comprehend the *character* of a cosmic mind whose purposes are fully revealed by the strange mixture of goods and evils that we find in this actual world's particulars. Or rather we cannot by any possibility comprehend it. The mere word "design" by itself has no consequences and explains nothing.

Frost's poem argues against this position on several grounds. It redeploys "design" designingly as the potent and the loaded word, and not as the "blank cartridge" which William James goes on to accuse it of having become. The word has huge consequences, and has itself become an explanation because, notwithstanding James's warning, it is prepared to make inferences about the designer's "*character*" based on observations of "this actual world's particulars." Most tellingly, "Design" ignores that which has "grown so vast as to be incomprehensible to us humans" and focuses, instead, on the microcosmic tableau described in the octave.

That tableau seems to provoke a crisis of representation. The word "like" occurs four times in the opening stanza—which is one time fewer than "In White" had managed, but still betrays the extent of the poem's reliance on simile. The moth attracts two similes: it is held up "Like a white piece of rigid satin cloth" and its "dead wings [are] carried like a paper kite." Both serve as avoidance strategies, moving away from horror toward the domestic and the man-made. Similarly, "the ingredients of a witches' broth" is a phrase which conveys a storybook iniquity, with nothing of the particular dreadfulness which the scene in its unembellished state might provoke. Poirier detects the language of advertising in line 5: "Mixed ready to begin the morning right" carries, he claims, a submerged reference to advertisements for breakfast cereal, and the "fat" and "dimpled" spider has the characteristics of the healthy babies who might appear in such advertisements (Poirier, 256). Poirier is right to notice the strategic mismatch between what is being described and the language used to describe it. The line "Assorted characters of death and blight" fails to take itself entirely seriously. Death and blight may be somber enough, but "Assorted characters" implies a lightheartedness, if not an offhandedness, on the poet's part. The "snow-drop spider" sounds harmless, even beautiful. And the identification of the flower as a "heal-all" seems to relish its own irony.

If "Design" were to end after line eight, it would read as a naturalist's grim joke. "I found a ball of grass among the hay," begins one of

John Clare's poems, and Frost starts in a similar vein. For all the critics' talk of fear, this is, after all, a description of a spider having caught a moth. The language may not want to face the horror, but even such evasions have their humor because horror is so small-scale and (in one sense) ordinary: trapping and eating insects is what spiders do. "Read the poem called 'Design' and see if you sleep the better for it," Lionel Trilling famously remarked, as he explained to an audience that Frost's universe is "terrifying" (Trilling, 157). But there is really nothing so frightful in the octave as to cause nightmares. As for the sestet, its leading questions are driven by a crueler irony; they seek to trap the reader as the spider trapped the moth.

In an earlier poem of design, William Blake had asked the tyger, "What immortal hand or eye / Dare frame thy fearful symmetry?" (Blake may also be lurking in Frost's lines 11–12, which seem to borrow images from "The Sick Rose.") Frost, like Blake, uses unanswered questions to encourage inferences about the artist responsible for framing the scene described: "What had that flower to do with being white?" Only at this point does the reader understand that more is at stake than the death of a moth. Spider, moth, and flower were all emphatically white, but the last of those—"The wayside blue and innocent heal-all"—should not have been. Whiteness is more normally the color of innocence and purity, but now it signifies deception and death. The flower which should heal is "kindred" to the predatory spider, and complicit in the moth's demise. Only in the penultimate line is the horror of the poem's chiaroscuro realized: it is the design of darkness to "appall," a word which, as several scholars have noted, has its origins in the French meaning "make pale." The blue heal-all has been made white by the darkness, and the spider has been sent to the appropriate height, in order to bring about the moth's death. Frost's final line breaks the iambics with a hurried afterthought— "If design govern in a thing so small"—as if to diminish its own drama with a shrug of the shoulders: like the sonnet itself, titled "Design" and governed by the poet's design, the scene is "a thing so small." Yet the reader is invited to assume that design governs larger things, like human affairs. Perhaps the horrific choreography of spider, moth, and flower is inspired by the same dark force which steers our lives; perhaps that dance of death is merely and coincidentally analogous to it. Either way, the poem implies that larger things than these are governed by darkness's design.

The Silken Tent

She is as in a field a silken tent
At midday when a sunny summer breeze
Has dried the dew and all its ropes relent,
So that in guys it gently sways at ease,
And its supporting central cedar pole,
That is its pinnacle to heavenward
And signifies the sureness of the soul,
Seems to owe naught to any single cord,
But strictly held by none, is loosely bound
By countless silken ties of love and thought
To everything on earth the compass round,
And only by one's going slightly taut
In the capriciousness of summer air
Is of the slightest bondage made aware.

~ ❧ ~

This Shakespearean sonnet revisits a favorite theme in Frost's work: the interrelationship between liberty and limitation. Frost described freedom as "feeling easy in your harness" (Vogel, 327), making it plain that true liberty can be realized only through the existence of constraints. For that matter, life is dependent on constraint: Frost's often-voiced observation that all life is cellular, writ large in a poem like "Mending Wall," serves as a reminder that boundaries *create* identities. By analogy, these beliefs fed Frost's long-standing disapproval of free verse: "tennis with the net down" is not tennis. So Frost's poetry both addresses and formally enacts the engagement of liberty with what "The Silken Tent" calls "ties."

Here, as so often elsewhere, Frost would have found a ready exemplar in Emerson, whose ambition was "to write such rhymes as shall not suggest a restraint, but contrariwise the wildest freedom." The wild freedom of "The Silken Tent" is the sheer technical panache displayed by its syntactical structure: the single sentence relishes its own performance by demonstrating a recklessness within accepted rules. The poem, like the tent, owes "naught to any single cord." This may be a Shakespearean sonnet, but in respect of its argument it is radically different from Shakespeare's practice. "I read this poem in its entirety since it's difficult not to," Paul Muldoon has remarked of "The Silken Tent" (Muldoon, 109). Typically, Shakespeare's sonnets mark a pause after each quatrain, and end with a complete rhyming couplet, but Frost's syntax gives no such opportunity for hesitation. The poem has what Frost calls elsewhere "its undeviable say" (*CPP&P*, 329). It insists on being read in its entirety because there is nowhere to stop.

That seamless beauty is much more than a syntactical effect. "The Silken Tent" takes its place among Frost's best work—and therefore among the best of modern poetry—because of its aural sensitivity. The poem's sibilance makes a series of silken ties which run from first line to last, and reach their peak, appropriately, at the "supporting central cedar pole." This dominant sound pattern exists alongside a proliferation of /n/ sounds, ensuring that the "silken tent" is always aurally present, and also alongside more local alliterative effects: "dried the dew," "ropes relent," "pole . . . pinnacle," and so on. The poem's modulating vowel music loosens and tightens as required: for example, the short vowels of "strictly held" play against the long and more languorous "loosely bound," as sound becomes obviously mimetic. (The oxymoron "loosely bound" is another version of "feeling easy in your harness.") These countless silken ties of sound and sense are the poem's greatest performance. For all that it makes a binding commitment to the sonnet tradition, and to one major subtradition within it, "The Silken Tent" never allows the reader to experience this formal bond as a form of "bondage."

Whatever the biographical inspiration, Frost was able to draw on the Song of Solomon for his conceit of the woman as a tent: "I am black, but comely, O ye daughters of Jerusalem, as the tents of Kedar, as the curtains of Solomon" (Song of Solomon 1:5). The language of erotic devotion in the Song of Solomon makes it a suitable source for Frost's poem. So does the binding connection between lovers, as pointed out by

John Hollander (Hollander 1988, 56), in Keats's "I Stood Tip-Toe": "the soft numbers, in that moment spoken, / Made silken ties, that never may be broken." Yet Paul Muldoon's claims to detect a strongly sexualized undercurrent in the poem—"I cannot but, can't but, hear a 'cunt' in the 'sil*ken* tent'" (Muldoon, 117), never mind the reference to "going slightly taut"—seem like a hint ingeniously taken where none was intended, even from a poet as thoroughgoingly ulterior as Frost.

The terms in which the woman's strength is celebrated have more in common with "Birches": her "supporting central cedar pole, / That is [the tent's] pinnacle to heavenward / And signifies the sureness of the soul" recalls the birch tree climbed "*Toward* heaven" (Frost's italics). In each case, the trunk allows the divine to be approached; it is, Poirier notes, "not only a point of terminus but a pointer" (Poirier, xv). The swinger of birches is allowed "to get away from earth awhile / And then come back to it and begin over." The woman in "The Silken Tent" takes the birch's role in acting as a go-between in the relationship of earth and heavens: she holds and is held, being "loosely bound . . . To everything on earth" and raising all those "silken ties" heavenward through "the sureness of [her] soul." Yet there is one difference. Whereas a tree sustains itself through its roots, this tent raises those "countless silken ties" and is reliant on them. Not a single one of them seems to be crucial, as that phrase "slightly taut" (like "loosely bound" and "slightest bondage") would suggest. Together, they keep the tent in place, playing their part in a mutually beneficial relationship. They award the woman her freedom; she is liberated because she is tied by "love and thought." She "gently sways at ease," only occasionally noticing the "slightest bondage" as she is described at the height of her powers: at noon on a sunny summer day. Appropriately, the rhyme of "air" and "aware" recognizes hers as the most ethereal of constraints.

The Most of It

He thought he kept the universe alone;
For all the voice in answer he could wake
Was but the mocking echo of his own
From some tree-hidden cliff across the lake.
Some morning from the boulder-broken beach
He would cry out on life, that what it wants
Is not its own love back in copy speech,
But counter-love, original response.
And nothing ever came of what he cried
Unless it was the embodiment that crashed
In the cliff's talus on the other side,
And then in the far distant water splashed,
But after a time allowed for it to swim,
Instead of proving human when it neared
And someone else additional to him,
As a great buck it powerfully appeared,
Pushing the crumpled water up ahead,
And landed pouring like a waterfall,
And stumbled through the rocks with horny tread,
And forced the underbrush—and that was all.

"He thought he kept the universe alone." "Just that one line could be a whole poem," Frost told his audience at a lecture in the last year of his life (*CPP&P*, 904). On its own, the line smacks of hubris: we may never find out where or when the poem is set, or who the protagonist is, but there is something presumptuous about the word "universe." The "island," or perhaps the "world," would be excusable semantically, although not rhythmically. Anyone who thinks that they keep the "universe" alone makes an arrogant theological claim. In that same lecture, Frost drew attention to the line's extravagance—an extravagance which he extended to the entire poem. "The Most of It" is extravagant, not only in the sense that Frost considered poetry itself to be extravagant, but also because it gestures so grandly from the local to the universal: "How stirring it is, the sun and everything. Take a telescope and look as far as you will. . . . How much of a universe was wasted just to produce puny us" (*CPP&P*, 902). The poem explores the relationship between the puny individual and the universal wastes surrounding him.

"Strongly spent is synonymous with kept," Frost famously argued. Notwithstanding that the "universe" of the poem seems to have been weakly and extravagantly spent, the opening line suggests that it is still "kept." To keep the universe is to possess and control it. That control is plotted in some of Frost's most heavily iambic lines, where variance is disallowed because it would imply disruption. The strange phrasing of the title establishes the iambic beat, which then goes almost unchallenged through the echoing repetitions until line 6, when the human cry itself disturbs the regulated world ("He would crý oút on lífe"). The prior "mocking echo" had already implied a threat to the individual's authority, but it was a threat generated by his own actions and therefore expressed in the same iambic beat. His complaint against life marks a momentary disturbance, before the iambs assert themselves once more.

The poem's story, then, is more than usually one of rhythm and rhyme. Rhyme is itself a mocking echo, as captured in that least perfect of the poem's rhymes: "wants" / "response." Rhyme's response may be *literally* unoriginal, but it does not quite amount to repetition, either. Its echo contains a surprise and a deviation, and it therefore sits between "copy speech" and the "original response" which the buck represents. What the protagonist "wants" is neither echo nor originality but rhyme, and in that sense, the poem provides for the reader the formal accomplishment which is denied to the lonely human. Rhythms work similarly, with the "greát búck" crashing as an unmetrical "embodiment" through the poem's iambic patterns. The disruption is simply too great to hold meaning for the quester, on whom the poem plays a cruel joke: he is mocked by echo, and then he is mocked by difference.

What does the "embodiment" embody? The reader learns its identity no sooner that the protagonist, so that it approaches through the water as something indeterminate but emphatically physical, "crash[ing]" and "splash[ing]." This force becomes manifested as a "great buck," yet the phrasing leaves little doubt that the buck's form is only one representation of a larger truth: "As a great buck it powerfully appeared," with the implication that it might as easily have appeared as something equally magnificent. "The Most of It" knows when to be specific, and when to be imprecise: "*some* tree-hidden cliff," "*Some* morning." The great buck, however, is both specific and beside the point. It is merely the "embodiment" of a nonhuman life which challenges egotism. He thought he kept the universe alone, but the buck's appearance is both meaningless and (therefore) potent with meaning: far from being central or unique, the human must acknowledge other kinds of existence to which he is irrelevant.

That the "embodiment" is the most peculiarly Frostian presence in "The Most of It" is proven by the poem's engagement with its Romantic precursor. Frost's poem is itself an example of "counter-love, original response," because it answers William Wordsworth's "There Was a Boy." The boy in that poem "stand[s] alone / Beneath the trees or by the glimmering lake," and he blows "mimic hootings to the silent owls / That they might answer him":

> And they would shout
> Across the watery vale, and shout again
> Responsive to his call, with quivering peals
> And long halloos, and screams, and echoes loud
> Redoubled and redoubled—a wild scene
> Of mirth and jocund din! And when it chanced
> That pauses of deep silence mocked his skill,
> Then sometimes in that silence while he hung
> Listening, a gentle shock of mild surprise
> Has carried far into his heart the voice
> Of mountain torrents; or the visible scene
> Would enter unawares into his mind

With all its solemn imagery, its rocks,
Its woods, and that uncertain heaven, received
Into the bosom of the steady lake.

Not for the first time, Frost borrows the setting and all the paraphernalia of Wordsworthian Romanticism in order to confute it. Here, he incorporates the solitary male protagonist, the lake, the mocking, the trees, the call for a response, and the boulders ("rocks" in Wordsworth's poem). Yet Wordsworth's boy interacts with the natural world, and provokes a delighted echo. He inspires the owls, and in those "pauses of deep silence" the noises and sights of his environment are received into his "heart" in the same way that the "steady lake" receives "that uncertain heaven." Frost, by contrast, stresses the rarity of the response, as the owls' echo of Wordsworth's poem is transformed into the mocking echo of his own. When it does finally come, the response is of an unconnected and bestial power. Nature, far from being a comforter, remains supremely indifferent to isolated man. It has no meaningful answer to the human cry. And so the poem moves relentlessly from "The Most of It" to "that was all"—from a shrugging acknowledgment that there is very little more to add, to a firm statement that everything relevant has been said.

The Subverted Flower

She drew back; he was calm:
"It is this that had the power."
And he lashed his open palm
With the tender-headed flower.
He smiled for her to smile,
But she was either blind
Or willfully unkind.
He eyed her for awhile
For a woman and a puzzle.
He flicked and flung the flower,
And another sort of smile
Caught up like finger tips
The corners of his lips
And cracked his ragged muzzle.
She was standing to the waist
In goldenrod and brake,
Her shining hair displaced.
He stretched her either arm
As if she made it ache
To clasp her—not to harm;
As if he could not spare
To touch her neck and hair.
"If this has come to us
And not to me alone—"
So she thought she heard him say;
Though with every word he spoke
His lips were sucked and blown
And the effort made him choke
Like a tiger at a bone.
She had to lean away.
She dared not stir a foot,
Lest movement should provoke

The demon of pursuit
That slumbers in a brute.
It was then her mother's call
From inside the garden wall
Made her steal a look of fear
To see if he could hear
And would pounce to end it all
Before her mother came.
She looked and saw the shame:
A hand hung like a paw,
An arm worked like a saw
As if to be persuasive,
An ingratiating laugh
That cut the snout in half,
An eye become evasive.
A girl could only see
That a flower had marred a man,
But what she could not see
Was that the flower might be
Other than base and fetid:
That the flower had done but part,
And what the flower began
Her own too meager heart
Had terribly completed.
She looked and saw the worst.
And the dog or what it was,
Obeying bestial laws,
A coward save at night,
Turned from the place and ran.
She heard him stumble first
And use his hands in flight.
She heard him bark outright.
And oh for one so young
The bitter words she spit

Like some tenacious bit
That will not leave the tongue.
She plucked her lips for it,
And still the horror clung.
Her mother wiped the foam
From her chin, picked up her comb
And drew her backward home.

Lawrance Thompson relays Frost's account that an early version of "The Subverted Flower" had been ready in time for *A Boy's Will* (1913), but that he had delayed publication through a fear that "it might seem too daring and too revealingly autobiographical" (Thompson 1966, 512). Thompson surmises that Elinor Frost would not have allowed the poem to be published in her lifetime. *A Witness Tree* (1942), which collected "The Subverted Flower," was Frost's first book to appear after his wife's death.

Although often cited, this biographical information helps very little with what is one of Frost's stranger and more recalcitrant poems. Like "Home Burial" before (or, it would seem, *after*) it, "The Subverted Flower" switches perspective between man and woman as their failure to communicate successfully leads each to fear the other. Again like "Home Burial," the poem tempts readers to take sides while both protagonists are suffering. Yet rather than expose one side as culpable or inadequate, "The Subverted Flower" finds disaster in mutual misunderstanding, with nothing of the choreographed decorousness of a poem like "Meeting and Passing."

The title has a literal and a metaphorical significance: the "tender-headed flower" is used aggressively as a "lash" and then discarded by the man; and the flower which is, figuratively, the girl's sexuality is subverted by her own "too meager heart." (Although he takes her for "a woman and a puzzle," he is a "man" and she is a "girl," with these hierarchies underlining the status of predator and prey.) Without intending it, each acts in exactly the way which the other will find distressing.

The fact that "power" rhymes and is closely associated with "flower" enhances the devastating force of the poem's various subversions. Neither of the protagonists has power over the other; at least, not the kind of power they would wish. It is *this*—a flower symbolizing a force beyond both of them—"that had the power." And they are equally victims of that power.

The poem's trimeter keeps action and description terse. She is silent throughout; his three lines of speech amount to just eighteen words. The third-person narrative viewpoint switches its sympathies as it switches perspectives. Occasionally, the narrator will report something which would have otherwise gone unremarked; but more often, the narrative voice is limited to the sights and insights of the protagonists themselves: "He eyed her"; "Made her steal a look of fear / To see if he could hear"; "She looked and saw the shame"; "A girl could only see"; "But what she could not see"; "She looked and saw the worst." In the absence of dialogue, this emphasis on the visual is, by extension, an acute attention to body language, as the characters study and try to puzzle out each other's behaviors. The man wants the girl to mirror him in response: "He smiled for her to smile." But his actions—the lashing of palm with "tender-headed" flower—can already be interpreted as intimidating, and his physical intervention in "stretch[ing] her either arm" only exacerbates that sense of danger: not for nothing does the narrator have to reassure us that the intention is "not to harm." The man finds the scene erotically charged, as she stands "to the waist / In goldenrod and brake, / Her shining hair displaced," so that he is overwhelmed by the need to touch her. At the same time, she and the narrator see him transformed into bestiality. He is a "brute" with a "ragged muzzle," a "paw," and a "snout," ready to pursue and pounce, and choking "Like a tiger at a bone." The more "bestial" he becomes, the weaker she seems, with a "too meager heart": the narrative voice criticizes each through the other's eyes.

The girl's understanding is presented as imperfect: she could not see "that the flower might be / Other than base and fetid." Nor does she understand that her own heart had completed what the flower began.

This connects the girl's unconscious sensuousness with the flower's: she is responsible for the man's reaction. The risks inherent in that attitude are plain enough, but they are offset throughout by the stress on male bestiality as observed by the narrator as well as the girl. On one level, she is herself the subverted flower—subverted in the man's imagination. Angel cannot traffic with beast. But paradoxically, the extreme terms under which they part betray a likeness which may augur future union. She has become like him, a beast "spit[ting]" "bitter words," her "bit" holding her tongue. He may have been transformed into a barking dog, but she herself seems to be foaming at the mouth.

The mother's call had issued from the safe domestic world—"From inside the garden wall"—and she is taken back out of threateningly sexualized nature and into that refuge at the poem's end. The last lines imply resistance to that return:

> Her mother wiped the foam
> From her chin, picked up her comb
> And drew her backward home.

To be drawn is not to be dragged, and yet "backward" shows no great willingness. The poem ends with subtle variations on where it began: "She drew back; he was calm." Now, she must be drawn back, and all sense of calm has gone, to be replaced by a fallen "comb" which is a symbol of the struggle.

The Gift Outright

The land was ours before we were the land's.
She was our land more than a hundred years
Before we were her people. She was ours
In Massachusetts, in Virginia,
But we were England's, still colonials,
Possessing what we still were unpossessed by,
Possessed by what we now no more possessed.
Something we were withholding made us weak
Until we found it was ourselves
We were withholding from our land of living,
And forthwith found salvation in surrender.
Such as we were we gave ourselves outright
(The deed of gift was many deeds of war)
To the land vaguely realizing westward,
But still unstoried, artless, unenhanced,
Such as she was, such as she would become.

More than almost any other of Frost's poems, "The Gift Outright" is
linked with a particular political and historical moment. First collected
in *A Witness Tree* (1942), it came to worldwide prominence in 1961 when
Frost read it at John F. Kennedy's inauguration. Frost had written "For
John F. Kennedy His Inauguration" especially for the occasion, but
found the sun's blinding glare on the snow and the white paper too much
for elderly eyes, so he spoke "The Gift Outright" from memory. There
has been speculation that Frost had planned the substitution in advance,
knowing the superiority of the older poem. That seems borne out by his
having discussed "The Gift Outright" with Kennedy beforehand; they
had agreed that the final clause should read "such as she *will* become"
(my italics). Frost emphasized the point at the Inauguration, by adding
as if ad libbing: "such as she would become, has become—and, for this

occasion, let me change that to *will* become." That uncertainty about goals and destinations brings the poem into conflict with the occasion which recruits it: if the project is complete, what can a new presidency achieve? Frost's supplement indulges in the paradox that the project is complete *and yet* ongoing.

"The Gift Outright" partakes of mythmaking and nation building: in proper Frostian fashion, its words have the ambition to become deeds. Altering the poem to stress that these processes of Americanization are still unfolding, Frost gives Kennedy's presidency and his own poetic work a fillip. A land which had been "artless" is here celebrated through art, as the processional iambs of the opening line formally convey the progress from east to west and from the colonial to a proud independence. This provides, of course, a brief and selective history lesson, which is vulnerable to protests that Frost's view of a united nation requires the exclusion of disruptive truths. The poem is concerned with one group's Manifest Destiny, at least insofar as that philosophy celebrated westward expansion; and the concern is stressed in its insistence on the pronoun "we"—nine times in sixteen lines—and its use of "ours," "our," "ours," "ourselves," "our," "ourselves." Native America and, in a different way, black America are passed over, unless their tragedies are understood as present in that catch-all aside: "(The deed of gift was many deeds of war)." *They* were not "we," and *their* history was not "our" history. The poem leaves unbroached the question of whether, through conquest and assimilation, those other groups have now qualified as full members of the poem's imagined community, or whether they continue to stand outside the nation-building project as described by Frost.

A politically skeptical reading which stressed these potential exclusions would follow Walter Benjamin's oft-quoted aphorism that there is no document of civilization which is not at the same time a document of barbarism. Frost's parenthetical aside acknowledges as much: the nicety of the legal phrase "deed of gift" is ironic, as nations are forged out of "many deeds of war." Yet even while admitting the barbarism, Frost's poem makes an irresistible case for its own civilization through the force of its rhetoric: having read "The Gift Outright" at Dartmouth in 1944,

Frost waxed lyrical about his nation as one of the world's wonders, a "sudden apparition of power and greatness."

Several critics have claimed that it is possible to think of "The Gift Outright" as a sixteen-line sonnet, but more than just arithmetic counts against that designation. It is extremely unusual, although not *quite* unprecedented, for Frost to have written a short lyric in unrhymed blank verse; and the poem's argument progresses without the volta which a sonnet might provide. "The Gift Outright" garners its solemn authority through a language which aims to sound inevitable, or at least uncontroversial, because it remains "unenhanced" by ostentatious flourishes such as rhyme. This is, nevertheless, far from an "everyday level of diction," as a word like "forthwith" and phrases like "land of living" or "salvation in surrender" indicate: simplicity and formality are here united. Declarative sentences proceed without the opportunity for dissent, and even Frost's parenthesis seems like a cunning way of silencing criticism by preempting it.

The opening line—"The land was ours before we were the land's"—provides a microcosm of Frost's strategies. It stands as a statement of fact, hiding a complex idea in repeated monosyllables and trustworthy iambs. The "land" will appear five times (or six, if "Eng*land*'s" can be allowed), and joins with those reiterated indicators of group membership—"we," "our," "ours," "ourselves"—as well as other repeated words: "still," "possessed," "found," "deed," "more," "outright," "gift." Phrases return, subtly changed: "we were the land's" becomes "we were England's"; "Such as we were" becomes "Such as she was"; and in the light of this tendency, even "surrender./Such as we were" seems like a hidden recapitulation. These echoes are complemented by several lines—the opening line included—which maintain a poise reminiscent of classical rhetoric: "In Massachusetts, in Virginia"; "Possessing what we still were unpossessed by,/Possessed by what we now no more possessed"; "(The deed of gift was many deeds of war)"; "Such as she was, such as she would become." The combined effect is of a tessellated strength built from a small number of basic and recurring linguistic patterns.

The apparent reasonableness of the poem's rhetoric hides more than a potential to exclude groups with different histories. The doctrine of "salvation in surrender," here reported as fact, dresses itself in the language of Christian theology even though God is a conspicuous absence throughout the poem. The "colonials" possessed the land, and themselves continued to be possessed by an overseas power; only when they successfully rejected that power, in what was presumably one of those "many deeds of war," were they able to "surrender" to the feminine land which is the poem's only deity. That "outright" sacrifice makes salvation possible, as the pioneers follow the land "vaguely realizing westward": the phrase is a memorable paradox, in which the clarity of the realized land meets the uncertain prospect of journeying across it. The rhythmical journey is similarly unsure compared with the sturdy iambs of the opening lines.

"The Gift Outright" never stops to explain how, in practice, one surrenders to the land, nor what the ensuing "salvation" might amount to. Nationhood is understood in such sacred terms that it seems ineffable, as the poem's final line admits in the sonority of its parting gesture: "Such as she was, such as she would become." The reader is not meant to understand that she both was *and* would become "unstoried, artless, unenhanced"—all those negatives have been made positive in the intervening period. Yet the grammar seems at odds with the rhetoric. What, exactly, has the land "become?" Even the logic of grammar, Frost seems to suggest in a sweeping gesture to the greatness of his nation, cannot override the self-evident answer to that.

Directive

Back out of all this now too much for us,
Back in a time made simple by the loss
Of detail, burned, dissolved, and broken off
Like graveyard marble sculpture in the weather,
There is a house that is no more a house
Upon a farm that is no more a farm
And in a town that is no more a town.
The road there, if you'll let a guide direct you
Who only has at heart your getting lost,
May seem as if it should have been a quarry—
Great monolithic knees the former town
Long since gave up pretense of keeping covered.
And there's a story in a book about it:
Besides the wear of iron wagon wheels
The ledges show lines ruled southeast northwest,
The chisel work of an enormous Glacier
That braced his feet against the Arctic Pole.
You must not mind a certain coolness from him
Still said to haunt this side of Panther Mountain.
Nor need you mind the serial ordeal
Of being watched from forty cellar holes
As if by eye pairs out of forty firkins.
As for the woods' excitement over you
That sends light rustle rushes to their leaves,
Charge that to upstart inexperience.
Where were they all not twenty years ago?
They think too much of having shaded out
A few old pecker-fretted apple trees.
Make yourself up a cheering song of how
Someone's road home from work this once was,
Who may be just ahead of you on foot
Or creaking with a buggy load of grain.

The height of the adventure is the height
Of country where two village cultures faded
Into each other. Both of them are lost.
And if you're lost enough to find yourself
By now, pull in your ladder road behind you
And put a sign up CLOSED to all but me.
Then make yourself at home. The only field
Now left's no bigger than a harness gall.
First there's the children's house of make believe,
Some shattered dishes underneath a pine,
The playthings in the playhouse of the children.
Weep for what little things could make them glad.
Then for the house that is no more a house,
But only a belilaced cellar hole,
Now slowly closing like a dent in dough.
This was no playhouse but a house in earnest.
Your destination and your destiny's
A brook that was the water of the house,
Cold as a spring as yet so near its source,
Too lofty and original to rage.
(We know the valley streams that when aroused
Will leave their tatters hung on barb and thorn.)
I have kept hidden in the instep arch
Of an old cedar at the waterside
A broken drinking goblet like the Grail
Under a spell so the wrong ones can't find it,
So can't get saved, as Saint Mark says they mustn't.
(I stole the goblet from the children's playhouse.)
Here are your waters and your watering place.
Drink and be whole again beyond confusion.

Often considered to be the last of Frost's major poems, "Directive" offers itself as a *summa poetica* because it runs through so many of the motifs which have sustained his work. "You come too," his persona had encouraged the reader at the start of *North of Boston* and in every subsequent collected and selected edition. "Directive" is less inviting and less reassuring—as its rather chilly title suggests—in that the guide is a trickster who "only has at heart your getting lost." Yet it completes the journey begun by "The Pasture." "You come too" had beckoned the willing traveler outside into Frost's hinterland. Now the traveler is given directions back to the start and the source, a return journey in space and time out of the present and into a past "made simple by the loss / Of detail," as that line break emphasizes the damage done by the intervening years. The past which the poem figures is a lost and only partially retrievable world. It is also a childhood world, incorporating some of the rhythms of nursery rhyme ("There is a house that is no more a house," and so on), in which the phrase "Once upon a time" is evoked even as it is skirted around: "Back in a time . . . Upon a farm."

Acknowledging Wordsworth's complaint that "The world is too much with us," Frost's poem signals its agreement by seeking refuge in a "simple" time. Nevertheless, the recourse to the sustaining rhythms of earliest childhood exists alongside a fiercely complex syntax. As Ellen Bryant Voigt observes of the opening line—"Back out of all this now too much for us"—"'this' functions grammatically as a demonstrative pronoun standing in for an elided referent . . . but 'this' also appears in our lexicon and our grammar as an adjective; so its placement . . . seems to press the adverb that follows (*now*) into service as a noun" (Voigt, 25). Is it that "all this" is "now too much," or that "all this now" is "too much?" The uncertainty befits a poem which journeys through ruined present and pristine past simultaneously, keeping each visible and allowing dominance to neither. The logical contradiction in the "house that is no more a house" exemplifies this dual status: summoned by poetic will, the past both exists and is lost, as the fourfold reiteration of "now" insists on the inescapability of the present. Yet that present is itself scarred by geological time as well as by recent human history: a glacier's "chisel work" is visible, putting into perspective "the wear of iron wagon wheels." A "belilaced cellar hole" marks the site of the house, and (in a wondrous simile) even that hole is "Now slowly closing like a dent in dough." Human scars on the landscape will not last long.

Besides these wounds, one formal way in which the past irrupts into the present is through allusion. "Directive" is among the most allusive of Frost's poems, and more often than not its sources are his own earlier poems (among others, "Ghost House," "The Mountain," "The Generations of Men," The Sound of the Trees," "After Apple-Picking," "Hyla Brook"). The journey, then, is mapped through the music and landscapes of his own work, although the guide's unreliability is reminiscent of the comment made by Frost in 1927 about what he called his "innate mischievousness":

> My poems [. . .] are all set to trip the reader head foremost into the boundless. Ever since infancy I have had the habit of leaving my blocks carts chairs and such like ordinaries where people would be pretty sure to fall forward over them in the dark. Forward, you understand, *and* in the dark. I may leave my toys in the wrong place and so in vain. (*SL*, 344)

Those toys have become "playthings" by the time of "Directive," and "getting lost" does not initially sound as dangerous as "fall[ing] forward over them in the dark," but Frost's innate mischievousness still confounds the quest for understanding. Small wonder that the poem should allude to Christ's comment in Mark's Gospel about the need to speak in parable: "Unto you it is given to know the mystery of the kingdom of God: but unto them that are without, all these things are done in parables: That seeing they may see, and not perceive; and hearing they may hear, and not understand; lest at any time they should be converted, and their sins should be forgiven them" (Mark 4:11–12). Having always stated the ambition to write for all sorts of readers, Frost in "Directive" seems at first to express a clear preference: those who miss the ulteriority of his parables "can't get saved." Salvation comes from being a good reader.

If only it were that simple. For all their promises, the poem's final lines remain remarkably duplicitous, as Frost toys with the reader's immortal soul. The guide who has at heart our "getting lost" may be referring to eschatology as much as geography. The intimacy of his invitation is beguiling: he invites us to drink from the brook which—although we may hesitate to identify it definitively as Hyla Brook—is represented throughout his work as the source of inspiration. (Frost wryly compliments his own achievement when he describes the brook as "Too lofty and original to rage," and criticizes lesser talents as "valley streams" which, when "aroused," do nothing but leave an unsightly mess.) We become initiates, knowing to look in the "instep arch / Of an old cedar" because we recognize the phrase from "After Apple-Picking": "My instep arch not only keeps the ache . . ." There we find a "broken drinking goblet like the Grail," so that a successfully redemptive end to our quest seems to have been achieved. Poetic power and religious power merge, and the "wrong ones" who have not made the same journey cannot share that power with us. Yet Frost's final lines require an urgent reconsideration of our souls:

> (I stole the goblet from the children's playhouse.)
> Here are your waters and your watering place.
> Drink and be whole again beyond confusion.

As metaphor is a kind of "make believe"—a plaything of the imagination, albeit in earnest—it is fitting that a goblet alleged to be like the Grail should have been stolen from that "children's playhouse." Salvation which relies on theft is a false salvation; but then again, Christ urges us to become like children in order to reach the kingdom of heaven, and Frost's confession is itself complicated by the issue of whether a broken and abandoned goblet can be "stolen" at all. Are we damned as thieves or saved as children?

The poem's final line seems to draw on the same inspiration as

Frost's oft-quoted aphorism that poetry can offer "a momentary stay against confusion" (*CPr*, 132). Frost's master, Emerson, speaks in his Channing Ode of the "angry Muse" which would put "confusion in [his] brain" if he were to let politics draw him away from study. The Muse, in the guise of poetry, brings Frost back from the confusion of such concerns, if only temporarily. However, the phrase "momentary stay" verges on the paradoxical: that which lasts only for a moment can hardly be said to "stay." In "Directive," Frost promises a potentially lasting refuge from "confusion," a restorative wholeness which is more than a shoring of fragments against one's ruins. Even so, "confusion" seems like a strange choice of word for such a watery poem: etymologically, to confuse is to pour together, and Frost's promise of wholeness amounts to a blending of "waters and . . . watering place[s]." The poem's final line, sitting with tonal uncertainty between invitation and command, risks bringing about the very confusion from which it claims to redeem us.

In the biblical tenor of the poem's final lines, there is one more lurking allusion. Once detected, it prompts a reassessment of all that has gone before: not just the poem, but the corpus of Frost's writings. The allusion is to Proverbs 9, in which women representing wisdom and foolishness compete to attract "passengers who go right on their ways." The decision made by those travelers determines the fate of their soul. Those who choose wisely, and "go in the way of understanding," will eat of the bread and drink of the wine which Wisdom has mingled; those who choose foolishly are attracted by the promise that "Stolen waters are sweet, and bread eaten in secret is pleasant." Which road has the traveler through Frost's work chosen? Wisdom serves mingled wine, but Frost's guide promises a wholeness "beyond confusion." Foolishness tempts with "stolen waters," while Frost's guide provides "waters" and a stolen drinking goblet. Proverbs spells out the cost to the traveler who chooses foolishly: "He knoweth not that the dead are there; and that her guests are in the depths of hell." Frost's most devastating joke on his readers is that he leaves us with reason to be fearful over whether, by becoming his disciples, we have been saved or damned.

Bibliography

Adams, Mary. 2001. "'Acquainted with the Night.'" In Tuten and Zubizarreta 2001, 1–2.

Bacon, Helen. 2001. "Frost and the Ancient Muses." In Faggen 2001a, 75–100.

Barron, Jonathan N. 2001. "'Desert Places.'" In Tuten and Zubizarreta 2001, 73–74.

Barry, Elaine. 1973. *Robert Frost.* New York: Frederick Ungar.

Bleau, N. Arthur. 1978. "Robert Frost's Favorite Poem." In *Frost: Centennial Essays III,* ed. Jac L. Tharpe, 174–177. Jackson: University Press of Mississippi.

Bloom, Harold. 1993. *The American Religion: The Emergence of the Post-Christian Nation.* New York: Simon and Schuster.

Bromwich, David. 1989. *A Choice of Inheritance: Self and Community from Edmund Burke to Robert Frost.* Cambridge: Harvard University Press.

———. 2001. *Skeptical Music: Essays on Modern Poetry.* Chicago: University of Chicago Press.

Brower, Reuben. 1963. *The Poetry of Robert Frost: Constellations of Intention.* New York: Oxford University Press.

Buell, Lawrence. 2001. "Frost as a New England Poet." In Faggen 2001a, 101–122.

Burnshaw, Stanley. 1986. *Robert Frost Himself.* New York: George Braziller.

Cook, Reginald Lansing. 1956. "Frost on Frost: The Making of Poems." *American Literature* 28 (1): 62–72.

———. 1974. *Robert Frost: A Living Voice.* Amherst: University of Massachusetts Press.

Cramer, Jeffrey S. 1996. *Robert Frost among His Poems: A Literary Companion to the Poet's Own Biographical Contexts and Associations.* Jefferson, N.C.: McFarland.

Faggen, Robert. 1997. *Robert Frost and the Challenge of Darwin.* Ann Arbor: University of Michigan Press.

———, ed. 2001a. *The Cambridge Companion to Robert Frost.* Cambridge: Cambridge University Press.

———. 2001b. "Frost and the Questions of Pastoral." In Faggen 2001a, 49–74.

Ferry, Anne. 2005. "Frost's Design." *Literary Imagination* 7 (3): 313–329.

Francis, Lesley Lee. 2004. *Robert Frost: An Adventure in Poetry, 1900–1918.* New Brunswick, N.J.: Transaction. Originally pub. Columbia: University of Missouri Press, 1994.

Frost, Robert. 1963. *The Letters of Robert Frost to Louis Untermeyer.* Ed. Louis Untermeyer. New York: Holt, Rinehart and Winston.

———. 1964. *Selected Letters of Robert Frost.* Ed. Lawrance Thompson. New York: Holt, Rinehart and Winston.

———. 1995. *Collected Poems, Prose, and Plays.* Ed. Richard Poirier and Mark Richardson. New York: Library of America.

———. 2006. *The Notebooks of Robert Frost.* Ed. Robert Faggen. Cambridge: Belknap Harvard.

———. 2007. *The Collected Prose of Robert Frost.* Ed. Mark Richardson. Cambridge: Belknap Harvard.

Hamilton, Ian. 1973. Introduction to Robert Frost, *Selected Poems*, 11–23. London: Penguin.

Hardy, Florence Emily. 1973. *The Life of Thomas Hardy, 1840–1928.* Rpt. in 1 vol. Originally pub. as 2 vols., London: Macmillan, 1928–1930.

Heaney, Seamus. 1996. "Above the Brim." In Joseph Brodsky, Seamus Heaney, and Derek Walcott, *Homage to Robert Frost,* 61–88. New York: Farrar, Straus and Giroux.

Hollander, John. 1975. *Vision and Resonance: Two Senses of Poetic Form.* New York: Oxford University Press.

———. 1988. *Melodious Guile: Fictive Pattern in Poetic Language.* New Haven: Yale University Press.

———. 1997a. Foreword to Robert Frost, *Poems*, 11–13. New York: Knopf.

———. 1997b. *The Work of Poetry.* New York: Columbia University Press.

Jarrell, Randall. 1952. "To the Laodiceans." *Kenyon Review* 14 (4): 535–561.

———. 1985. *Randall Jarrell's Letters: An Autobiographical and Literary Selection.* Ed. Mary Jarrell. Boston: Houghton Mifflin.

Kearns, Katherine. 1994. *Robert Frost and a Poetics of Appetite.* New York: Cambridge University Press.

Kilcup, Karen L. 1998. *Robert Frost and the Feminine Literary Tradition.* Ann Arbor: University of Michigan Press.

Klein, Amelia. 2008. "The Counterlove of Robert Frost." *Twentieth-Century Literature* 54 (3): 1–26.

Lathem, Edward Connery, ed. 1966. *Interviews with Robert Frost.* New York: Holt, Rinehart and Winston.

Lentricchia, Frank. 1975. *Robert Frost: Modern Poetics and the Landscapes of Self.* Durham: Duke University Press.

Marcus, Mordecai. 1976. "The Whole Pattern of Robert Frost's 'Two Witches': Contrasting Psycho-Sexual Modes." *Literature and Psychology* 26: 69–78.

Mertins, Louis. 1965. *Robert Frost: Life and Talks-Walking.* Norman: University of Oklahoma Press.

Meyers, Jeffrey. 1996. *Robert Frost: A Biography.* New York: Houghton Mifflin.

Monteiro, George. 1988. *Robert Frost and the New England Renaissance.* Lexington: University Press of Kentucky.

Muldoon, Paul. 1998. "Getting Round: Notes Towards an Ars Poetica." *Essays in Criticism* 48 (2): 107–128.

Oster, Judith. 2001. "Frost's Poetry of Metaphor." In Faggen 2001a, 155–177.

Parini, Jay. 1999. *Robert Frost: A Life.* New York: Henry Holt.

Parker, Blandford. 2001. "Frost and the Meditative Lyric." In Faggen 2001a, 179–196.

Plato. 1993. *Republic.* Trans. Robin Waterfield. Oxford: Oxford University Press.

Poirier, Richard. 1977. *Robert Frost: The Work of Knowing.* New York: Oxford University Press.

Richardson, Mark. 1997. *The Ordeal of Robert Frost: The Poet and His Poetics.* Urbana: University of Illinois Press.

———. 2001. "Frost's Politics of Control." In Faggen 2001a, 197–219.

Rotella, Guy. 2001. "'Synonymous with Kept': Frost and Economics." In Faggen 2001a, 241–260.

Sergeant, Elizabeth Shepley. 1960. *Robert Frost: The Trial by Existence.* New York: Holt, Rinehart and Winston.

Smith, Newton. 2001. "'The Need of Being Versed in Country Things.'" In Tuten and Zubizarreta 2001, 225–226.

Spencer, Matthew, ed. 2003. *Elected Friends: Robert Frost and Edward Thomas to One Another.* New York: Handsel.

Steele, Timothy. 2001. "'Across Spaces of the Footed Line': The Meter and Versification of Robert Frost." In Faggen 2001a, 123–153.

Thompson, Lawrance. 1966. *Robert Frost: The Early Years, 1874–1915.* New York: Holt, Rinehart and Winston.

———. 1970. *Robert Frost: The Years of Triumph, 1915–1938.* New York: Holt, Rinehart and Winston.

Trilling, Lionel. 1962. "A Speech on Robert Frost: A Cultural Episode." In *Robert Frost: A Collection of Critical Essays,* ed. James M. Cox, 151–158. Englewood Cliffs, N.J.: Prentice-Hall.

Tuten, Nancy Lewis, and John Zubizarreta, eds. 2001. *The Robert Frost Encyclopedia*. Westport, Conn.: Greenwood.

Vogel, Nancy. 2001. "'The Silken Tent.'" In Tuten and Zubizarreta 2001, 326–328.

Voigt, Ellen Bryant. 2009. *The Art of Syntax: Rhythm of Thought, Rhythm of Song*. Minneapolis: Graywolf.

Wakefield, Richard. 2001. "'The Vanishing Red.'" In Tuten and Zubizarreta 2001, 394.

Walsh, John Evangelist. 1988. *Into My Own: The English Years of Robert Frost, 1912–1915*. New York: Grove.

Woznicki, John R. 2001. "'The Cow in Apple Time.'" In Tuten and Zubizarreta 2001, 67.

Index

Abercrombie, Lascelles, 246
Abrams, M. H., 358
Adams, Mary, 342
Arnold, Matthew, 355

Bacon, Helen, 206, 214
Barron, Jonathan N., 350
Benjamin, Walter, 374–375
Berryman, John, 339
Blake, William, 341, 360
Bloom, Harold, 18
Bridges, Robert, 9–10
Bromwich, David, 170, 230
Brooks, Cleanth, 350
Brower, Reuben, 114–115, 207, 235,
    244, 329, 347–349, 356
Browning, Robert, 109–110, 243
Buell, Lawrence, 239, 326

Catullus, Gaius Valerius, 68, 313,
    324–325
Clare, John, 359–360
Coleridge, Samuel Taylor, 28, 188–
    190, 238

Dante (Dante Alighieri), 180, 313,
    341

Eliot, T. S., 313–314
Emerson, Ralph Waldo, 9, 335, 352,
    355–356, 362, 383

Faggen, Robert, 50, 207
Ferry, Anne, 357
Ford, Ford Madox, 45
Francis, Lesley Lee, 315–316
Frost, Elinor (RF's wife), 326, 371
Frost, Isabelle Moodie (RF's
    mother), 10, 29
Frost, Robert: and the Classics, 6,
    32–34, 46, 47, 51, 61, 68, 167, 206,
    313, 324–325; and education, 5,
    273, 275–276; and England, 9–10,
    45, 180, 219, 229–231, 315–317; and
    the First World War, 180, 221,
    228–231; and freedom, 18, 34–35,
    81, 148, 170, 215, 346, 363–364; and
    the language of poetry, 5–6, 21, 26,
    46, 68, 154, 171, 175, 203–204, 315–
    318; and meter and rhythm, 7–8, 9,
    68, 120–121, 146, 274–275, 324–
    325; and nationhood, 5, 8–9, 207,
    208–209, 220–221, 374–377; and
    his readership, 3–4, 5, 48, 182, 320,
    383; and religion, 33, 96, 215, 326,
    350–353, 358, 360–361, 365–366,
    377, 381–383; and rhyme, 42, 101,
    366; and society, 18, 20, 38, 42–43,
    170, 174–175, 287, 308–311, 345–
    349; and "the sound of sense," 7,
    8, 243, 304; and speech, 6, 7, 21,
    26, 46, 70, 89, 101, 109–110, 121;
    and ulteriority, 3–4, 8, 24–25, 27–

Frost, Robert (*continued*)
29, 89, 256–257, 265–269, 319–321,
340
Frost, Robert, books by: *A Boy's
Will,* 6, 10, 13–14, 17, 177; *A Further
Range,* 339; *Mountain Interval,*
14; 177–178, 186, 199, 239, 247, 251;
New Hampshire, 251–252, 328,
339; *North of Boston,* 14, 16, 45–
46, 79, 89, 114–115, 120–122, 134,
154, 176, 178, 186, 199, 229, 239,
251, 303; *Steeple Bush,* 339; *West-
Running Brook,* 339; *A Witness
Tree,* 339, 371
Frost, Robert, poems by: "Ac-
quainted with the Night," 339,
340–342; "After Apple-Picking,"
46, 101, 113–116, 381–382; "The
Axe-Helve," 229, 247, 270–276,
279, 301; "Beyond Words," 313;
"Birches," 211–215, 247, 364; "The
Black Cottage," 90–97, 111, 144;
"Blueberries," 98–103; "The Bon-
fire," 225–231, 248; "Christmas
Trees," 166, 183–186, 247; "The
Code," 109, 115, 117–123, 279;
"The Cow in Apple Time," 219–
221; "The Death of the Hired
Man," 6, 45, 54–63, 134; "Desert
Places," 339, 350–353; "Design,"
123, 339, 357–361; "Directive,"
4, 14, 21, 335, 339, 378–383; "A
Dream Pang," 202–203; "An En-
counter," 222–224, 247, 310; "The
Fear," 149–155, 308; "Fire and
Ice," 312–314; "For John F. Ken-
nedy His Inauguration," 374; "For
Once, Then, Something," 324–
327; "Genealogical," 242; "The

Generations of Men," 14, 21, 115,
122, 124–135, 144, 381; "Ghost
House," 14, 15, 19–22, 292, 335,
381; "The Gift Outright," 339,
374–377; "Good Hours," 46, 101,
115, 169, 173–176, 247, 341; "The
Grindstone," 251, 277–281; "The
Gum-Gatherer," 237–240, 247;
"A Hillside Thaw," 331–333;
"The Hill Wife," 154, 308; "Home
Burial," 82–89, 94, 111, 144, 154,
234, 292–293, 371; "The House-
keeper," 136–148; "A Hundred
Collars," 72–81, 111, 122; "Hyla
Brook," 205–207, 208, 381–382;
"In a Disused Graveyard," 292;
"In the Home Stretch," 41, 191–
201; "Into My Own," 14, 15, 16–18,
38, 41, 247, 310, 320; "The Line-
Gang," 222; "Maple," 4, 247, 251,
260–269, 303; "Meeting and Pass-
ing," 202–204, 208, 371; "Mending
Wall," 46, 49–53, 79, 115, 169, 219,
256, 279, 362; "The Most of It,"
339, 342, 364–368; "The Moun-
tain," 64–71, 109, 122, 205–206,
303, 381; "Mowing," 14, 15, 27–29,
38, 166, 217, 347; "The Need of
Being Versed in Country Things,"
334–337; "Neither Out Far Nor In
Deep," 123, 339, 354–356; "New
Hampshire," 251; "La Noche
Triste," 242; "An Old Man's Win-
ter Night," 177–178, 187–190, 238,
352; "The Onset," 328–330, 332;
"'Out, Out—,'" 167, 232–236, 279;
"The Oven Bird," 208–210; "The
Pasture," 16–17, 46, 47–48, 79, 169,
173, 247, 380; "Paul's Wife," 247,

251, 266, 282–289; "The Pauper Witch of Grafton," 306–311; "Place for a Third," 290–295; "Putting in the Seed," 216–218; "Reluctance," 14, 40–43, 247; "The Road Not Taken," 4, 174, 179–182, 247, 336, 340; "Rose Pogonias," 14, 15, 23–26; "The Self-Seeker," 156–167, 169, 185, 279; "A Servant to Servants," 103–112, 115, 144, 154, 308; "The Silken Tent," 339, 362–364; "Snow," 177; "The Sound of the Trees," 246–249, 310, 381; "A Star in a Stone-boat," 252–259, 281; "Stopping by Woods on a Snowy Evening," 319–323, 328, 340, 341, 351; "The Subverted Flower," 217, 339, 369–373; "The Telephone," 222; "There Are Roughly Zones," 220; "A Time to Talk," 221; "To E. T.," 252, 315–318, 330; "Tree at My Window," 247; "The Trial by Existence," 15, 30–35; "The Tuft of Flowers," 14, 15, 36–39, 51, 166, 171, 185, 347; "Two Look at Two," 251; "Two Tramps in Mud Time," 52–53, 102, 166, 339, 343–349; "Two Witches," 296–311; "The Vanishing Red," 122, 167, 241–245, 279; "The Vantage Point," 38, 292; "The Witch of Coös," 251, 296–304, 308; "The Wood-Pile," 46, 115, 168–172, 310

Ginsberg, Allen, 86
Graves, Robert, 9

Hamilton, Ian, 95, 170–171
Hardy, Thomas, 5, 208–209

Heaney, Seamus, 234, 325
Hollander, John, 9, 62, 116, 210, 316–317, 363–364
Homer, 33, 102
Horace (Quintus Horatius Flaccus), 206

James, William, 358–359
Jarrell, Randall, 20, 86, 204, 214, 251, 269, 310, 341, 354–355
Jefferson, Thomas, 96
Joyce, James, 302

Kavanagh, Patrick, 102
Kearns, Katherine, 266–267, 320
Keats, John, 115, 208, 214, 322
Kennedy, John F., 339, 374–375
Kilcup, Karen L., 87
Klein, Amelia, 326

Lentricchia, Frank, 52, 70, 134, 320, 329, 341
Longfellow, Henry Wadsworth, 13
Lowell, Amy, 122

Marcus, Mordecai, 302
Marvell, Andrew, 26, 28
Meyers, Jeffrey, 314
Milton, John, 224
Monteiro, George, 229
Muldoon, Paul, 178, 363–364

Oster, Judith, 213

Parini, Jay, 28, 234, 316, 339
Parker, Blandford, 166
Pascal, Blaise, 188, 352
Pinsky, Robert, 217
Plath, Sylvia, 63

Plato, 32–34
Poirier, Richard, 26, 60, 70, 87, 133,
154, 173, 209, 213, 217, 248, 320,
358–359, 364
Pope, Alexander, 17
Pound, Ezra, 9, 14

Richardson, Mark, 62, 81, 217
Robinson, Edwin Arlington, 200

Sergeant, Elizabeth, 322
Shakespeare, William, 17, 28, 89,
133, 135 174, 202–203, 233–234,
287–288
Shapley, Harlow, 312
Shawshank Redemption, The, 3
Shelley, Percy, 190, 208, 214, 231, 256
Stein, Gertrude, 257

Tennyson, Alfred, 206, 209
Thomas, Edward, 9, 45, 180, 252,
315–318

Thompson, Lawrance, 153, 177,
179, 217, 228, 229, 326, 342, 345,
371
Trilling, Lionel, 5, 122, 123, 354–355,
360

Vaughan, Henry, 26
Virgil (Publius Vergilius Maro), 46,
47–48, 51, 101
Voigt, Ellen Bryant, 380

Wakefield, Richard, 242–243
Warren, Robert Penn, 350
Whitman, Walt, 8–9, 208–209
Wordsworth, William, 5–6, 32–33,
52, 68, 94, 171, 220, 238–240, 288,
347–348, 367–368, 380
Woznicki, John R., 220
Wyatt, Thomas, 313

Yeats, W. B., 14, 21